Facts On File
**NATIONAL
PROFILES**

The
Benelux
Countries

FACTS ON FILE
NATIONAL
PROFILES

The
Benelux
Countries

G<small>EORGE</small> T<small>HOMAS</small> K<small>URIAN</small>

Facts On File National Profiles: The Benelux Countries

copyright © 1989 by George Thomas Kurian

Facts On File, ® Inc.
460 Park Avenue South
New York, New York 10016

Library of Congress Cataloging-in-Publication Data

Kurian, George Thomas.
    Facts on File national profiles. The Benelux countries/George Thomas Kurian.
        p.   cm.
    Bibliography: p.
    Includes index.
    ISBN 0-8160-2026-4
    1. Benelux countries.   2. Netherlands.   3. Belgium.
    4. Luxembourg.   I. Title.   II. Title: Benelux countries.
DH18.K87   1989
949.2—dc20   89-33079

British CIP data available on request

Facts On File books are available at special discounts when purchased in bulk
quantities for businesses, associations, institutions or sales promotion. Please contact
the Special Sales Department of our New York office at 212/683-2244 (dial
800/322-8755 except in NY, AK or HI).

Composition by Logidec
Printed in the United States of America

10 9 8 7 6 5 4 3 2 1

CONTENTS

INTRODUCTION

The Benelux Countries is the first of a series of national profiles, derived from the larger Encyclopedias of the 1st, 2nd and 3rd Worlds, that will cover the major regional groupings of the world. Each profile will provide a comparative survey of over 30 key areas of national life in the region's constituent countries.

Regions are the building blocks of international relations. Geographical proximity creates political and economic linkages, often reinforced by common linguistic, religious and cultural legacies. The scope of conflict is strongest among neighbors, but so also is the scope for cooperation. Competing nationalism, historic rivalries and memories of past hostilities have to be overcome before forging a viable and harmonious regional alliance. Yet, more regional groupings have been formed since the end of World War II than during all the centuries preceding it. Smaller nations have found that their national interests are better served by and more effectively pursued through regional organizations.

Benelux, historically known as the Low Countries, is a prime example of such a region. The three countries—Belgium, Luxembourg and the Netherlands—are bound in a symbiotic relationship like Siamese triplets. They share the same historical and political heritage and have common liguistic, religious and cultural roots. Historically, all the three were, at one time or another in their history, part of the same empire or nation. In the 15th century they came under the rule of the dukes of Burgundy, and later the Habsburg Empire and the Spanish Empire of Philip II. They were reunited briefly by the Congress of Vienna in 1815. The ducal family of Luxembourg is of Dutch descent and is related at present by marriage to the royal family of Belgium. Politically, all three countries are constitutional monarchies. Geographically, the Low Countries occupy the northwestern corner of Europe served by two of the great natural harbors of the Continent, Antwerp and Rotterdam. Having few natural resources, all the three became trading nations. Belgium and the Netherlands became masters of empires several times the size of their national territories. The three countries also share common legal systems. Even denominational and linguistic differences within each country have only served to demonstrate the unity of the larger whole.

Because of the natural unity of the Low Countries, their historical evolution into three separate entities is an anomaly. It is one of the few instances in European history where artificial boundaries were imposed by stronger neighboring powers without reference to natural ethnic and geographical divisions. Belgium and Luxembourg particularly are entirely artificial creations, representing, in one sense, the detritus of modern historical events. Thus the Benelux Union was an effort to transcend the forces that broke up the political unity of the region and to repair and renew its natural linkages.

The origins of the Benelux Union can be dated from 1930, when Belgium, Luxembourg and the Netherlands concluded a convention with Denmark, Norway, Sweden and Finland, setting forth a joint intention to reduce customs autonomy. In 1932 the Belgium-Luxembourg Economic Union and the Netherlands concluded the Convention of Ouchy by which the three governments agreed not to increase reciprocal customs duties, to reduce import duties and to eliminate as soon as possible existing commercial restrictions. In October 1943 the three governments in exile concluded in London an agreement designed to regulate payments and to strengthen economic relations after the war. In September 1944 the three signed a Customs Convention, which was implemented in 1947. In June 1953 the three governments adopted a protocol embracing social as well as economic policies and an additional protocol on commercial policy. Thus the Benelux Treaty of 1958 served primarily to codify agreements that had already been reached.

The governing bodies of the Union are the Committee of Ministers, the Interparliamentary Consultative Council, the Council of the Economic Union, the Economic and Social Advisory Council and the College of Arbitration. The Benelux Court of Justice was established in 1974.

The emergence of the European Community and its full-scale integration by 1992 have diminished the political and economic role of the Benelux Union. Yet, the region deserves study as a fascinating melting pot of Franco-German cultures and as one of the most developed economic zones in Europe.

BELGIUM

BELGIUM

BASIC FACT SHEET

OFFICIAL NAME: Kingdom of Belgium (Koninkrijk België; Royaume de Belgique; Konigreich Belgien)

ABBREVIATION: BE

CAPITAL: Brussels

HEAD OF STATE: King Baudouin (from 1951)

HEAD OF GOVERNMENT: Prime Minister Wilfried Martens (from 1981)

NATURE OF GOVERNMENT: Constitutional monarchy

POPULATION: 9,873,066 (1987)

AREA: 30,540 sq. km. (11,781 sq. mi.)

MAJOR ETHNIC GROUPS: Flemings and Walloons

LANGUAGES: Dutch and French

RELIGION: Roman Catholicism

UNIT OF CURRENCY: Belgian franc

NATIONAL FLAG: Tricolor of black, yellow and red vertical stripes

NATIONAL EMBLEM: A lion rampant on a shield forms the central design of the coat of arms. The lion is in gold emblazoned on a black field. Encircling the shield is the ornate collar of the Order of Leopold. Behind it, golden scepters form a saltire or diagonal cross. A royal gold and red crown tops the design, and a gold and white ribbon decorates it. The national motto in gold letters on a red riband at the base appears in both French and Dutch. The English translation reads, "Union Provides Strength."

NATIONAL ANTHEM: "La Brabançonne" (The Song of Brabant)

NATIONAL HOLIDAYS: National Independence Day (July 21); National Dynasty Day (November 15); Labor Day; January 1; all major Catholic festivals

NATIONAL CALENDAR: Gregorian

PHYSICAL QUALITY OF LIFE INDEX: 96 (on an ascending scale with 100 as the maximum)

DATE OF INDEPENDENCE: October 4, 1830

DATE OF CONSTITUTION: 1981

WEIGHTS & MEASURES: Metric

GEOGRAPHICAL FEATURES

Located in northwestern Europe, Belgium occupies an area of 30,514 sq. km. (11,781 sq. mi.), extending 278 km. (173 mi.) SE to NW and 181 km. (112 mi.) NE to SW. Its borders are formed by the North Sea and the neighboring states of France, West Germany, the Netherlands and Luxembourg. The length of the total border is 1,446 km. (899 mi.) of which that with the Netherlands is 450 km. (280 mi.); that with West Germany, 162 km. (101 mi.); that with Luxembourg, 148 km. (92 mi.); and that with France, 620 km. (385 mi.). The length of the coastline is 66 km. (41 mi.), with a territorial sea limit of 4.8 km. (3 mi.).

Belgium has no natural frontiers. the Belgian Lorraine is a continuation of the French Lorraine and Luxembourg, the high plateau is a continuation of West Germany's Eifel uplands, and the Kempenland continues into the Netherlands, which also shares the coastal polders and deltas of the Schelde and Rhine rivers. The present-day borders are more or less those of the 19th-century Austrian Netherlands, the bishopric of Liège and the duchies of Brabant and Luxembourg. The border with the Netherlands dates from the Peace of Westphalia of 1648, the border with France from the Treaty of Utrecht of 1713 and the border with Luxembourg from that country's independence in 1857. The German-speaking cantons on the eastern border with West Germany were acquired in 1919 as war reparation included in the Treaty of Versailles.

PRINCIPAL TOWNS (Population on December 31, 1983)	
Bruxelles (Brussel, Brussels)	982,434*
Antwerpen (Anvers, Antwerp)	488,425†
Gent (Gand, Ghent)	235,401
Charleroi	213,041
Liège (Luik)	203,065
Brugge (Bruges)	118,146
Namur (Namen)	101,861
Mons (Bergen)	91,216
Mechelen (Malines)	76,670
Kortrijk (Courtrai)	75,592
Oostende (Ostend)	69,039
Hasselt	65,503
* Including Schaerbeek, Anderlecht and other suburbs.	
† Including Deurne and other suburbs.	

The capital is Brussels, which became the administrative as well as the financial and business hub of the country in the 19th century. Close to one-tenth of Belgium's population lives in the capital. Brussels' rival in economic importance and architectural beauty is Antwerp, one of the world's largest ports and the capital of Flemish culture. The port lends a cosmopolitan atmosphere to this otherwise medieval and baroque town. Liège is the capital of Wallonia, at the junction of the Meuse and Ourthe rivers. Ghent, in Flanders, is the scene of some of the bloodiest events in Belgian history. Provincial centers include Mechlin, the ecclesiastical capital; Louvan; Tournai, the oldest town; Bruges; Namur; and Mons. Few provincial cities have more than 100,000 inhabitants.

Almost one-fifth of the country was reclaimed from the North Sea between the eighth and the 13th centuries. Salt marshes became rich plowland behind a lengendary barrier of dikes for which Dante himself expressed admiration in the *Inferno*. A coastal strip of a depth of 48 km. (30 mi.) was thus added to the country; at the same time rivers like the Schelde, which had spread out in broad, shallow deltas, were made navigable.

Belgium can be divided into three topographic zones: the northern lowlands, the central low plateaus and the southern hilly region. It is drained by two rivers, the Meuse and the Schelde, both of which rise in France and flow into the sea through the Netherlands. Most Belgian waterways drain toward the northeast, although a few streams in the eastern Ardennes flow to the Rhine, and the IJzer River cuts through the dunes in West Vlaanderen Province. All waterways are linked through a system of canals to the port of Antwerp.

The western part of the northern lowlands is divided into maritime Flanders (the coastal fringe of beaches, dunes and the belt of polders) and interior Flanders (the gently rising terrain of West Vlaanderen, Oost-Vlaanderen, northern Hainaut and northern Brabant provinces). The coastline is nearly straight, and the beach is white; practically free of pebbles; and stabilized by fences called groins, which reach from the higher beach into the water. Behind the beach lie the dunes and behind them the polders. Access of coastal cities to the sea has been affected by constant silting. Both Ghent and Brugge, once coastal cities, are now reached by canals.

The eastern part of the northern lowlands, called Kempenland, is bounded by the Meuse, Schelde, Demer, Rupel, and Dijle rivers. It consists of sparsely populated, barren heathlands. Industry has developed near the Kempen coalfield because of its proximity to coal, cheap land, the Albert Canal and the port of Antwerp.

The gently undulating central low plateaus include northern and southern areas. The northern section covers southern Brabant and Hainaut provinces; the Plateau of Hesbaye; the mixed region that follows the Demer River Valley; and the Pays de Herve, east of the city of Liège. The region includes Brussels. Midway through the central low plateaus runs the Sambre-Meuse Valley, which divides the northern from the southern section. The valley contains the industrial cities of Mons, Namur, Liège and Charleroi. The southern plateau, including the Entre-Sambre-et-Meuse region, is slightly higher than the northern one and has more forests and pastureland. To the east of this region lies the broken hill country of Condroz Plateau, which sometimes is considered part of the Ardennes. Its northern edge is defined by the Famenne Depression.

The thinly populated southern hilly region consists of the high plateau of the Ardennes and the Belgian Lorraine. The highest points of the region are in the Hautes Fagnes near the German border. Although an important dairying area, one-half of the Ardennes still is forested, as are the scarplands of the Belgian Lorraine at the southern end of the country.

As in other developed countries, water supply is being overburdened by excessive use. Belgium has an annual supply of some 800 million cu. m. (612 million cu. yd.) of groundwater, but three-quarters of the supply originates from the southern half of the country. About 80% of the water is being consumed, and the amount is steadily rising. Water pumped from underground sources accounts for three-quarters of total supplies; the remainder is surface water from rivers, canals, basins and barrages. The Meuse is by far the most important source of surface water, along with its tributaries, the Semois, the Sambre and the Ourthe.

CLIMATE & WEATHER

Climatically, northwestern Belgium belongs to the Flemish oceanic region and the rest of the country to the West European continental region. Regional variations result from the division of the country into uplands and lowlands. Lowland Belgium has a climate similar to that of Britain because of the passage of air depressions, which result from a combination of tropical and polar air masses. They cause characteristic weather features such as changing winds, summer thunderstorms, winter drizzle and overcast skies. the Flemish oceanic region has a mild climate because of the warm waters of the North Atlantic Drift, which is responsible for fogs. The fogs are made worse by industrial pollution. The interior has more extreme summers and winters, while the uplands have more severe frost and more cold and rain. The average temperatures are highest in July and lowest in January. They range from 24.7°C to -0.8°C (76.5°F to 30.6°F) at 100 mi. (328 ft.) above sea level near Brussels in interior Flanders; from 23.3°C to -1.1°C (73.9°F to 30°F) at 8 m. (26 ft.) above sea level in Brugge in maritime Flanders; from 24.4°C to -3°C (75.9°F to 26.6°F) at 39 m. (128 ft.) above sea level in Kempenland; and from 23.8°C to -4.2°C (74.8°F to 24.4°F) at 190 m. (623 ft.) above sea level in the Ardennes.

The arrival of the first frost varies from early October in the Ardennes to the second week of November in Brussels and mid-November in Oostende. Rainfall also varies. The Northwest is relatively dry, varying according to the distance from the coast, while the Southeast is wet, cloudy and variable because of greater altitude and exposure. As a result, north of the Sambre and Meuse rivers, the rainfall averages 510 to 760m. (20 to 30 in.) per year, rising to 1,200m. (47 in.) in the hills of the South. Snow is less frequent than rain, melts quickly and varies in amount from year to year; the coast receives an average of at least five days of snowfall per year, while the Ardennes get up to 50 days.

POPULATION

In 1986 the population of Belgium was estimated at 9,868,000 on the basis of the last census, in 1981, when the population was 9,848,647. The population is expected to reach 9,890,000 by 1990 and 9,925,000 in 2000.

DEMOGRAPHIC INDICATORS

Population: 1987: 9,873,066
Year of last census: 1981
 Males (000): 4,865   Females (000): 5,059
 Sex ratio: 962 males per 1,000 females
Population trends (million)
 1930: 8,129   1960: 9,153   1990: 9,860
 1940: 8,301   1970: 9,690   2000: 9,890
 1950: 8,639   1980: 9,859   2020: 9,854
Population doubling time in years at current rate: Over
    100 years
Hypothetical size of stationary population (million): 9
Assumed year of reaching net reproduction rate of 1:
    2020
Age profile (%)
 0–14: 19.4   30–44: 20.0   60–74: 13.0
 15–29: 23.6   45–59: 18.1   Over 75: 5.9
Median age (years): 35.3
 Age groups in 2000 (000):
 0–14: 1,474   15–64: 6,604   Over 65: 1,581
Density per sq. km.: 324
Annual growth rate (%)
 1950–55: 0.52   1965–70: 0.36   1980–85: 0.04
 1960–65: 0.67   1970–75: 0.33   1985–90: 0.02
                 1975–80: 0.13
Vital statistics
 Crude birth rate 1/1,000: 11.9
 Crude death rate 1/1,000: 11.4
 Dependency (total): 47
 Infant mortality rate 1/1,000: 11
 Child (0–4 years) mortality rate 1/1,000: Insignificant
 Natural increase 1/1,000: -0.1
 Total fertility rate: 1.60
 General fertility rate: 50
 Gross reproduction rate: 0.78
 Marriage rate 1/1,000: 5.8
 Divorce rate 1/1,000: 1.6
 Life expectancy, males (years): 70.1
 Life expectancy, females (years): 76.7
 Average household size: 2.7
 % Illegitimate births: 5.2
Youth
 Youth population 15–24 (000): 1,500
 Youth population in 2000 (000): 1,000

```
┌─────────────────────────────────────────────────┐
│         DEMOGRAPHIC INDICATORS (continued)        │
│ Women                                             │
│  Of childbearing age 15–49 (000): 2,400           │
│  Children per: 1.6                                │
│  % women using contraception: 81                  │
│  % women married 15–19: 7                         │
│ Urban                                             │
│  Urban population (000): 8,818                    │
│  % urban 1965: 93    1985: 96                     │
│  Annual urban growth rate (%)                     │
│  1965–80: 0.5    1980–85: 0.4                     │
│  % urban population in largest city: 14           │
│  % urban population in cities over 500,000: 24    │
│  Number of cities over 500,000: 2                 │
└─────────────────────────────────────────────────┘
```

Belgium is one of the most densely populated and urbanized nations in the world. The average reported density for the country is 836.7 per sq. km. (323.1 per sq. mi.). It reaches 6,149 persons per sq. km. (2,374 persons per sq. mi.) in Brussels, 916 persons per sq. km. (354 persons per sq. mi.) in Antwerp, 662 persons per sq. km. (256 persons per sq. mi.) in Brabant Province, 418 persons per sq. km. (161 persons per sq. mi.) in Flanders and 191 persons per sq. km. (74 persons per sq. mi.) in Wallonia.

Nearly 89% of the population was urban in 1986 compared to 66% in 1960. The largest urban areas are Brussels, Antwerp, Liège, Ghent and Charleroi. However, urbanization data conceal an important feature of urban life. Often, instead of moving to another area, particularly a different language area, Belgians tend to commute by train, car, bus or bicycle. The exodus of Belgians from the rural areas to the big cities has been minimal because of this factor.

In the postwar period, only three provinces—Antwerpen, Brabant and Limburg—have shown an above-average population growth rate, accounting for almost three-quarters of total growth. Even so, within urban centers, as opposed to the suburbs, the population has been declining. Migration to Brussels dropped significantly in the 1970s, while communes of 5,000 to 25,000 people have grown consistently. About one-half of the population live in communes and another 49% live in communities of over 25,000 people.

Belgium shares some demographic similarities with Britain and France. Belgium was the first continental country, after France, to experience a decline in birth rate following industrialization and the widespread use of contraceptives. By 1882 the marital fertility rate had declined to less than 10%. However, since then, the population growth has stabilized. In the 1960s Belgium had the highest death rate and the lowest birth rate of any country in Western Europe. By 1982 it was more or less on a par with other neighboring countries. Between 1975 and 1980 there was a slight increase in the birth rate, but during the next five years it fell again. In 1984 the World Bank estimated that the average annual growth rate was 0.8% during the period 1830–1900, 0.5% during the 1900–70 period and 0.2% during the 1970–82 period. Based on an extrapolation of these figures, the population is expected to reach 10 million by 2010.

Because the number of illegitimate births is relatively low in Belgium, nuptiality has a direct bearing on fertility. In the second half of the 19th century there was a change from late, nonuniversal marriage to earlier, more widespread marriage. Between 1852 and 1856 the mean age for marriage was 28.6 for women and 30.5 for men as opposed to six years younger for each sex in 1960. Similarly, in the mid-19th century three-quarters of the men aged 25 to 30 were single, but in 1970 over three-quarters were married. The population of either sex never having married by age 50 substantially decreased between 1829 and 1947. The proportion of married women between 15 and 50 years most sharply increased in western Belgium, in industrialized provinces and in wealthier areas, In general rural and Catholic Flemish areas had higher rates of marital fertility than Wallonia and Brussels. As a result, Flanders' share of the population increased after 1850 despite higher adult and infant mortality rates. The ratio of population of Flanders to Wallonia was 52 to 48 in 1866, 55 to 45 in 1910, 61 to 39 in 1947 and 64 to 36 after 1970. This changing population ratio remains the basis of heated political debates.

In 1983 the regional mortality rates were 13.4 per 1,000 for Brussels, 12.9 for Wallonia and 10.7 for Flanders. The three regions had almost the same birth rate: 12.1 per 1,000 for Flanders, 11.7 for Wallonia and 11.7 for Brussels. The population is aging in Wallonia because of a falling birth rate, smaller families and a longer life expectancy. In 1981 there were 1.4 million Belgians receiving retirement pensions.

Since World War II Belgium has turned to labor migrants or guest workers to offset the decline in economically active young people, recruiting a first wave from neighboring European countries and a second wave from Turkey and North Africa. After 1974 the immigration of workers stopped officially, but illegal immigrants continued to arrive. Although by 1983 there was a net outflow of guest workers, immigrants continued to bolster the national birth rate. The immigrant birth rate was 19.4 per 1,000 compared to 11.2 for Belgians. In 1977 some 47% of the births in Brussels were to foreign labor. Migrants and their families make up 8.8% of the national population, but there are regional variations: 4.3% in Flanders, 14.5% in Wallonia and 31.3% in Brussels. Wallonia contains one-half of all foreign migrants. To reduce the flow of immigrants to Brussels, a new law was passed in 1985 that gives municipalities in the Greater Brussels region the right to refuse to register new migrants—defined as citizens of non-EEC countries. Six municipalities have taken advantage of the new law.

Belgium is active in the area of women's rights. The consultative Commission for the Condition of Women, attached to the Ministry of Foreign Affairs, advises the government on women's issues. Several other commissions deal with women's education and working conditions. Women are well represented in the Parliament and the cabinet.

ETHNIC COMPOSITION

The original population of Belgium was of Celtic stock. The Celts were virtually wiped out during the Barbarian invasions of the early Christian era. The last tribe to settle in Belgium, during the fourth century, was the Salian Franks, who also constitute the basic racial stock of France. It is generally agreed that there are no ethnic differences between the Dutch- and the French-language groups.

Since the end of World War II, Belgium has acquired a sizable foreign population. In 1983 their numbers were as follows:

Italy	279,700	Algeria	10,796
Morocco	105,133	Portugal	10,482
Turkey	63,587	Zaire	8,575
Spain	58,255		

Of the total number of 878,577 foreigners, 529,265 are from EEC countries, 93,225 from non-EEC countries, 78,397 from Asia, 137,339 from Africa and 17,822 from the Americas. There are also 20,333 refugees and 1,843 stateless persons. Over 63% of the foreigners are between 15 and 64 years, and 32% are less than 14 years old. Most Africans and Asians have remained unintegrated into mainstream Belgian society.

LANGUAGES

Despite ethnic homogeneity, Belgium is characterized by linguistic cleavages that impinge on key areas of national life, as politics and education. The languages spoken in contemporary Belgium are Dutch, French and German. Linguistic and political boundaries do not coincide: German is spoken in the eastern part of the country bordering West Germany; Dutch in the northern area bordering the Netherlands; and French in the southern and western areas bordering France. The provinces of West Vlaanderen, Oost-Vlaanderen, Antwerpen, Limburg and northern Brabant constitute the Dutch-speaking Flanders, while those of Liège, Luxembourg, Hainaut, Namur and southern Brabant constitute the French-speaking Wallonia. The German speakers, using Low German and Franco-Mosellan dialects, live in the eastern cantons of Eupen and

Malmedy, but they account for less than 1% of the population. Only in certain areas, such as Brussels, are minorities given special status in a bilingual context. Technically, Walloons speak any of the Romance-language dialects called Picard, Gaumais and Walloon (itself split into central, western and eastern dialects), and the Flemings speak any of the Germanic dialects called Brabant, Limburg, and West Flemish. Although the Flemish and Walloon dialects are not necessarily mutually intelligible, the broad labels form the standards in the linguistic battles.

Because of French influences and traditions, Parisian French has set the standard for Walloon speakers. On the other hand, Flemish and Brabant dialects dominated Flanders until the 16th century, when the dialects of the Netherlands began to set the standard. The Flemish speakers, cut off from Netherlands by politics, adopted Amsterdam Dutch as their written and spoken language in the mid-19th century. Linguistic purists call the language of the Flemings "Netherlandic" in contrast to the Hollandic or Dutch spoken exclusively in the Netherlands.

A poll conducted by the Catholic University of Louvain in the early 1980s investigated the language preferences of Belgians. Dutch was used frequently in at least one-half of public utilities and private enterprises in Wallonia. English and German also were used, to a lesser extent. In Brussels, French was most popular. In Flanders, French was employed in almost all private enterprises and public utilities and English and German in about 80% of private enterprises and 50% of public utilities. French university students were weaker in Dutch than Dutch-speaking students in French. Only 30% of the enterprises in Wallonia considered the linguistic qualifications of applicants when hiring, compared with 60% in Flanders. In both regions, an average of 20% of jobs in public services required dual language proficiency. These rates contrasted with 90% of private enterprises and 75% of the public services in Brussels. Outside Brussels students could choose which second language to study. In Wallonia, some 50% of the students chose Dutch and 36% chose English, while in Flanders some 91% opted to learn French and 9% English. At the same time, a majority of the 18-year-olds in Wallonia said they would like to study English, while 18-year-olds in Flanders were equally divided between French and English.

The term "Wallonia" was coined in 1844 by the poet Joseph Grandgagnage and applied to the French region after 1850. Those who came to be called Flemings had earlier been variously called Brabanters or Belgians and their language as Low German or Flemish.

Historically, French was the language of the elite during the Spanish, Austrian and French regimes and of the ruling class for many years after independence. It was the language of public administration, judicial proceedings, the church and education. Flemish was commonly used only to speak to servants or at the lowest levels of government and by the local clergy. It was associated with the illiterate masses while French was the language of culture, diplomacy, the civil service and commerce.

As well as dialects, there are Belgian variations of standard French and Dutch along with differences in accents. Since 1864, when Dutch was adopted as the standard by royal decree, there have been numerous, less than successful efforts to coordinate spelling, grammar and pronunciation. Since World War II standard Dutch has gained ground, especially among the younger generation. Nevertheless, archaisms and regional elements have survived in the national speech.

Switching between dialects and the standard language exists on a variety of levels. Dialect is less common in more public and formal situations but very common in rural areas and informal situations, as in speaking to members of one's own family. Social values also play a part in choosing whether to speak the standard or the dialectal form.

Officially, Brussels is a bilingual region, but the proper status for the two languages has posed a sensitive problem. Brussels began as a Flemish city; in 1846 some 67% of the population spoke Flemish dialects or Dutch. By 1910 the percentage of French speakers had risen to 49%, by 1930 to 59% and by 1960 to 85%.

Bilingualism became a political issue in the 1950s as the Flemings began to feel threatened by the increasing Gallicization of Belgian culture. The younger generation of Flemings became Flamingant (militantly conscious of their Flemish heritage). The controversy spilled over into politics, where new loyalties were forged on the basis of language. No language census has been held in Belgium since that of 1947, which found that 51% spoke Dutch, 1% German, 33% French and 15% Dutch and French. To the French-speaking Belgians, linguistic identity is a matter of self-definition, whereas to the Flemings it is a matter of cultural loyalty. For the Flemings language is not only a part of their heritage but also a romantic and mystical matter reflecting communal bonds. To defend their language, the Flemings have obtained the passage of laws defining language affiliations by territoriality—i.e., those who live in Flanders should speak Dutch and those who live in Wallonia should speak French. The question of Brussels has not been settled to anyone's satisfaction.

The political consequences of the language conflicts have been equally divisive. The Christian Socialists are split into Flemish and Walloon factions while the Liberal Party is troubled by a splinter Brussels group, the Bruxellois. The existence of two extremist groups, the Flemish Volksunie and the French Rassemblement Walloon, further complicates matters. The greater fertility of the Flemings gives them a growing superiority in the language struggle.

RELIGIONS

Belgium has no state church, and the Constitution grants state aid to officially recognized religions. These include Catholicism, Anglicanism, Judaism and Islam.

Catholicism is the dominant religion, and the church receives state subsidies for the maintenance of the clergy and the upkeep of church buildings. In return, the church recognizes that religious marriages must be validated by civil ceremonies; gives up the legal right of priests to attack the government; and submits to government approval for certain public activities, such as the creation of new parishes. The church was formally associated with the Christian Bloc until 1945 and before that took openly political stands. There are eight Catholic episcopal sees in Belgium, of which only the archdiocese of Malines-Brussels is bilingual.

The most significant cleavage in religious politics is between Catholics and nonbelievers. The struggle between the two groups follows the fortunes of the church. The oft-made assertion that Catholicism is on the decline has come under reexamination as the church exhibits areas of strength, to the despair of its critics. In Western civilization, Catholicism is not merely a set of dogmas but is also interwoven with the fabric of social and intellectual life and ethical systems and worldviews. It intervenes in lives through its many rites of passage— baptisms, funerals, marriages, Holy Communions and other sacraments. It plays a significant role in private education. It also influences worldviews that inspire politics and economics, perhaps more unconsciously than consciously. As a result, nonbelievers who had believed that they had won the war against the Catholic Church by the middle of the 20th century are finding that the struggle is far from over. Two factors are involved in the church's continued vitality. The first is that there has been a general weakening in secular ideologies and a diminution in their aggressive stances against the church. Second, the church itself is able to adopt new and innovative programs and practices that appeal to those increasingly disillusioned with secular society. As a result, a new Catholicism has emerged that is more ecumenical on the one hand and more individualized on the other. Religious adherence is stronger in Belgium as compared with neighboring countries when measured by increasing enrollment in Catholic schools, increases in pilgrimages to Catholic shrines, a high proportion of those receiving Holy Communion and other sacraments, and a low proportion of those getting divorces. According to Gottfried Cardinal Danneels, Belgian Catholicism is not completely conventional but rather "popular." He noted that prayer and devotion to the Virgin Mary are the most significant features of the new Catholicism in Belgium. It is significant that the last appearances of the Virgin Mary recognized by the Catholic Church occurred in 1932 and 1933 at Beauraing in the province of Namur and Banneaux in the province of Liège.

The major crisis for the church is the scarcity of secular and religious clergy and members of religious orders. In 1978 there were 13,635 priests, or one for every 718 inhabitants. Seminary enrollments and ordinations are also declining. In 1978 there were only 87 students entering seminaries and 51 priests ordained as against 165 priests ordained and 202 students entering seminaries in 1963. As a result, the average age of priests has risen to 55 years, and less than 10% are under 40. Statistics for religious orders are hard to procure. Data for 32 of the 60 female contemplative orders showed that during the 1967–77 period, 157 women entered and 88 left. To offset this trend, the church is ordaining lay deacons, called pastoral workers in Flanders and animators in Wallonia.

Overall there are fewer practicing Catholics than in the past. In the 1950s about 50% of the Catholic population attended Mass regularly. By 1980 this had fallen to 29%. However, other indicators show that the church still exerts a considerable influence on the life events of believers, such as in marriages, baptisms and funerals.

Surprisingly, the second-largest religious group is Sunni Muslim, mostly migrants from Turkey and North Africa. In 1974 Islam was recognized as an official religion, and it receives subsidies for building mosques. The Jewish community has dwindled from a prewar high of 90,000 to 35,000. Protestants and Orthodox Christians are found in scattered communities.

HISTORICAL BACKGROUND

Belgium is named after the Belgae, a Celtic people whose land was conquered by Julius Caesar in 57 B.C. and constituted as Gallia Belgica, a province of the Roman Empire. In the fifth century it was overrun by the Franks and in the eighth century it became a part of the Carolingian Empire. When the empire fell apart on the death of Charlemagne, several independent principalities emerged, including the counties of Flanders, Hainaut and Namur, the duchy of Brabant and the prince-bishopric of Liège. During the following three centuries, the towns of Flanders, particularly Bruges, Ypres and Ghent, became prosperous through trade. In the 15th century, all of the present Benelux countries came under the rule of the Dukes of Burgundy and later, through the marriage of Mary of Burgundy with Archduke (later Emperor) Maximilian, under the Habsburg crown. When Maximilian's grandson Emperor Charles V divided his empire, the Benelux territories were united with Spain under Philip II, whose energies were devoted to the suppression of Protestantism. This led to a Protestant revolt ended only by the Treaty of Westphalia (1648), which granted independence to the northern Protestant provinces. The southern half remained Catholic under Spanish rule.

For the next century and a half, the southern Low Countries became a pawn in Franco-Austrian rivalries. The territory was lost to France until the 1713 Peace of Utrecht, which concluded the War of the Spanish Succession and returned it to the Habsburgs. The country was again occupied by the French during the War of the Austrian Succession (1744) and restored to Austria by the Treaty of Aix-la-Chapelle (1748). Austrian rule became increasingly unpopular under the successors of Maria Theresa, Joseph II and Leopold II. French armies invaded Belgium in 1792 for the third time in a century and annexed it, by the 1797 Treaty of Campo Formio. Belgium was reunited with the Netherlands by the Congress of Vienna, an action that led to widespread discontent and a series of uprisings. The Dutch were compelled to retreat, and on October 4, 1830, Belgium was declared independent and the Congress of Vienna meeting in London a year later recognized its independence. However, William I, king of the United Netherlands, invaded Belgium and was repulsed by the French army. In 1839 he was forced to accept the Treaty of XXIV Articles by which Belgian independence was irrevocably guaranteed under King Leopold of Saxe-Coburg-Gotha. His successor, Leopold II, financed the exploration and settlement of the Congo Basin, thereby laying the foundations of Belgium's colonial empire, which eventually extended to Rwanda and Burundi.

Belgium was invaded by Germany during World Wars I and II and suffered extensive damage. After the capitulation of Germany in 1945, a constitutional crisis rose over the return of King Leopold III. Although 57.7% of the Belgian electorate favored his return, opposition by Socialists and Liberals and a rash of strikes, riots and demonstrations led to his abdication, and in 1951 his son Baudouin I was formally proclaimed king. In 1960 the Belgian Congo was granted independence followed by two years of bitter civil war involving Belgian mercenaries. In 1962 Rwanda and Burundi also were granted independence.

Postwar Fleming-Walloon conflicts have dominated domestic politics. In 1974 Flanders, Wallonia and Brussels became semiautonomous regions within the kingdom, but the continuing rivalry between Dutch-speakers and French-speakers posed serious threats to the country's stability and future.

CONSTITUTION & GOVERNMENT

Belgium is a constitutional monarchy. Enshrined in the 139 articles of the Constitution of 1831 are some of the liberal principles current in the early part of the 19th century. The twenty articles gathered together in Chapter 2 provide constitutional guarantees for all of the classic personal liberties, including freedom of association, press, worship and education. The inviolability of the home and of property, the right of petition and the equality of all in the eyes of the law are also guaranteed. The Constitution provides for a unitary form of government having regional provincial, arrondissement and communal levels of administration.

The original document has proved remarkably durable. By 1971 there had been only two amendments, both concerned with franchise qualifications. In 1893 universal male suffrage with plural voting (based on tax, property and education) was introduced; in 1921 plural voting was eliminated and women were allowed to vote on a limited basis for the first time. It was not until 1948 that full female franchise was established.

In 1971 the Constitution was again amended to accommodate growing Flemish and Walloon pressures for cultural, administrative and economic autonomy. The amendment provided for the creation of three cultural communities: French-speaking, Dutch-speaking and German-speaking. Only the first two were vested with legislative competence. It also established three regions: Flemish, Walloon and Brussels, each having a legislative body composed of elected deputies. The deliberate ambiguity of these provisions has led to political instability, frequently precipitating crises of what came to be known as "immobilism" at the national and regional levels.

In 1980 the Constitution was amended again to address the thorny problem of regionalization. "The Reform of the State," as this amendment came to be known, established community institutions on the one side and regional bodies on the other. The former were to be responsible for cultural and personalized matters, whereas the regional bodies were authorized to deal with economic and social matters. It did not affect the status of Brussels, the most intractable of all issues dividing the Flemings and the Walloons.

The procedures for amending the Constitution are complex. The amendment process begins with a declaration by Parliament of the need for a revision followed by a dissolution of both houses of Parliament, the calling of a general election within 40 days, a two-thirds majority vote by the newly elected members of Parliament in favor of the proposed amendment and the assent of the king. The Constitution may not be amended in time of war or other circumstances, such as a regency.

The Constitution established a monarchical form of government and vested the crown in the descendants of Leopold I in the male line by order of primogeniture, with the perpetual exclusion of women. In default of male heirs, the monarch nominates his successor with the consent of Parliament. If the successor is a minor upon the death of the king, Parliament meets in joint session to arrange for the regency and guardianship of the new king until he reaches 21 years.

The king is the head of state and commander in chief of the armed forces. Technically, executive power is vested in the crown, but it is exercised by the cabinet. Under the Constitution, the king is "irresponsible"—i.e., his acts must be countersigned and covered by a responsible minister. Although the king appoints and dismisses his ministers, the outgoing prime minister must countersign his successor's appointment. One would therefore suppose that the role of the crown in Belgium is purely symbolic. However, the reverse is true. The king plays a key role in the formation and resignation of governments. The "ungovernability" of Belgium since the 1950s has made that role frequently necessary and more difficult, calling for greater royal discretion and sagacity. Since most postwar governments have been coalition governments, the king guides and directs the rounds of consultations before they are formed. After an election, the king generally names an *informateur,* who will conduct negotiations and report to the king. The gravity and length of recent political crises have complicated the king's task, forcing him into more imaginative and interventionist procedures. Once an agreement is reached, the role of the king is over. The king finally appoints the cabinet; the prime minister then makes his policy statement (*déclaration gouvernementale*) to each house and seeks a vote of confidence.

The king must, with the countersignature of his ministers, sign all bills and subordinate legislation of importance. This royal sanction, known as *arrêté royal,* is more of a formality in modern times. The king has no veto and may not act against the advice of the cabinet.

The chief executive organ is the cabinet, or the government, as it is more commonly known in Belgium. The Constitution devotes only six articles (Nos. 86 to 91) to the cabinet. There are no special requirements for a cabinet minister except that he or she be a citizen, either native-born or naturalized, and not a member of the royal family. Ordinarily ministers are drawn from either house of the bicameral Parliament and retain their legislative seats and privileges while serving in the cabinet, although sometimes exceptionally distinguished outsiders may be appointed. The number of ministers varies, depending on the exigencies of coalition politics, but the usual range is from 20 to 30, including the prime minister and two or three vice prime ministers. The ministers are aided by junior ministers, formally known as secretaries of state or simply state secretaries. Since 1970 there has been a requirement for parity between Flemish and Walloon ministers (with the exception of the prime minister). The principle of legislative equality does not apply to junior ministers who, upon appointment, must relinquish their parliamentary seats. When named to the cabinet, political party leaders must give up their party offices.

The cabinet operates with a series of committees. Some governments have set up a *kernkabinett* or inner cabinet, while others have created two inner committees, Comité de Politique Générale and Comité de Coordination Sociale et Économique. The cabinet does not take votes but reaches its decision by consensus. This does not mean unanimity, but those who disagree with the government position must resign.

The cabinet is collectively responsible to Parliament, which has the power of oversight over the executive branch. Cabinet members may participate on their own initiative or at the insistence of Parliament in deliberations of either house but may vote only in the house to which they belong. Generally, the cabinet initiates more bills than the legislature.

In a constitutional sense, the cabinet assumes responsibility for all acts of the king, and countersigns all his acts, except military decisions made by the king in his capacity as commander in chief. The prime minister is only a first among equals, and his actual influence depends on the makeup of a given coalition government. The post of prime minister only gradually came into existence and was not mentioned in the Constitution until 1970. In the early years he was known as the *formateur,* and the king presided over the cabinet from time to time. The prime minister's office was formally established by the Constitutional reform of 1970. He alone may present the government's resignation or propose the dissolution of Parliament. He also signs the cabinet minutes and countersigns the *arrêtés royaux* nominating or dismissing ministers. One of his most important tasks is to mediate interparty disputes in a coalition government. The power of the Belgian prime minister has grown in recent years, but even so is less than that of the British prime minister. Constitutionally, the cabinet is not a collegial body. Although the law requires all *arrêtés royaux* "to be discussed in cabinet," there is no legal provision for collegiate decision-making.

In the years since World War II the formation of governments has evolved into a major political exercise. The multiparty system, under the rule of proportional representation, has contributed to the splintering of the electorate, and no single party has been able to capture outright a majority of the national vote. Thus each government represents a marriage of convenience between or among the two or three major parties arranged through hard bargaining and compromise.

RULERS OF BELGIUM

Regent

Feb.–July 1831	Erasme Surlet de Chokier

Kings

July 1831–Dec. 1865	Leopold I
Dec. 1865–Dec. 1909	Leopold II (*son*)
Dec. 1909–Aug. 1914	Albert (*nephew*) (1st)
(Aug. 1914–Nov. 1918	German occupation)
Nov. 1918–Feb. 1934	Albert (2nd)
Feb. 1934–May 1940	Leopold III (*son*) (1st)
(May 1940–Sept. 1944	German occupation)

Regent

Sept. 1944–July 1950	Prince Charles (*brother*)

Kings

July 1950–July 1951	Leopold III (2nd) (abdicated)
July 1951–	Baudouin (*son*) (Prince Royal Aug. 1950–July 1951)

Prime Ministers

Sept. 1830–Feb. 1831	Charles Rogier (1st)
Feb.–July 1831	Erasme Surlet de Chokier
July 1831–Oct. 1832	Charles de Brouckère
Oct. 1832–Aug. 1834	Charles Rogier (2nd)
Aug. 1834–Aug. 1840	Barthélémy Theux de Meylandt (1st)
Aug. 1840–April 1841	Joseph Lebeau (Cler. P.)
April 1841–June 1845	Jean-Baptiste Nothomb
June 1845–March 1846	Sylvain van de Weyer (Lib. P.)
March 1846–Aug. 1847	Barthélémy Theux de Meylandt (2nd) (Cler. P.)
Aug. 1847–Sept. 1852	Charles Rogier (3rd) (Lib. P.)
Sept. 1852–March 1855	Henri de Brouckère (Lib. P.)
March 1855–Oct. 1857	Pierre de Decker (Mod. Cler. P.)
Oct. 1857–Jan. 1868	Charles Rogier (4th) (Lib. P.)
Jan. 1868–July 1870	Hubert Frère-Orban (1st) (Lib. P.)
July 1870–Dec. 1871	Jules d'Anethan (Cler. P.)
Dec. 1871–Aug. 1874	Barthélémy Theux de Meylandt (3rd) (†) (Cler. P.)
Aug. 1874–June 1878	Jules Malou (1st) (Cler. P.)
June 1878–June 1884	Hubert Frère-Orban (2nd) (Lib. P.)
June–Oct. 1884	Jules Malou (2nd) (Cler. P.)

RULERS OF BELGIUM *(continued)*

Oct. 1884–March 1894	Auguste Beernaert (Mod. Cler. P.)
Feb. 1896–Jan. 1899	Paul de Smet de Nayer (1st) (Cler. P.)
Jan.–Aug. 1899	Julius van den Peereboom (Cler. P.)
Aug. 1899–May 1907	Paul de Smet de Nayer (2nd) (Cler. P.)
May 1907–Jan. 1908	Jules de Trooz (Cler. P.)
Jan. 1908–June 1911	François Schollaert (Cler. P.)
June 1911–Aug. 1914	Charles de Broqueville (1st) (Cler. P.)
(Aug. 1914–Nov. 1918	German occupation)
Nov. 1918	Gerhard Cooreman
Nov. 1918–Nov. 1920	Leon Delacroix
Nov. 1920–Dec. 1921	Henri Carton de Wiart (Cath. P.)
Dec. 1921–May 1925	Georges Theunis (1st) (Cath. P.)
May–June 1925	Alois van der Vyvere (Cath. P.)
June 1925–May 1926	Prosper Poullet (Cath. P.)
May 1926–June 1931	Henri Jaspar (Cath. P.)
June 1931–Oct. 1932	Jules Renkin (Cath. P.)
Oct. 1932–Nov. 1934	Charles de Broqueville (2nd) (Cath. P)
Nov. 1934–March 1935	Georges Theunis (2nd) (Cath. P.)
March 1935–Nov. 1937	Paul van Zeeland (Cath. P.)
Nov. 1937–May 1938	Paul Janson (Lib. P.)
May 1938–Feb. 1939	Paul-Henri Spaak (1st) (Soct. P.)
Feb. 1939–May 1940	Hubert Pierlot (1st) (Cath. P.)
(May 1940–Sept. 1944	German occupation)
Sept. 1944–Feb. 1945	Hubert Pierlot (2nd) (Cath. P.)
Feb. 1945–March 1946	Achille van Acker (1st) (Soct. P.)
March 1946	Paul-Henri Spaak (2nd) (Soct. P.)
March–Aug. 1946	Achille van Acker (2nd) (Soct. P.)
Aug. 1946–March 1947	Camille Huysmans (Soct. P.)
March 1947–Aug. 1949	Paul-Henri Spaak (3rd) (later Secretary-General of NATO) (Soct. P.)

RULERS OF BELGIUM *(continued)*

Aug. 1949–June 1950	Gaston Eyskens (1st) (Chr. Soct. P.)
June–Aug. 1950	Jean Duvieusart (Chr. Soct. P.)
Aug. 1950–Jan. 1952	Joseph Pholien (Chr. Soct. P.)
Jan. 1952–April 1954	Jean van Houtte (Chr. Soct. P.)
April 1954–June 1958	Achille van Acker (3rd) (Soct. P.)
June 1958–April 1961	Gaston Eyskens (2nd) (Chr. Soct. P.)
April 1961–July 1965	T. Lefèvre (coalition)
July 1965–March 1966	P. Harmel (coalition)
March 1966–June 1968	P. van den Boeynants (coalition)
June 1968–Jan. 1973	G. Eyskens (coalition)
Jan. 1973–April 1974	E. Le Burton (coalition)
April 1974–Oct. 1978	L. Tindemans (coalition)
Oct. 1978–April 1979	P. van den Boeynants (coalition)
April 1979–April 1981	W. Martens (coalition)
April 1981–Dec. 1981	M. Eyskens (coalition)
Dec. 1981–	W. Martens (coalition)

CABINET LIST

King	Baudouin I
Prime Minister	Wilfried Martens
Vice Prime Minister	Melchior Wathelet
Vice Prime Minister	Philippe Moureaux
Vice Prime Minister	Jean-Luc Dehaene
Vice Prime Minister	Willy Claes
Vice Prime Minister	Hugo Schiltz
Min. of Cooperation and Development	André Geens
Min. of Education (Francophone)	Yvan Ylieff
Min. of Employment and Labor	Luc Van Den Brande
Min. of Finance	Philippe Maystadt
Min. of Foreign Affairs	Leo Tindemans
Min. of Foreign Trade	Robert Urbain
Min. of Interior, Modernization of Public Services, Science Institutions and Culture	Louis Tobback
Min. of National Defense	Guy Coeme
Min. of Pensions	Alain Van Der Biest
Min. of Post, Telephones and Telegraphs	Freddy Willockx
Min. of Public Functions	Michel Hansenne

CABINET LIST *(continued)*	
Min. of Public Works	Paula d'Hondt-Van Opdenbosch
Min. of Social Affairs	Philippe Busquin
Sec. of State for Brussels Region (Francophone)	Jean-Louis Thys
Sec. of State for Brussels Region (Flemish)	Jef Valkeniers
Sec. of State for Energy	Elie Deworme
Sec. of State for Environment and Social Emancipation	Miet Smet
Sec. of State for European Affairs and Agriculture	Paul De Keersmaeker
Sec. of State for European 1992	Anne-Marie Lizin
Sec. of State for Finance (Small/Medium Enterprises)	Herman Van Rompuy
Sec. of State for Institutional Reform	Norbert De Batselier
Sec. of State for Middle Class and Veterans	Pierre Mainil
Sec. of State for National Education	Luc Van Den Bossche
Sec. of State for Pensions	Leona Detiege
Sec. of State for Public Health and Handicapped Policy	Roger Delizee
Sec. of State for Scientific Policy	Marcel Colla
Governor, National Bank of Belgium	Jean Godeaux

FREEDOM & HUMAN RIGHTS

Belgium is a constitutional monarchy, and respect for human rights is provided for in the Constitution and observed in practice. However, Belgium contends with serious internal pressures resulting from Fleming-Walloon rivalries on the one hand and a large immigrant population on the other. In 1984 and 1985 the country was plagued by a series of terrorist attacks and bombings by the Belgian CCC (Communist Combat Cells), but they ceased with the arrest of CCC leaders in 1986. In recent years there have been some reports of police brutality in arrests and detention of suspects. Aged prisons and discrimination in the treatment of prisoners is another long-standing issue. Prisoners in two large penitentiaries rioted in 1987 because British subjects extradited to Belgium for trial on offenses related to the 1985 Heysel Stadium riot were housed in better facilities. Pretrial detention sometimes is abused, according to human rights activists.

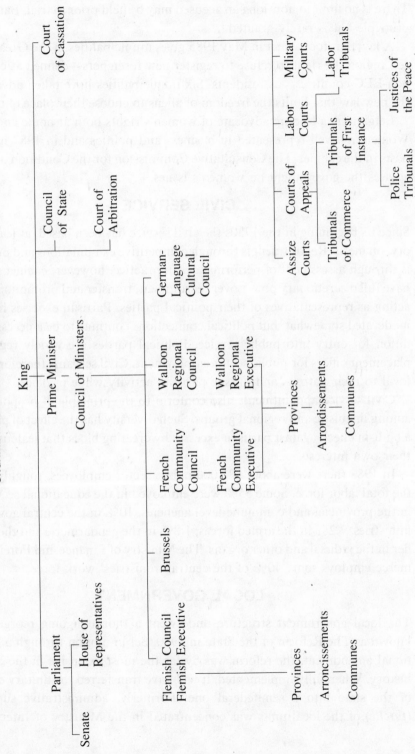

ORGANIZATION OF BELGIAN GOVERNMENT

King

Parliament — Prime Minister — Court of Cassation

Senate

House of Representatives

Council of Ministers

Council of State

Court of Arbitration

Brussels

French Community Council

French Community Executive

Walloon Regional Council

Walloon Regional Executive

German-Language Cultural Council

Flemish Council
Flemish Executive

Provinces

Arrondissements

Communes

Provinces

Arrondissements

Communes

Assize Courts

Courts of Appeals

Labor Courts

Military Courts

Tribunals of Commerce

Tribunals of First Instance

Labor Tribunals

Police Tribunals

Justices of the Peace

There is no limit to how long an accused may be held prior to trial. Bail exists in principle but is rarely granted.

A law that took effect in May 1985 gives municipalities in the Greater Brussels region the right to refuse to register new foreigners—defined as citizens of non-EEC countries—as residents. Six municipalities have taken advantage of the new law that limits the freedom of aliens to choose their place of residence.

Belgium is a leading advocate of women's rights both at home and abroad. Women are well represented in business and politics and in 1987 held three posts in the cabinet. The Consultative Commission for the Condition of Women advises the government on women's issues.

CIVIL SERVICE

Since its beginning in the 1930s the civil service has been based, at least in theory, on merit. Recruitment is through competitive examinations and promotion is through assessment of performance. In practice, however, cabinet members have full discretionary power over recruitment, transfer and promotion, usually acting as representatives of their political parties. Partisan excesses have been moderated somewhat, but political connections continue to be a necessary condition for entry into public service. Political parties are widely regarded as placement offices for public sector employment. Civil servants therefore remain loyal to their patrons and pursue partisan activity while in office.

Civil service appointments also conform to the principle of proportionality among linguistic and regional groups. Such diversity has the effect of producing a built-in check against partisan excesses by creating blocs that jealously guard their own interests.

In 1983 there were about 885,000 public sector employees, roughly 21% of the total labor force. Some 55% were employed in the educational sector, 23% in the provincial and commune-level agencies, 10% in the central government ministries, 7.2% in the armed forces, 1.8% in the gendarmerie and the remainder in the judicial and other organs. The Ministry of Finance and Foreign Commerce employs some 40% of the central ministries' work force.

LOCAL GOVERNMENT

The local government structure underwent a thoroughgoing reorganization known as The Reform of the State in 1980. Set in motion through a constitutional amendment, the reform was by far the most extensive in the country's history. When fully implemented, it will have transferred the unitary character of the state into a semifederal one. Formerly, administrative supervision (*tutelle*) of the local units was concentrated in the Ministry of Interior. This power has now been given to the regional authorities, sidestepping the complicated question of the status of Brussels.

In the Reform of the State, the term "community" refers to a linguistic and cultural unit. Thus the Flemish community comprises all the Dutch-speaking people in the four traditionally Flemish provinces of Antwerpen, Limburg, Oost-Vlaanderen and West Vlaanderen, and the Leuven and Halle-Vilvoorde arrondissements in the province of Brabant. The French community embraces French-speakers in the provinces of Hainaut, Liège, Luxembourg, Namur and the arrondissement of Nivelles in Brabant. Brussels is bilingual.

The term "region" is a geographical and territorial concept applicable to Flanders and Wallonia but not Brussels. The 1980 law did not formally recognize Brussels as a third region on a par with either Wallonia or Flanders. Thus legislative competence is granted only to the community and regional bodies of Flanders and Wallonia.

The concept of regionalization was established by the constitutional amendment of 1971 that introduced the concepts of cultural communities and regions. It laid a framework for the recognition of three language-based communities—Dutch, French and German—each with its own separate cultural council. However, legislative competence was granted only to the Dutch-speaking and French-speaking councils, which were to be composed of their respective linguistic groups in Parliament. These councils were to be empowered to legislate over cultural matters, education and labor relations. The composition and power of the council for the German-speaking community were to be determined by separate legislation.

The 1971 amendment also paved the way for the creation of three regional legislatures composed of elected representatives in Flanders, Wallonia and Brussels. These bodies were to have the power to legislate on social and economic matters. Unlike the cultural councils that had begun to function on a limited scope after the early 1970s, the regional legislatures were slow to evolve because of continuing partisan discord over the details of reorganization. A comprehensive package on regionalization was devised in 1977 by a four-party coalition cabinet led by Leo Tindemans. Known as the Community Pact or Egmont Pact, it called for the establishment, among other things, of elective regional councils with additional powers to deal with so-called personalized matters—health care, social assistance, family and youth policy, education and vocational training. The Egmont Pact, however, was stillborn, as the Council of State determined that it violated certain provisions of the Constitution. This led to a declaration by Parliament in 1973 proposing a revision of the Constitution to enable the reforms. In July 1980 the Constitution was amended and two enabling bills were enacted—the Special Law on Institutional Reforms and the Ordinary Law on Institutional Reforms.

Under these reforms the cultural councils were renamed community councils and their administrative arms became executives. Both Flanders and Wallonia were granted identical councils and executives. However, the Flemings opted for one rather than two seperate institutions for the community and the region. Thus the Flemish Council and the Flemish Executive were to exercise the powers vested in the regional council and the regional executive in Flanders. On the other hand, the French-speakers chose to have two separate institutions—the French Community Council and the French Executive Council and the Walloon Regional Council and the Walloon Regional Executive.

The community councils are composed of the directly elected members of both houses of Parliament, including those elected in Brussels. The latter, however, are not allowed to vote on any regional matters. The councils are empowered to deal with cultural and personalized matters as called for by the Egmont Pact. They share legislative initiative with the executives, who are collectively accountable to the councils. One of the executive members must be from Brussels but has no vote on regional issues. The executives are headed by chairmen who are elected by and from among the executive members in proportion to the partisan composition of the regional councils. Election of the chairman as well as decision-making are by consensus. Decrees of the councils or the executives have the force of parliamentary laws and are not subject to countermand by the central government.

Regional councils are composed of the same representatives as the community councils. They have wide legislative powers over social and economic matters, including land development, urban renewal, industrial location, environmental protection, rural development, irrigation, flood control, housing, hydraulic engineering, exploitation of natural resources, regional planning and economic development, aid to industrial and agricultural enterprises, tourism, energy, employment, research and supervision of provincial and communal authorities.

The activities of the community and regional institutions are financed under the terms of the Ordinary Law on Institutional Reforms of 1980. The financial resources include rebates on national taxes equal to about 10% of the national budget.

Jurisdictional disputes involving community and regional bodies are to be resolved by a court of arbitration, under an enabling bill of 1983. Such conflicts may also be handled by the Council of State and the Court of Cassation. Public claims for damages against the communal or regional bodies are settled by a conciliation committee chaired by the prime minister.

German-speaking Belgians are also given community status under the Constitution. This council is composed of twenty-five elected members who hold office for four years. The council is competent to deal with cultural and personalized matters but not economic and social ones. Because it has no executive, council decisions are carried out by the national ministries.

The status of Brussels as a third region remains a frozen issue. Instead of a regional council, Brussels has a metropolitan council elected by proportional representation and an executive whose members are divided equally between Dutch-speaking and French-speaking communities. The council does not have legislative competence, and its competence is limited to matters having little or no political implications. On matters where the council is unable to reach a consensus decision, the national government's authority prevails. In cultural, educational and health matters, the Flemish and French councils have extraterritorial jurisdiction in Brussels.

Below the regions are the nine provinces and the 43 arrondissements. Four provinces are Flemish, four French, and the province of Brabant—the home province of Brussels—is bilingual. Each province has a legislative council composed of 50 to 90 members directly elected for four-year terms. The council meets for a total of 15 days annually, extendable for a maximum of four weeks. Its principal duties are to elect its executive body, called the permanent committee, elect senators to Parliament, endorse the provincial budget and supervise communes. The six-member permanent committee functions as the executive when the council is not in session. The chief provincial executive officer is the governor, who is formally appointed by the king on life tenure based on the recommendation of the cabinet and the advice of the Minister of Interior (whose full title is Minister of Interior, Modernization of Public Services, Science Institutions and Culture). The governor serves as the principal agent and liaison of the central government in provincial administration and is responsible for the execution of the provincial council's decisions. The governor has the right to suspend the decisions of the permanent committee and to invoke the intervention of the central government. The governor's principal assistant is the provincial registrar.

Brabant is in a category by itself. It has two separate community councils: one for the Dutch-speaking arrondissements of Halle-Vilvoorde and Leuven and one for the French-speaking arrondissement of Nivelles. These councils have jurisdiction only in cultural and personalized matters. Social and economic matters are regulated by the central government, represented by a governor. There is also a vice governor, who enjoys the same legal and administrative status as the governor and who serves as the commissioner or chief executive officer of the 19 communes of Brussels and the six Flemish communities bordering on Brussels.

The arrondissement is a subdivision of the province and has no self-governing status. It is headed by a commissioner who is responsible for general administration, law and order, and communal matters (for communes having fewer than 5,000 inhabitants).

The lowest administrative subdivision is the commune, also called municipality or borough. Since 1976 there have been only 580 communes, in contrast to 2,300 before that year. The reduction was achieved through mergers in an attempt to reduce administrative costs.

Each commune has a direct elected council of from nine to 55 councillors, serving six-year terms. The council adopts regulations in accordance with the community, regional and provincial guidelines in the areas of finance, social affairs, police, culture, education, roads and licenses, subject to the scrutiny of the community and regional and provincial authorities, who have the right to suspend or annul the council's decisions. The administrative arm of the communal council is an executive composed of a burgomaster (or mayor) and two to 10 aldermen. The burgomaster is appointed by the central government from among the communal council members. He is assisted by a functionary called the commune secretary. The Constitution provides for the agglomeration of communes in the larger cities. There are five such agglomerations, in Brussels, Antwerp, Liège, Ghent and Charleroi. Communal expenditure is financed from its share in the *fonds des communes,* direct state and provincial aid and additional levies or taxes, such as dog and vehicle licenses.

AREA AND POPULATION				
		area		popu-lation
Prov-inces	**Capitals**	sq. km.	sq. mi.	(1983 est.)
Antwerp	Antwerp	2,867	1,107	1,577,000
Brabant	Brussels	3,358	1,297	2,221,000
East Flanders	Ghent	2,982	1,151	1,332,000
Hainaut	Mons	3,787	1,462	1,292,000
Liège	Liège	3,862	1,491	996,000
Limburg	Hasselt	2,422	935	724,000
Luxembourg	Arlon	4,441	1,715	223,000
Namur	Namur	3,665	1,415	409,000
West Flanders	Brugge	3,134	1,210	1,084,000
TOTAL		30,518	11,783	9,858,000

Source: Official government figures.

FOREIGN POLICY

Several articles of the Constitution refer to foreign policy and place its conduct in the hands of the crown rather than Parliament. The king signs treaties, declares war, makes peace and leads the armed forces in war. However, he may not cede, add to, or exchange any Belgian territory without consent of Parliament. Executive agreements, which have taken the place of formal treaties, may be concluded by officials or ministers without parliamentary approval if they do not involve measures over which Parliament has constitutional oversight. Since 1980 the community councils are empowered by Article 59 of the Constitution to conduct international cooperation in relation to cultural and personalizable matters.

The Foreign Ministry, earlier called the Department of Foreign Affairs, was one of the original five departments of state. For some time the ministry was combined with the Ministry of Foreign Trade and Development. The most powerful official in the ministry is the secretary-general. The third important agency in the conduct of foreign affairs is Parliament, through its foreign affairs committees in the House and the Senate.

Since the end of World War II Belgium has abandoned its former policy of passive neutrality and opted for a policy of active international cooperation. This core principle of Belgian foreign relations was stated by Leo Tindemans, former foreign minister and prime minister, in 1982: ". . . a small country, because of its powerlessness to act alone in a world that has no rules of law, is forced to resort to alliances, in which it enjoys certain prerogatives. If it avails itself of those rights, if it defines its own position and upholds it consistently, it can carry weight in the decision-making process. In other words, a small country acting alone—which, outside of alliances, leads to impotence—may, within such alliances, exert a certain amount of influence."

Alliances are thus the key to Belgian foreign policy. It is a founding member of the United Nations, NATO, the Benelux Union, the EEC and all of the major Western European regional organizations. Significantly, the EEC, NATO and the Benelux Union are headquartered in Brussels. Belgium has given consistently strong support to NATO, and one of its best-known statesmen, Paul Spaak, served as its secretary-general during the critical 1957–61 period.

In the early 1980s Belgium maintained diplomatic relations with more than 140 countries, 124 of which had resident embassies or legations in Brussels. A number of foreign ambassadors stationed in Brussels are accredited to Luxembourg and the Netherlands as well.

Belgian foreign relations have a marked economic slant, and they are closest with West Germany, France and the Netherlands, the three most important trading partners, both as suppliers and customers. With Luxembourg, relations are conducted virtually on a domestic rather than a foreign level, and trade statistics of the Belgium Luxembourg Economic Union (BLEU) are reported together.

Relations with the United States are close and friendly for historical reasons. The United States plays a significant role in the Belgian economy, accounting for 39% of all foreign investments, compared to 34% for all EEC members. Political relations, however, have often sagged under the pressure of some sensitive issues, such as technology transfer to Communist and certain terrorist countries, such as Libya. Another irritation concerned the stationing of intermediate-range cruise missiles on Belgian soil. According to Tindemans: "In the best of circumstances, there will always remain a difference in sensitivity, reactions and interests between the Europeans and the United States. . . . The average citizen on both continents tends to see [NATO] as a sort of protectorate; the United States as protector calls the tune and defines policies, which have to be followed in essence, willy-nilly, by the Europeans. This wrong image brings difficulties on both sides. In America, a reluctance to underwrite a defense guarantee for the benefit of ungrateful protégés, and in Europe the sense of not being masters of their own fate, of being brought into disputes that are not entirely their own. . . ." Tindemans maintained that ". . . military power is not and cannot be good in itself; it is only a somewhat repellent necessity. While for most Americans problems have to be solved by direct action (and, if they are not, Washington is somehow deemed not to be entirely equal to its task), the Europeans tend to circumvent problems, to negotiate them away, or simply to try to outlive them."

Belgium regards Africa as the gateway into the Third World. The new emphasis on diversifying Belgian relations with the African states of the entire continent represents a shift from Belgium's previous policy based on special relationship to Zaire, Rwanda and Burundi, its former colonies. In the 1960s the three former colonies absorbed nearly all of the bilateral aid from Belgium. By 1967 the share was reduced to 78%, remaining at that level for many years before declining to 48% in 1980. Another 23% went to other African countries, 15% to Asia and 5% to Latin America.

PARLIAMENT

The Belgian legislature is a bicameral Parliament consisting of the House of Representatives and the Senate. According to the Constitution, the powers of Parliament include enactment of bills, oversight of the executive and impeachment of ministers. The House of Representatives (the lower house) has 212 deputies directly elected for four-year terms. The Senate has 181 members. The king's sons or the princes in the line of succession are senators by right at age 18, although they are not allowed to vote or speak in chamber until they are 25. The members of both houses are representatives of their respective electoral constituencies, representatives of their language group and, finally, representatives of the whole Belgian nation.

Despite its constitutional supremacy, parliamentary powers have slowly eroded in the postwar era, making it little more than a *chambre d'enregistrement,* a rubber-stamping body. Most of its former legislative initiatives have shifted to the executive branch because of the increasing volume of legislation, increasing state intervention in all spheres of national life and the highly technical nature of legislative drafting. Under the Constitution, Parliament may waive its supervisory functions in certain circumstances and for specified periods so the executive may deal expeditiously with certain problems. This is done under provisions for delegation of special powers. The major function of Parliament is as an electoral college from which the executive emerges, although the election results are often so ambiguous that coalition politics almost seem to run counter to the verdict of the electorate.

Although bicameralism was originally introduced to mitigate the "dangers of radicalism in the lower house," the Senate's composition has come to be a carbon copy of that chamber. As such, the Senate has ceased to be a politically independent revising body, and there is no conflict between the two houses. The Reform of the State finally deprived the Senate of its *raison d'être* and left it with no further role except in revision of the Constitution and election of community and regional assemblies.

Parliament is elected for four years, but the king may dissolve it earlier. In recent years, few legislatures have served their full terms. Most dissolutions occur because of dissensions in the ruling coalition.

Each house is chaired by a president and two vice presidents elected from among its members. Both chambers convene in October for a regular session that lasts a total of 60 to 80 days, extending through the following September. With certain exceptions, the two chambers have equal powers. All legislation must be passed in the same form by both chambers. Financial appropriations acts must pass through both houses, although they must be initiated in the lower house first. The two houses meet in joint session to decide issues relating to succession to the throne. The lower chamber is generally considered to be superior body and the true representative of the people. Thus governments seek first a vote of confidence in the lower house, which alone may impeach ministers before the Court of Cassation.

Each house has a bureau made up of the president, vice president and secretaries, plus the chairmen of recognized political groups. In the Senate there is a college of quaestors responsible for financial and administrative matters. The parliamentary agenda is fixed by another body, called the Conference of Presidents, composed of the president, the vice president and the president and one member of each political group. The prime minister or his representative may attend the conference proceedings. The proposed order of business is ratified by the House of Representatives.

The two houses have 13 permanent committees each session, the most important being Foreign Affairs, Defense, Economic Affairs, Finance, Legal Affairs, Social Affairs and Employment in the lower house and Social Affairs, Economic Affairs, Finance, Infrastructure, Internal Policy, Legal Affairs, External Relations and Defense in the upper house. Both houses are also divided into sections—six in the House of Representatives (External Relations, Internal Affairs, Economic, Social, Cultural and Infrastructure) and four in the Senate (Social, External Affairs, Internal Affairs and Economic Affairs). These sections are subparliaments that consider bills up to the final stage, which takes place only in plenary sessions. Special committees may be set up to deal with particular bills. As well as working on bills, committees exercise control functions. They may hear statements from ministers. Committee membership is proportional. The author of a bill under consideration may always attend, as may one member per group not represented on the committee. Any member of either house may make written statements to a committee.

Parliamentary control over the executive is exercised through several means. Members may table written questions, and these are to be answered within 15 days. There is also an hour-long questions time on Wednesdays. In addition, members may table interpellations, which permit longer questions and a debate on the minister's reply and a motion of no confidence. Speaking time always is limited, except for ministers and *rapporteurs*. The longest allocation is 30 minutes in the general debate on a bill. The author of an interpellation may speak for 15 minutes.

With the exception of special powers bills, which are issued only in times of war or national emergencies, laws fall into three categories: framework laws, program laws and planning laws. Framework laws or *lois cadres* are very general laws or directives that allow the government wide powers to implement them. Program laws and planning laws deal with infrastructure plans. These three kinds of laws have increased the powers of the executive beyond the intentions of the framers of the Constitution. Government bills are called *projets de loi* and have priority in Parliament. Private members' bills are called *propositions de loi* and often are refused even at first reading. Almost all government bills are passed. Before a bill is submitted to Parliament, it is referred to the legislative section of the Council of State for an advisory opinion. Although supposedly nonbinding, this opinion often decides the fate of a bill. All bills except government bills must have the support of at least five members and a favorable vote on its first reading. At this stage the president may refer the bill to a committee, where ministers or their representatives appear to defend their proposals. Each committee reports via a *rapporteur*. The committee reports to the full house with its proposed changes, if any. To forestall adverse effects on government operations, the principal budget bills must be voted out by December 25 and lesser appropriation bills by March 30. Each house follows the same procedure and must agree to the same text. No provisions exists to break deadlocks, nor even for conciliation by the houses. However, in practice the Senate gives way.

Article 131 provides for amendments to the Constitution. The procedure begins with a *déclaration de revision,* which is considered by Parliament and then voted upon. Once a declaration is accepted, Parliament is automatically dissolved and new elections are held. The new Parliament may then amend the Constitution by a two-thirds majority.

Since 1981 Belgians may vote on reaching age 18. However, candidates must be at least 25. Since 1893 voting has been compulsory, and fines of BF1 to BF25 may be levied on those who do not comply. As a result, the percentage of nonvoters has never been higher than 10% in recent years. Voters must vote in their communes but can do so in certain cases by proxy. Campaigns are spirited and highly competitive, lasting up to 40 days. Radio and television time is made available to candidates of all parties. Transportation to the polls is provided free of charge for all political parties. Generally, elections are fair and free of violence or fraud.

Elections take place every six years for communal councils and every four years for Parliament. New elections must be held within 40 days of the dissolution of Parliament or provincial councils.

Article 44(2) lays down that elections to the House of Representatives shall take place "by a system of proportional representation." However, the Belgian system is not completely proportional, since according to Article 48 of the Constitution, the arrondissements and the provinces are the basic units of electoral law. The Belgian system is a list system. The law allows lists to form alliances within a given province or provinces and permits a second distribution of seats for lists that have obtained for the House of Representatives 66% of the electoral quotient in the arrondissement and 33% of the quotient for the Senate.

In each election the parties may table lists supported by at least 200 to 500 electors or three members of Parliament. The list may contain candidates up to the maximum number of seats to be filled and an equal number of candidates as *suppléants,* or alternates. The order of the candidacy is determined by the party. Voters may cast their vote in four ways: (1) for the list as a whole, (2) for a given candidate by preference, (3) for a given candidate and alternate by preference and (4) for an alternate by preference. Each list then receives a number of lists in accordance with the d'Hondt system, invented by a Belgian professor in the 19th century. The distribution of seats and the election of candidates are arrived at using the following four steps:

1. In each arrondissement an electoral divisor is calculated as follows:

$$\frac{\text{Total votes cast}}{\text{Seats to be filled}} = A$$

For each party an electoral quotient is calculated:

$$\frac{\text{Votes cast for that list}}{A} = B$$

The first distribution allocates a seat or seats to each list having an electoral quotient of one or more.

2. Those lists with an electoral quotient of 0.66 in an arrondissement may participate in the second division. For each qualified list, the number of votes cast in the *whole province* is divided successively by the number of seats already won plus one, then two, then three and so on. The quotients thus obtained are classified in descending order.

3. To allocate the second distribution of seats to an arrondissement, local quotients are calculated for each list as follows:

$$\frac{\text{Electoral quotient in the arrondissement}}{\text{First distribution of seats plus } 1, 2, \ldots}$$

4. The final stage is the election of candidates to fill the seats allocated to each list. A list quotient is calculated:

$$\frac{\text{Votes obtained}}{\text{Seats to be filled} + 1}$$

Preference votes usually upset the list order at the middle, not at the top, which is rarely affected.

The Senate was originally designed as an apolitical body to represent regional interests. But over the years the Senate has become as politicized as the House of Representatives. The political composition of the House of Representatives thus rarely varies from that of the Senate.

The most recent reform of the Senate—Article 56 of the Constitution adopted in 1921—imposed higher qualifications for senators, including better education, and professional experience. None of these qualifications is imposed on provincial senators (introduced in 1893) and co-opted senators (introduced in 1921). There are three categories of senators:

CHAMBER OF REPRESENTATIVES			
General election, December 13, 1987			
	Votes	%	Seats
CVP	1,194,687	19.45	43
PS	961,429	15.66	40
SP	913,975	14.88	32
PVV	709,137	11.55	25
PRL	577,897	9.41	23
PSC	491,839	8.01	19
VU	494,229	8.05	16
Agalev	275,307	4.48	6
Ecolo	157,985	2.57	3
FDF	71,340	1.16	3
Vlaams Blok	116,410	1.90	2
PCB/KPB	51,074	0.83	0
PvdA/PTB	45,162	0.74	0
Others	80,741	1.31	0
Total	6,141,212	100.00	212

SENATE			
General election, December 13, 1987			
	Votes	%	Seats
CVP	1,169,539	19.20	22
PS	958,760	15.74	20
SP	896,114	14.71	17
PRL	564,221	9.26	12
PVV	686,608	11.27	11
PSC	474,708	7.79	9
VU	494,432	8.12	8
Agalev	299,051	4.91	3
Ecolo	168,381	2.76	2
Vlaams Blok	122,925	2.02	1
FDF	77,596	1.27	1
PCB/KPB	52,322	0.86	0
PvdA/PTB	43,381	0.71	0
Others	84,522	1.39	0
Total	6,092,560	100.00	106

In addition, the Senate has 50 members elected by provincial councils, a further 25 co-opted by the elected members and one senator by right, the heir to the throne.

- Directly elected senators, of whom there are 106 elected on the basis of universal suffrage.

- Provincial senators, of whom there are 50. Each province is allocated at least three senators—one senator for 200,000 inhabitants and one for any excess over 125,000. These senators may not belong to the provincial councils that elect them and must not have been members of the council in the two years preceding their election.
- Co-opted senators, of whom there are 25. They are elected by the other senators. The number of co-opted senators must always be half the number of provincial senators. The Constitution provides for a fourth category of ascriptive senators who are sons of the reigning king or princes of the royal family.

POLITICAL PARTIES

Political parties play a central role not only in political life but in social and economic life as well. They constitute an extensive network of linkage between the elites and the masses and as distributors of the spoils of office. Parties provide cultural, medical, educational and social services for their members and function as extrastate organizations performing vital intermediary services between the state and the masses. As such they receive state subsidies in proportion to the number of deputies and senators in Parliament.

Unlike many other countries with a proportional system of representation, there is no great multiplicity of parties in Belgium. The three traditional political groupings—the Social Christians, the Socialists and the Liberals—have remained dominant in this century. In the 1981 general elections these three groupings accounted for 80% of the lower parliamentary chamber seats and 71% of the national vote. These percentages have declined by only about 10 points since 1960. Because coalition cabinets have been the rule in postwar Belgium, compromise and harmony guided their policies. The premium was on pragmatism and cooperation rather than on radical departures from tradition. As a result, immobilism has been elevated to a national ideology, emphasizing concerted action rather than solutions to complex problems.

The party system changed radically in the 1960s with the emergence of the language issue. Community parties with French and Flemish labels succeeded in winning 20% of the vote in 1971, but their support dwindled to 14% in 1981 and 9% in 1985. The conflict also forced the traditional parties to split into two separate linguistic parties.

In 1945 the Christian Bloc, as it was then called, renamed itself the Social Christian Party (Parti Social Chrétien, PSC) in an effort to move away from its strict confessional appeal and to recast itself as a mass organization. Dating back to the 1880s, the Social Christians played a leading role in coalition governments for all but a few years (1946–47 and 1954–58). In 1968 the party formally split into two separate parties, one French (PSC) and the other Flemish, the Christian People's Party (Christelijke Volkspartij, CVP). However, there still is close liaison between them and they share the same party headquarters in Brussels. Each has an identical organization, with the national congress as the supreme policy-making body. In practice, the most powerful party organ is the bureau, chaired by the party president. The bureau members are elected by the national council chosen earlier by the national congress. The congress, council and bureau organs also exist at the provincial, arrondissement and communal levels. Interparty cooperation at the national level is maintained through a liaison group. For the purpose of coalition-building, the two parties present themselves as a single CVP/PSC bloc. As the larger of the two, the CVP has provided all the prime ministers since 1968 except in 1978–79, when the prime minister was from the PSC.

The CVP is the dominant party in Flanders, where it draws its support from the farmers and workers, the middle classes and Catholics. Trying to broaden its appeal, the CVP has adopted more or less centrist positions on many issues. The diversity of socioeconomic positions to which it appealed had its predictable consequence in the creation of left-wing and right-wing schisms within both the CVP and the PSC.

In Wallonia the PSC is a minority party overshadowed by the Socialists. The PSC's electoral base is spread evenly among farmers, workers, the middle class and Catholics. For years the PSC was given to more internal schisms than the CVP. On its right wing is the aggressively probusiness Political Center for Independents and Christian Cadres, and on its left wing the Christian Democrats and the Federation of Belgian Christian Trade Unions.

Both the CVP and the PSC remain committed to "Christian Personalism" and "Economy in the Service of Man." They favor policies of social responsibility and justice, a high level of employment, free enterprise, cuts in public spending, reduced state intervention, adequate family allowances and social services. On education and abortion they side with the church, and in foreign policy they strongly support NATO.

The CVP has the largest membership organizations in Belgium, claiming 186,000 members drawn from the heavily Catholic grass roots. At the local level, it is supported by a number of powerful organizations, such as the Farmers League, the Christian Workers Movement and the National Association of Christian Middle Classes, all with strong ties to the Catholic Church.

The Belgian Socialist Party (Francophone: Parti Socialiste Belge, PSB/ Flemish: Belgische Socialistische Partij, BSP) is the youngest of the three traditional parties. The BSP/PSB was founded in 1885 as the Belgian Workers' Party and rose to prominence by winning universal male suffrage. By 1920 it had displaced the Liberals as the second largest political party. It adopted the name Socialist in 1944. Except for 15 days in 1946, when they formed an all-Socialist government, the Socialists have been junior coalition partners with the other two traditional parties. As the language crisis heated up, the party split into the BSP in Flanders and the PSB in Wallonia. Separate organizations are maintained at national, provincial, arrondissement and communal levels. Regional federations enjoy relative autonomy, especially in the selection of parliamentary candidates. The highest party organ is the national congress, whose policy-making functions are performed by a general council between sessions. The executive arm of the congress and the council is the bureau. The Walloon Socialists are more left of center than the Flemish socialists because of a long history of political activism among workers in the region's older industrial cities.

Democratic socialism based on a strong social welfare system and a humanized free-enterprise economy remains the goal of both the PSB and the BSP. The Socialist platform also calls for economic planning, state employment, a more equitable tax system and the nationalization of key industrial sectors. On social issues it advocates legalized abortion, better health care and housing, and environmental and consumer protection. In foreign affairs the Socialists support NATO but not nuclear deployment in Europe.

The Liberal Reform Party (Parti Reformateur Liberal, PRL)/Freedom and Progress Party (Partij voor Vrijheid en Vooruitgang, PVV). The Liberals were the first organized political party in Belgium, and, along with the Catholics, dominated the political scene from 1830 to 1894, when the Socialists wrested a place for themselves. The original Liberals were strongly anticlerical and pro-enterprise and individual rights. The anticlerical bias was toned down in the 1950s, and in 1962 the party adopted its present name. The linguistic and communal conflicts eventually caught up with the Liberals, and the party split up into two autonomous wings. The Dutch-speaking wing retained its old name, while the French-speaking one adopted a new one.

The right-of-center Liberals advocate greater private enterprise, leaner bureaucracy and state enterprise, reduced public spending, rational management of the Social Security system, restraint on trade union pressures and a stronger defense. Like the Social Christians and the Socialists, the Liberals have separate national organizations but collaborated for coalition bargaining. The national organizations are the congress, the bureau (for the PRL), the political committee (for the PVV) and the executive. The two parties share the services of a political research institute, the Paul Hymans Study Center.

Minor parties include:

People's Union (Volksunie, VU), founded in 1954 to promote Flemish nationalism and maximum autonomy for Flanders. The party's political base is mostly in Flanders, with a small following in Brussels. Although unabashedly nationalist, the VU is a centrist party, eschewing extremism. It advocates a federal state, fiscal discipline and economic policies more equitable for Flanders.

Walloon Rally (Rassemblement Wallon, RW) is the Walloon mirror image of the VU. The RW was formed in 1968 to counter the rise of Flemish nationalism. By 1971 it had become the second-largest party in Wallonia. It is more a regional party than a linguistic one and it differs from the Socialists in its greater appeal to practicing Catholics. In foreign affairs it stands left of center, demanding reduced defense spending and dismantling of nuclear arms.

The Democratic Front of Francophones (Front Démocratique des Francophones, FDF) was founded in 1964 as a party of French-speakers in Brussels supporting the claims of the capital city as a third region on par with the other two. It is closely allied to the RW and generally wins about a third of the Brussels vote.

Communist Party of Belgium (Kommunistische Partij van Belgie, KPB; Parti Communiste de Belgique, PCB) was formed in 1921 as a breakaway from the Workers' Party. In 1985 it won only 1.18% of the vote, and it is voiceless in the legislatures at any level. Its strongest support comes from the industrial cities of Wallonia.

Democratic Union for the Respect of Labor (Union Démocratique pour le Respect du Travail/Respekt voor Arbeid en Democratie, UDRT/RAD), founded in 1978, is an antitax protest party. It won one seat in 1985.

Flemish Bloc (Vlaamsche Blok, VLBL) was founded in 1978 as an extremist breakaway offshoot of Volksunie.

Ecological Party (Ecolo-Agalev), the «green» party founded in 1978, has been able to capture a greater share of the vote at each election since then.

Party of German-Speaking Belgians (Partei der Deutschsprachigen Belgier, PDB).

Party of Labor (Partij der van Arbeid, PvA) is a Marxist-Leninist Party more radical than the Communist Party.

A multitude of other nonpolitical groups exert significant influence on policy-making and national debates. These include the Catholic Church, the Société Générale de Belgique, the Farmers' League, the Belgian Agricultural Alliance and the three major trade unions.

ECONOMY

Belgium's advanced industrial economy is based essentially on the manufacture of finished and semifinished goods from imported materials and the provision of financial and transportation services associated with its location at the cross-roads of Western Europe. Its highly efficient and intensive agriculture provides about 80% of its domestic needs. Given its small domestic market and lack of significant natural resources, the country is extremely dependent on foreign trade and highly sensitive to developments in international markets. This accounts for Belgium's ardent support of free trade and European integration.

The major problems of the Belgian economy system from its antiquated industrial structure, increasingly buffeted by aggressive competition; high labor costs, which have discouraged investment; the growing public sector deficits caused, at least partially, by the burden of an extensive social welfare system; and excessive foreign borrowing.

The global recession of 1979 shook the economy to its core. The balance of payments showed a record deficit in 1981, and economic growth was stagnant. Regional rivalries and lack of coherent economic leadership impeded recovery until 1982, when Parliament granted the government emergency powers to enact measures to restore corporate competitiveness, control public expenditures and boost employment. As part of its program, the government suspended wage indexation and devalued the Belgian franc, actions that had until then been considered politically risky. By the mid-1980s the economy had largely recovered sufficiently, although further progress depended on export demand and continued fiscal and wage restraints. Labor is still restive over wage concessions that have not produced significant gains in employment. The constitutional process of regionalization also portends additional strains on the economy. The decreasing sense of solidarity between the regions as economic difficulties mounted has generated pressures for further devolution of economic powers.

In one sense, Belgium is trying to adjust to the dislocations caused by the demise of its industrial power based on coal mining and heavy industry along the Sambre-Meuse and Wallonia. In the late 19th century, Wallonia was one of the most prosperous regions on the continent. Belgium recovered quickly from the ravages of world wars, partly as a result of the benefits of cheap raw materials from the Congo. However, by the late 1940s the aging industrial structure was unable to compete with newer producers, and growth slowed to below the European average in the 1950s. The economy was saved by making the successful transition to a transnational European economy and the rollback in trade restrictions. Investments in the 1960s were particularly strong and approached one-quarter of the GNP. The economy remained buoyant until the mid-1970s, growing by 5% annually between 1960 and 1973. Unemployment reached a low of 1.6% in 1965, and foreign workers had to be imported to fill vacancies in industry.

Meanwhile, a virtual revolution had taken place in industrial geography. With the replacement of coal by petroleum, the Walloon areas had lost their predominance and the Brussels-Antwerp axis had become the country's economic core. The rise of port-based manufacturing, particularly in steel and petrochemicals, had fostered employment throughout Oost-Vlaanderen. The expansion of the modern service industries—the tertiary sector—had also favored the Flemish region. Rising standards of living conducive to the intensification of financial and commercial activities, banking, transportation and research had brought more than one-half of the labor force into the tertiary sector.

Flanders also benefited from state support and foreign investment. It has a large supply of youthful labor released from agriculture. In establishing a new industrial base in the region, Flanders received 50% more in state subsidies and grants than Wallonia during the 1960s. New industries shunned the antiquated infrastructure and more militant labor of the traditional industrial areas and preferred the new industrial parks in Flanders. Foreign investment in Flanders between 1959 and 1969 accounted for 80% of all investment. Thus industry was bifurcated into two sectors: a modern sector in Flanders, comprising automobiles, electric and electronic products, synthetic fibers and petroleum derivatives, controlled by large multinationals; and a traditional sector in Wallonia, controlled by a small group of powerful domestic holding companies. Both sectors became increasingly dependent on neighboring countries both as marketing outlets and as sources of new technology. Even greater internationalization of the economy led to the decline in interregional trade, making the country more vulnerable to exogenous developments.

The uninterrupted boom since 1958 was finally broken by the shocks of the two oil crises in 1973 and 1979, and the resultant global recession had severe repercussions for the small export-oriented economy. External competitiveness declined as the changing conditions of international demand brought internal structural weaknesses to the fore. By 1983 the economic indicators were all bleak: The GNP growth rate had dwindled to 0.5%, inflation had risen to 7.7% and 14% of the labor force was out of work.

A number of adverse factors, some economic and some political, had contributed to precipitate the crisis. The traditional industrial activities had a drag effect on the economy. Second, the traditional export markets were themselves experiencing slow growth, and Belgian exporters did not take advantage of new and rapidly growing markets, such as in the Middle East. Third, wages, pensions and Social Security had been protected from inflation by indexation. Although indexation took the heat off of labor relations, it led to a surge in real costs, far in excess of productivity gains.

Official economic policy also was complicated by linguistic and regional rivalries, which became intense at about this time. As industrial loci shifted to Flanders and as coalition governments tried to balance regional interests, political considerations prevailed over economic ones. Government support for the ailing Walloon steel industry became a divisive political issue that virtually immobilized economic development. Almost all economic policy issues soon degenerates into debates on an equitable distribution of economic aid and the relative fiscal burdens borne by the Flemish and Walloon regions. Major public projects for one region had to be matched by funds for the other, even if they were not viable. Ideological differences between political parties on social welfare and state intervention also have hindered policy-making. In coalition governments, the Flemish parties represented the right and center while the Socialists represented the left, and the mediation of these interests resulted in economic compromises that failed to resolve the issues. With conflicting mandates, these governments often adopted stopgap measures and partial reforms. The formation of Wilfried Martens' fifth government (Martens V) in December 1981 finally broke this vicious circle. The center-right coalition of Social Christians and Liberals adopted an economic policy line directed toward an improvement in the entrepreneurial climate. Their initiatives included a restrictive wage policy, devaluation of the Belgian franc, generous corporate tax concessions and reduced social expenditures. At the same time, the government defused some of the opposition to these unpopular measures by yielding to pressures for greater regionalization.

Although the Belgian economy is a free-enterprise one, the state is an active partner in economic development. Particularly after 1959, the state began to support industrial expansion and conversion by granting financial aid and fiscal benefits to foreign and domestic companies. The 1970s brought the state a more active role in the restructuring of declining industries and the creation of a mixed economy. State intervention, however, remains discreet and has been primarily felt only in the weak sectors, with the exception of transportation and communication services, which are traditional state domains. Because economic organization is based on "concertation," government intervention in private industry is made only after consultation with bodies representing employee associations, trade unions and financial interests.

The first step toward an enhanced government role in the economy was the establishment of the Economic Planning Bureau within the Ministry of Economic Affairs in 1959. Its function is to formulate, after appropriate study, broad guidelines for economic expansion, including public investment, in the form of five-year plans. In 1962 its terms of reference were broadened to include regional planning, but with The Reform of the State, this responsibility has been devolved to the regions. The bureau is composed of representatives from the government, private industry, scientific research bodies and trade unions. A royal decree in 1967 included private holding companies in the planning process.

Each year private holding companies are required to submit to the bureau details of their planned investments within the country and abroad. From these data, the bureau makes important medium- and long-term economic forecasts and draws up a summary of market conditions and trends.

Industrial policy and planning objectives rest on the tenets of the Claes Plan, after Willy Claes, who was minister of economic affairs in 1958. The Claes Plan called for the modernization of declining industries, specialization and diversification of product lines, stimulation of technological research and export promotion. Special attention was given to small- and medium-sized enterprises. To promote industrial and commercial investment, the government has relied extensively on fiscal and financial incentives in the form of interest-free subsidies, capital or employment grants, tax relief and government guarantees on commercial loans. The scope of the first investment incentive law, the General Expansion Act of 1959, was broad and nationwide, while the Regional Expansion Act of 1970 provided incentives to specified development zones where economic problems are the most acute as well as new and dynamic sectors outside these zones. Depending on the project location, grant incentives in development zones could not exceed 15 or 20% of investment after tax. For implementing the incentives legislation, the government established the Fund for Economic Expansion and Regional Reconversion, capitalized through certain tax receipts. The approved development zones are in the Kempenland coal mining area in Wallonia and the Westhoek area in Flanders.

Since 1982 the government, guided by a more market-oriented approach, has gradually been replacing subsidies and other incentives by fiscal measures, such as reduction of corporate taxes from 48 to 45% and increased deductions for investment outlays. In addition, coordination centers and employment zones known as T-Zones were developed to encourage foreign investment. T-Zones were created in geographically delimited areas reserved for the establishment of new industrial or service facilities in advanced data processing, software technology, microelectronics, office automation, robotics, telecommunications and biotechnology. Facilities within these zones are exempt for corporate income tax for 10 years. Coordination centers offer a similar exemption, but their purpose is to encourage development of corporate research. Both domestic and foreign firms are qualified to avail themselves of these benefits if they meet specified size and employment conditions. In addition, foreign executives and researchers are exempt from work permit requirements and contributions to domestic Social Security.

The financial arm of the government's industrial policy is the National Investment Company (NIM/SNI), created in 1962. In addition to providing public venture capital for setting up, reorganizing or expanding both Belgian and foreign companies, NIM/SNI conducts all operations in financing and real estate, buys stock in private companies, and even creates public companies when the private sector fails to take desirable initiatives. The NIM/SNI is assisted by many specialized affiliates, such as the Belgian Company for International Investments, and the Office for Industrial Promotion. There are also three regional investment companies created by the Law of Economic Reorientation of 1978.

In 1982 the total value of NMI/SNI investments totaled BF15.5 billion, excluding restructuring operations. By 1983 it had a significant stake in more than 120 firms employing 22,000 persons, more than three-fifths of them export-oriented. Some 85% are small- to medium-sized companies unable to obtain bank capital, and slightly more than one-half are new companies.

A key element in the government's economic policy is regionalization. This has led to the establishment of separate ministerial departments for each region and, after the constitutional reform of 1970, to the recognition of regions as economic entities through the creation of regional economic councils and regional development corporations. The councils are vested with consultative powers as well as the development of regional plans to be forwarded to the Economic Planning Bureau. They receive annual endowments under the budget of the Ministry of Economic Affairs, equal amounts being allocated to Flanders and Wallonia.

The seven regional development corporations, one each for Brussels and Wallonia and five for Flanders, were set up in the form of public utilities. Each received an annual government subsidy. The regional councils set up in Flanders and Wallonia in 1980 are also empowered to deal with aid to industrial enterprises and investment promotion. However, the central government still sets the standards in these areas, and the regional council merely implement the decisions made at the national level. Moreover, the fiscal potential is severely limited at the regional level, estimated at less than 15% of the national budget.

Belgium is a member of the Development Assistance Committee (DAC) of the OECD. The volume of Belgian development aid is well above the average for DAC countries. Moreover, the grant element in the aid program averaged 95%. Development aid is administered by the Administration Générale de la Coopération au Développement. A major part of the aid is in the form of bilateral project aid, for which funds are derived from the net yield of the National

Lottery. Bilateral aid also includes technical assistance in the form of experts, military technical assistance, cultural scholarships, subsidies to Belgian universities and food aid. Belgium also extends soft loans to developing countries. Since 1977 no interest has been charged to the least developed countries, and for others the interest rate is only 2%. The term of maturity is 30 years, with no repayments or interest for the first 10 years. In principle these loans are to be used to purchase Belgian-made capital goods.

PRINCIPAL ECONOMIC INDICATORS, 1985

Gross National Product: $79.9 billion
GNP per capita: $8,100
GNP average annual growth rate: 1.1%
GNP per capita average annual
  growth rate: 2.8% (1965–85)
Average annual rate of inflation: 5.9% (1980–85)
Consumer Price Index: 1980=100
  All items: 142.33
Wholesale Price Index: 123.14
Average annual growth rate (1980–85)
  Public consumption: 0.2%
  Private consumption: 0.2%
  Gross domestic investment: -4.2%

PUBLIC FINANCE

Government fiscal policy is to stimulate the economy through public expenditure. In the process of doing so, it has incurred large deficits. The country has witnessed a great expansion of public services over the past few decades, as a result of which the state share of expenditure has represented an ever larger share of the GNP. By 1983 current and capital expenditures of the central government and local authorities represented 63.2% of the GNP compared to 48.5% for the EEC as a whole.

The formulation of the Belgian annual budget is a major political drama, given the vested interests of the various ministries and pressure groups. The budget is drawn up by the Ministry of Finance and Foreign Commerce based on the short-term forecasts made by the Ministry of Economic Affairs and the medium-term framework elaborated by the Economic Planning Bureau. The link between the plan and the budget is not so close as in France. Final approval of the budget is by Parliament, and sometimes passage may be delayed well into the fiscal year (which coincides with the calendar year). In general, the Ministry of the Budget handles central government expenditures while the Ministry of

---

GROSS DOMESTIC PRODUCT

GDP nominal (national currency): 4.812 trillion
GDP real (national currency): 3.604 trillion
GDP per capita ($): 8,121
Average annual growth rate of GDP, 1980–85: 0.6%

GDP by type of expenditure (%)
  Consumption
    Private: 66
    Government: 18
  Gross domestic investment: 16
  Gross domestic saving: 20

  Foreign trade
    Exports: 75
    Imports: -75

Cost components of GDP (%)
  Net indirect taxes: 10
  Consumption of fixed capital: 9
  Compensation of employees: 56
  Net operating surplus: 25

Sectoral origin of GDP
  Primary
    Agriculture: 2
    Mining: 1

  Secondary
    Manufacturing: 24
    Construction: 5
    Public utilities: 4
  Tertiary
    Transportation and communications: 8
    Trade: 20
    Finance: 5
    Other services: 20
    Government: 8

Average annual sectoral growth rate, 1980–86

  Agriculture: 3.1
  Industry: 0.5
  Manufacturing: 1.6
  Services: 1.1

Finance and Foreign Commerce handles revenue collections and the Treasury manages the public debt.

Not included in the budget are the capital expenditures of subordinate authorities—the communes and the provincial and regional authorities—and of various organizations such as subsidized housing associations and public investment institutions that operate within the framework of government programs.

BALANCE OF PAYMENTS, 1985 ($ million)

Current account balance: 671
Merchandise exports: 47,052
Merchandise imports: -47,534
Trade balance: -482
Other goods, services & income: 33,477
Other goods, services & income: -31,669
Other goods, services & income net: 1,808
Private unrequited transfers: -129
Official unrequited transfers: -527
Capital other than reserves: -265
Net errors & omissions: -56
Total (lines 1, 10 + 11): 350
Counterpart items: 505
Total (lines 12 + 13): 855
Liabilities constituting
    foreign authorities reserves: -426
Total change in reserves: -429

BUDGET (million Belgian francs)

Revenue	1986*	1987†
Direct taxation	885,250	901,834
Customs and excise	102,197	102,478
VAT, stamp, registration and similar duties	371,330	388,145
Other current taxes	65,503	56,494
Capital revenues	4,562	3,640
Total	1,428,842	1,452,591

Expenditure	1986†	1987†
Government departments	831,115	750,421
Public debt	428,642	403,393
Pensions	180,895	181,305
Education and cultural services	288,584	281,280
Defense	109,298	105,625
Other expenditure	134,400	133,124
Total	1,972,934	1,855,148

*Provisional.
†Official estimates.

The increased burden of public sector expenditures is both a cause and a result of the economic crises. Given the country's extensive social welfare system

---

CENTRAL GOVERNMENT EXPENDITURES, 1985
(% of total expenditures)

Defense: 5.1
Education: 12.9
Health: 1.7
Housing, Social Security, welfare: 42.7
Economic services: 13.8
Other: 23.8
Total expenditures as % of GNP: 55.9
Overall surplus or deficit as % of GNP: -10.6

CENTRAL GOVERNMENT REVENUES
(% of total current revenues)

Taxes on income, profit and capital gain: 38.0
Social Security contributions: 32.9
Domestic taxes on goods and services: 23.1
Taxes on international trade and transactions: 0
Other taxes: 1.9
Current nontax revenue: 4.1
Total current revenue as % of GNP: 45.8
Government consumption as % of GNP: 17
Annual growth rate of government consumption: 0.2
(1980–85)

---

and indexation practices, public expenditures rise in reverse proportion to economic growth and in direct proportion to unemployment. Lack of political procedures for arbitrating among the conflicting demands of various social groups and regions has also promoted expenditure growth.

In the central government budget for 1982, for example, the largest expenditure categories after wages, goods and services were Social Security transfers to individuals—including expenditures on unemployment benefits and employment programs—at 26% of the total budget and interest on the public debt at 17%. Over the 1970–82 period, expenditures on unemployment benefits and employment programs increased the most rapidly of all current expenditures, at an annual rate of 37.1%, followed by interest on the public debt, at 19.7%. Other expenditures that increased twice as rapidly as the GNP included rent and interest subsidies, loans to private companies and buying stock in enterprises. Only three categories showed a slower growth rate than the GNP: investments, transfers to foreign countries and subsidies to enterprises.

In an effort to keep pace with expenditures, taxes and Social Security contributions rose from 26% of the GNP to 40% in 1983. Excessive taxation led to widespread tax evasion, "black" (unreported) work and flight of capital. A Catholic University of Louvain economist estimated that the underground economy represented more than 15.2% of the official GNP in 1980. The government introduced a Social Security card in 1984 to curb black work and other fraud.

Since tax revenues did not keep pace with expenditures, public sector deficit and borrowing requirements rose steeply after 1975. By 1981 borrowing by central and local authorities rose to 16.2% of the GNP, the highest level in the OECD. Concurrently, the combined debt of central and local government authorities surged from 57.5% of the GNP in 1974 to 88% in 1981 and 96% in 1984.

Throughout the 1960s and early 1970s the public sector deficit was basically covered by medium- and long-term security issues on the Belgian market. Since 1977, the National Bank of Belgium also financed a modest share. Commencing in 1978, the authorities have increasingly relied on foreign borrowing. Foreign currency debt ballooned from zero in 1978 to BF942 billion in 1984. External financing reflected growing strains on the domestic money market. Since 1979 the public sector deficit has exceeded the domestic lending capacity, whereas it accounted for only one-half of this capacity in 1973. In 1982 and 1983 more than one-third of the deficit was financed by borrowing abroad. Although originally the deficit was viewed as a temporary phenomenon, its economic consequences are bound to overshadow the Belgian economy for the whole decade of the 1980s.

Granted emergency powers by Parliament, the Martens V coalition government set to reduce the central government deficit to the EEC average of 7.5% by 1985. The already excessive burden of taxation limited room for maneuvering on the tax front, although the government raised the value-added tax (VAT) substantially in 1982. The government succeeded in reducing the deficit by 3% in real terms in 1983, but lower tax receipts and interest charges continued inexorably to push up the deficit. The cabinet then ratified a new three-year austerity program that called for salary reductions in the public sector, further wage restraint, reform of the Social Security system, tax concessions for modernizing industrial plants and a requirement that excess company profits be invested in Belgium or made available without interest to the Treasury. The program sought to elicit equal sacrifices by all and leave room for growth in employment. On the expenditure side, the government sought to maintain investment at its 1984 level.

The financial state of the subordinated, or local, authorities is not much rosier. Between 1977 and 1982 the communes experienced a 10.6% annual growth in expenditures compared with a 7.8% increase in income. Communes used to depend for 30% of their ordinary revenue on the Municipal Fund, financed by the Ministry of the Interior and Public Office. Since 1979 these subventions have declined while the obligations have expanded as a result of wage increases, and social services were expanded. Altogether 527 of 589 communes had deficits in their budgets in mid-1983, adding up to a total debt of BF400 billion. As the problem of municipal indebtedness became politicized and threatened to interfere with the regional economic programs, the Martens V coalition decided to extend the reform of public finance to the local level. It used its decree powers to rule that from 1988 the budgets of the municipalities would have to be balanced; otherwise, the central government would be able to intervene to step up revenue collection or cut expenditures. To this end, the 6% limit on the municipal surtax was abolished in 1983.

As the 1984 correction program had not succeeded in stanching the public deficit—the Treasury borrowing requirement still amounted to 12% of the GDP in 1985—a new correction program was launched in 1986 that aimed to cut borrowing requirements to 8% by 1987. It calls for a greater effort to manage public expenditures on a case-by-case basis by cutting nonessential items. Social expenditures are reduced by 10%. Transfers to households are reduced by BF82 billion, transfers to local authorities by BF16 billion and subsidies to public enterprises by BF16 billion. The procurement of goods and services by the central government is reduced by BF25 billion. When fully implemented, the program could reduce the general government borrowing requirement to 5.5% of the GNP by 1989, when the public debt/GNP ratio is expected to stabilize. Until then Belgium's massive public debt will constitute a major policy constraint.

CURRENCY & BANKING

The National Bank of Belgium (NBB), the nation's central bank, is charged with the conduct of the government's monetary policy. Its principal tool is the management of interest rates. Interest rate policy sought to maintain international financial equilibrium and defend the exchange rate while attempting to keep interest rates as low as possible to promote economic activity. The Treasury, even though it clears interest rates on its security issues with the NBB, exerts a heavy influence on these rates because of the volume of its offerings.

Belgium is a developed free-market economy in which the dominant sector is private.

The national currency unit is the Belgian franc (BF) or franc belge. The Belgian franc is divided into 100 centimes (centiemen). Coins are issued in denominations of 1, 5, 10, 20 and 250 francs and notes in denominations of 50, 100, 500, 1,000 and 5,000 francs.

Belgium actively pursues and encourages foreign investment and treats foreign investors on a par with its own nationals. There are no restrictions on the

THE BELGIAN FRANC-DOLLAR EXCHANGE RATES, 1982–87					
1982	1983	1984	1985	1986	1987
46.920	55.640	63.080	50.360	40.410	305.270

import of foreign capital. Many firms entering the market, however, resort to BLEU sources for financing.

Several factors contribute to a healthy investment climate: stable political and social conditions, a high standard of living, a qualified and productive labor force, a stable and developed financial infrastructure and little government interference. Brussels' role as headquarters of the EEC and NATO are additional attractions.

Foreign investment is led by the United States, which is represented by over 1,200 companies with a total investment of over $5 billion. About 40% of the companies are engaged in trading and sales, some 30% in manufacturing and the remainder in services, including shipping, advertising, transportation, insurance, accounting and hotel and food chains.

The establishment of a business enterprise in Belgium does not require specific government authorization. For certain business activities, however, the government is empowered to screen applications for new investment. Also, foreign companies with permanent operations in the country must have a responsible tax guarantor.

The Royal Decree of 1976 regulates the form and content of the annual accounts of large enterprises; companies are no longer required to publish annual accounts in the *Annexe au Moniteur Belge* but have to deposit them with the registry of the commercial court. Income and profits accruing to aliens may be repatriated without limitations and are guaranteed by the Institut Belgo-Luxembourgeois du Change (IBLC). Such a guarantee is not, however, granted if the funds are to be repatriated within a three-year period.

Belgium has enacted several laws designed to promote industrial investment and applicable to both foreign and domestic investors. The first, the General Aid Law of 1959, was followed by the 1970 Regional Expansion Law and the Law of Economic Reorientation of 1978. These incentives include interest rate subsidies, capital premiums, exemption from registration tax and real-property tax, accelerated depreciation and government guarantees of loan repayments.

Typically, interest rates are determined by adjusting the discount rate and the rediscount ceiling. There are no minimum reserve requirements, although at times the government used minimum portfolio holding requirements on securities and public bonds to avoid raising rates on securities. Quantitative restrictions are generally avoided for fear of a strong deflationary effect on overall domestic demand.

Because the balance of payments deficits in recent years have depleted liquidity, public deficit is financed by monetary creation through advances from the NBB and the Securities Regulation Fund, a parastatal body that regulates markets for government securities. In the early 1980s, nearly two-thirds of the deficit was financed through increases in the money supply, even though this contributed to the inflation. Since 1979, the margin for maneuver in monetary policy has been narrowed because of the upward trend in international rates and the weakness of the Belgian franc. Belgian interest rates are among the highest in OECD countries, depressing investment and increasing the burden of repayments. A strong currency policy has also contributed to high interest rates. The devaluation of the Belgian franc was avoided until 1982 to prevent higher import costs of raw materials and energy from being added to the price of exports.

Since 1922 Belgium and Luxembourg have been linked in the Belgium-Luxembourg Economic Union. There is no exchange control between the two countries, and the Belgian franc is on a par with the Luxembourg franc. In turn, the two countries participate together with other EEC members, excluding Britain, in the exchange rate and intervention mechanism of the European Monetary System (EMS), established in March 1979 as an outgrowth of the "snake" arrangement instituted in 1972 after the breakdown of the Bretton Woods system. Under the arrangement, Belgium maintains the spot exchange rates between the Belgian franc and the other EEC currencies within margins of 2.5% above or below the bilateral central rates.

Another feature of the Belgian exchange rate is the existence of two spot markets: the official or regulated market and the free market. Most current transactions are settled in the official market, where only official banks may carry out foreign exchange transactions. Speculative capital flows through the free market, thus taking the pressure off the currency and deterring the flight of capital. In 1982, the spread between the two rates reached a record 16%. The two-tiered system has helped to reduce the intervention of the NBB in the foreign exchange market.

The persistent weakness of the Belgian franc has adversely affected its monetary relations with its neighbors. When the Belgian franc was devalued in 1982, Luxembourg only reluctantly followed suit. To avoid such actions in the future, Luxembourg established its own Monetary Institute in 1983 to take over some of the powers formerly exercised by the NBB. Belgium also had to agree to calculate Luxembourg's balance of payments surplus separately in reporting the trade statistics of BLEU.

The financial sector is controlled by a small number of powerful holding companies through pyramiding of stockholdings and interlocking directorates. Bank holding companies, particularly the Société Générale de Belgique, have extensive holdings in major industries. Banking has one of the greatest concentration ratios in the economy. This has created an economic system in which there is less competition than in most other OECD countries. The domination of the Société Générale de Belgique by financiers rather than industrialists has imparted a conservative bias to both sectors and reduced venture capital to a secondary role.

Brussels has maintained its dominance in banking in this century. It is the ninth-largest financial center in the world and where two major clearing systems and an important reinsurance market are located. Until 1960 the banking system was composed of three kinds of specialized institutions. Deposit banks handled short-term business credit and international payments traffic; private savings banks catered to personal banking; and semiofficial credit institutions granted medium- and long-term credit to sectors insufficiently covered by the private sector banks. These lines of demarcation have become blurred since the 1960s.

The Banking Reform Law of 1935, as amended in 1967, recognized commercial banks as investment banks, thereby removing the prohibition on holding company bonds. Banks were permitted to hold shares for a limited period when underwriting public issues. Eventually, the Mammouth Law of 1975 widened the scope of the private savings banks and placed them, along with deposit banks, under the supervision of the Banking Commission, an autonomous body charged with implementation of banking legislation. It regulates the percentage of deposits that a bank must invest in government securities and issues an annual consolidated report on the financial position of the banks it oversees.

Even after 1975, private savings banks, of which there are 30, have remained loyal to their primary function as family bankers. Nearly four-fifths of their credit business is in mortgages and home loans. Mergers have reduced the number of Belgian-controlled commercial banks from 67 in 1960 to 28 in 1983. Within this group, three banks—Société Générale de Banque, Banque Bruxelles Lambert and Kredietbank—account for almost three-quarters of the total deposits of the commercial banking sector and over one-half of the loans extended to private borrowers. Foreign banks number 29, composed predominantly of multinational banks. In addition, some 25 banks have branches in Belgium but are under foreign jurisdiction. Foreign banking presence is bolstered by Brussels' role as the capital of the EEC and the lack of discriminatory practices against foreign banks under Belgian banking law. Belgium also maintains a strong banking presence abroad. Foreign transactions of Belgian banks represented 48% of their total balance sheet in 1981. Belgian banks have an extensive network of foreign branches and representatives.

Belgians have been pioneers in many innovative areas of banking, such as electronic transfer of funds (ETF) and the formation of banking consortia. Automatic check cashing facilities are located even at gas stations, supermarkets and retail outlets.

The main competition for commercial banks is from semipublic credit organizations in specialized areas as agriculture, mortgage and industry. In terms of deposits, they are as large as the banking sector, and important sources for medium- and long-term industrial loans and government bonds. They enjoy an advantage over commercial banks in that they are not subject to the same kind of government regulation. Other deposit-taking institutions include the Postal Check Service and a cooperative system of over 800 savings and agricultural credit organizations—the so-called Raiffeisen banks—under the sponsorship of the Belgische Boerenbond.

Belgians are good savers. Even with austerity measures in full force in the early 1980s, they saved at an average annual rate of 17%, and these savings largely underpinned the banking system for many decades. Nevertheless, significant funds are being diverted to Luxembourg and into various forms of investments.

The Belgian stock market is small by international standards, with only about 200 active issues. Barring a few dozen major securities, the majority represents small- and medium-sized companies whose limited-share capital is owned by a few families. To orient domestic savings to risk capital, a royal decree was issued in 1982 on share investments. Since then, the Belgian Bourse has witnessed a surge of activity, growing by 130% in two years to an all-time high of BF137.6 billion in 1983. The law made certain types of share purchases tax deductible and also allowed tax deductions for corporations on capital raised on the stock market.

The use of credit cards is becoming more widespread, and many banks offer cards that permit check-cashing privileges. However, these cards are less popular with older and more conservative Belgians.

In 1984 the market price of industrial shares (with 1980 = 100) was 154, the call money rate 9.47% and the yield of long-term government bonds 11.98%.

FINANCIAL INDICATORS, 1986

International reserves minus gold: $5.538 billion
  SDRs: 342 million
  Reserve position in IMF: 565
  Foreign exchange: $4.630 billion
Gold (million fine troy oz): 34.18

FINANCIAL INDICATORS, 1986 *(continued)*

Ratio of external debt to total reserves: 0

Central bank
Assets:
  Foreign assets: 77.9%
  Claims on government: 22.1%
  Claims on bank: 0
  Claims on private sector: 0
Liabilities:
  Reserve money: 100.6%
  Government deposits: 0
  Foreign liabilities: 0
  Capital accounts: 0

Money supply
Stock in billion national currency: 962.5
M^1 per capita: 97,430
U.S. liabilities to: $8.726 billion
U.S. claims on: $8.483 billion

Private banks
Assets:
  Loans to government: 24.9%
  Loans to private sector: 15.6%
  Reserves: 0.3%
  Foreign assets: 59.3%
Liabilities: deposits, of which BF7.87 trillion
  Demand deposits: 7.5%
  Savings deposits: 15%
  Government deposits: 0
  Foreign liabilities: 72.3%

GROWTH PROFILE (Annual Growth Rates, %)

Population, 1985–2000: 0.1
Crude birth rate, 1985–90: 12.1
Crude death rate, 1985–90: 12.2
Urban population, 1980–85: 0.4
Labor force, 1985–2000: 0.1
GNP, 1975–85:
GNP per capita, 1965–85: 2.8
GDP, 1980–85: 0.7
Inflation, 1980–85: 5.9
Agriculture, 1980–85: 3.4
Industry, 1980–85: 0.6
Manufacturing, 1980–85: 1.6
Services, 1980–85: 0.6
Money holdings, 1980–85: 6.2
Manufacturing earnings per employee, 1980–85: 3.0
Energy production, 1980–85: 14.5
Energy consumption, 1980–85: -1.3

GROWTH PROFILE
(Annual Growth Rates, %) *(continued)*

Exports, 1980–85: 3.4
Imports, 1980–85: 1.1
General government consumption, 1980–85: 0.2
Private consumption, 1980–85: 0.2
Gross domestic investment, 1980–85: -4.2

RANKINGS

1. Total land area: 123
2. Current population: 59
3. Annual population growth rate: 171
4. Birth rate: 181
5. Death rate: 84
6. Population density: 19
7. Urbanization: 25
8. Annual urban population growth rate: 120
9. Senior citizens in population: 7
10. Homogeneity Index: 87
11. Most powerful nations: 53 (Belgium-Luxembourg.)
12. Age of nations: 38
13. Civil Disorder Index: 67
14. Index of Democratization: 4
15. Foreign aid per capita: N.A.
16. Most powerful Milt. nations: 32
17. Men and women under arms: N.A.
18. Defense expenditures: 17
19. Defense expenditures as % of GNP: 59
20. Gross National Product: 18
21. GNP per capita: 10
22. Per capita GNP annual growth rate: 62
23. Average annual rate of inflation: 93
24. Strongest currency: 84
25. External public debt: N.A.
26. External public debt as % of GNP: N.A.
27. Balance of trade: 114 (Belgium-Luxembourg)
28. Exports per capita: 6 (Belgium-Luxembourg)
29. Imports per capita: 4 (Belgium-Luxembourg)
30. Terms of trade: 47
31. Share of food in imports: 58
32. Agriculture's share of GDP: 97
33. Agricultural Production Index: 77
34. Food Production Index: 46
35. Tractors: 31 (Belgium-Luxembourg)
36. Fertilizer consumption: 36 (Belgium-Luxembourg)
37. Production of roundwood: 90 (Belgium-Luxembourg)
38. Fish catch: 77
39. Industry's share of GDP: 32
40. Energy production: 56

RANKINGS *(continued)*

41. Energy consumption per capita: 18
42. Coal production: 20
43. Crude petroleum production: 20
44. Electrical energy consumption: 24
45. Economically active population: 59
46. Women in the labor force: 74
47. % of labor force in agriculture: 148
48. % of labor force in industry: 11
49. % of labor force in services: 14
50. Railway trackage: 4
51. Length of roads: 6
52. Passenger cars: 14
53. Inland waterways: 2
54. Cargo handled by ports: 20
55. Civil aviation: passengers: 25
56. Tourist arrivals: 15
57. Tourist receipts: 12
58. Male life expectancy: 29
59. Female life expectancy: 24
60. Physical Quality of Life Index: 12
61. Physicians: 7
62. Male literacy rate: 25
63. Female literacy rate: 20
64. Study abroad: 67
65. Educational expenditures as % of GNP: 38
66. Radio receivers: 39
67. Television sets: 11
68. Daily newspaper circulation: 30
69. Annual movie attendance: 64
70. Number of museums and attendance: 27

Source: *New Book of World Rankings.*

AGRICULTURE

Although 28% of the land area is cultivated, farming is limited by the high population density and the rapid absorption of land for nonagricultural use. Farming is characterized by many small, fragmented holdings, and farm activities are generally highly mechanized and intensive and oriented toward livestock production; dairy and meat products have typically accounted for two-thirds of the value of farm output. Agriculture is the bottom sector of the economy, contributing only 2% to the GDP and employing an equal proportion of the labor force. During 1980–86 its growth rate was 3.1%. In 1986 the value added in agriculture was $2.740 billion.

Since Belgium is a member of the EEC, Belgium's farm policies, with the exception of those relating to food and health requirements, are based on the

Common Agricultural Policy (CAP). Despite governmental efforts to achieve income parity between farmers and nonfarmers, the average income of wage and salary earners was over 25% more than that of farmers in 1984. Over the 1960–82 period the number of farms in the country dropped by 40%, as a result of which the average farm size increased from 62,000 sq. m. to 133,000 sq. m. (6.2 ha. to 13.3 ha.). Larger farms have led to remarkable productivity gains. Belgian farmers are among the most efficient in Europe, producing from 80 to 90% of domestic food needs and making the country self-sufficient in sugar, most dairy products, eggs, beef, veal, pork and fresh vegetables.

Of the agricultural land, 39% is devoted to crops and 3% to horticulture. Most of the remaining area consists of pasture on which livestock is raised, especially in the North, where the climate is favorable to raising dairy cows and hogs. Climatic conditions also favor the cultivation of root crops, green forage and industrial crops such as sugar beets, chicory and flax. Cereal grains are less favored, although certain adapted varieties and special cultivation techniques permit the growth of wheat and cereal fodder. The country contains a variety of soils. The most productive are the clay soils in the polders of the northern maritime plain and the loess soils that stretch across the country north of the Sambre and Meuse rivers. These soil areas account for almost half of the cultivated land. Regions of poorer soil include the sandy area in the Flanders plain, the Kempenland to the northeast and the Ardennes and the Belgian Lorraine in the South. Poorer soils are used mostly for cattle raising. Field cropping is predominant in Wallonia, whereas 90% of the horticultural production and pig and poultry raising is in Flanders. Horticultural production is concentrated in West Vlaanderen, Ghent and its environs, known for ornamental plants and flower bulbs, while Limburg and northeastern Brabant are noted for fruit growing.

By far, Flanders is the breadbasket of the country, accounting for 76% of the annual agricultural output with only 45% of the agricultural area and 65% of the agricultural labor force.

Most farm holdings are single-family operations employing only limited outside help. Tenancy is the primary form of farm tenure. Part-time farmers own about one-half of the land, while professional farmers own only one-quarter of the land they farm. Existing legislation protects tenants in regard to rental levels and termination of leases.

Belgium is a net importer of farm products. In 1984, farm imports were valued at $6.638 billion, 65% from other EEC countries and 12% from the United States. The major imports are wheat, citrus fruits, animal feeds and oil seeds. The major exports are fresh and processed vegetables, processed cereals, cocoa, sugar and confectionary items in addition to animal products, particularly pork.

About nine-tenths of all Belgian farmers are associated with one or more farm associations, which, in turn, are represented at the national level in the Green Front and at the EEC level in the Committee of Professional Agricultural Associations. The three principal associations are: the Farmers' League (Belgische Boerenbond), the National Federation of Professional Agricultural Unions of Belgium (Federation Nationale des Unions Professionalles Agricoles de Belgique, UPA) and the Belgium Agricultural Alliance (Alliance Agricole Belge, AAB). The Boerenbond is the largest and the most influential, and it is active mainly in Flanders. The other two operate only in Wallonia, the AAB being overwhelmingly Catholic.

The Boerenbond is believed to have more influence on agriculture than even the Ministry of Agriculture, especially in the provision of key services, such as fiscal and legal counsel, distribution, credit, insurance and education. Farmers are dependent on the Boerenbond, for it controls upstream and downstream activities in slaughtering, wholesaling, dairy processing, freezing and exporting. In addition, Boerenbond-affiliated banks lend credit to farmers on more favorable terms than the state-run National Institute for Agricultural Credit.

The three national farm programs are land consolidation, farm retirement and agricultural investment. The first began in 1956, but because of the complexity of the legal, financial and administrative procedures, only about 10% of the eligible land has been brought under consolidation. To encourage the elimination of marginal farms and to increase farm size, the farm retirement program was instituted in 1965, providing financial compensation to farmers who release nonviable holdings. Agricultural investment programs are undertaken by two public institutions: the Agricultural Fund and the Agricultural Investment Fund. The former supports structural aid measures, including aid for disadvantaged regions, improvement of infrastructure and markets, farm retirement and modernization and disease control. The latter provides financial assistance for increasing productivity and income through grants and low-interest loans. The Guidance Section of the EEC Common Fund for Agricultural Policy also provides direct assistance to Belgian farmers. Farm prices, subsidies, tariffs and levies affecting 90% of Belgian farm products are determined through decisions made by the EEC Council of Agricultural Ministers.

Forests cover about one-fifth of the country's land area, primarily in Wallonia. The most heavily forested regions are the province of Luxembourg, which encompasses part of the Ardennes Plateau and Lorraine scarplands, where nearly 44% is forested. In contrast, West Vlaanderen has only 2.4% under forest. Close to three-fifths of the productive forests are composed of deciduous species, such as oak, ash, beech and poplar, while the rest are coniferous, including spruce, larch and various kinds of pine. Nearly one-half of the entire forest area is under the management and control of the Belgian Forest Authority. The forests meet one-half of the country's timber requirements.

Belgium is not a major fishing nation. The average annual fish catch is less than one-tenth that of the Netherlands. The major fishing ports are Zeebrugge, Oostende and Nieuwport.

AGRICULTURAL INDICATORS

Agriculture's share of GDP: 2% (1986)

Average annual growth rate: 3.1% (1980–86)

Value added in agriculture: $2.740 billion (1986)

Cereal imports (000 tons): 4,047 (1986)

Index of agricultural production (1979–81=100): 105 (1983–85)

Index of food production (1979–81=100): 105 (1983–85)

Index food production per capita: (1979–81=100): 98 (1984–86)

Number of tractors: 115,000 (including Luxembourg)

Number of harvester-threshers: 9,600 (including Luxembourg)

Total fertilizer consumption: 452,000 tons

Fertilizer consumption per 10,000 sq. m. (1 ha.) (100 oz.) 5,223

Number of farms: 102,000

Average size of holding (ha.): 13.6

Size class %
  Below 1 ha.: 2.3
  1–5 ha.: 38.1
  5–10 ha.: 15.6
  10–20 ha.: 21.2
  20–50 ha.: 18.7
  50–over 200 ha.: 4.1

Tenure %
  Owner-operated: 27.7
  Rented: 71.5
  Other: 0.8

Activity %
  Mainly crops: N.A.
  Mainly livestock: N.A.
  Mixed: N.A.
% of Farms using irrigation: N.A.

Farms as % of total land area: 45.7

Land use %
  Permanent crops: 7.4
  Temporary crops: 92.6
  Fallow: N.A.
  Meadows and pastures: 34.2
  Woodland: 0.7
  Other: 2.3

```
┌─────────────────────────────────────────────────┐
│         AGRICULTURAL INDICATORS (continued)       │
│  Yields (kg/ha.)                                  │
│     Grains: 6,349                                 │
│     Roots and tubers: 33,674                      │
│     Pulses: 3,537                                 │
│     Milk kg./animal: 4,160                        │
│                                                   │
│  Livestock (000)                                  │
│     Cattle: 3,180                                 │
│     Horses: 35                                    │
│     Sheep: 147                                    │
│     Pigs: 5,593                                   │
│                                                   │
│  Forestry                                         │
│  Production of roundwood: 3,086,000 cu m.         │
│  (2,359,327 cu yd.)                               │
│     of which industrial roundwood %: 82.6         │
│  Value of exports ($ 000): 600,736                │
│  Fishing                                          │
│  Total catch (000 tons): 47.9                     │
│     of which marine %: 100                        │
│  Value of exports ($ 000): 87,200                 │
└─────────────────────────────────────────────────┘
```

MANUFACTURING

The Belgian manufacturing sector has suffered the loss of its bellwether role in the economy during the past two decades. Its contribution to the GDP has declined from 30% in 1965 to 24% and its growth rate during 1973–84 to 1.3%, from 7.4% during 1965–73. The oil crisis of 1973 was the turning point in the industrial history of modern Belgium, as it brought to the fore the latent weaknesses in the structure of the manufacturing sector. First, the traditional industries controlled by powerful financial interests were resistant to change. Second, traditional manufactures, as textiles, were labor-intensive but unable to compete with the lower costs in newly industrializing countries. Third, Belgium lost its major export markets without being able to find new ones to replace them.

There was a further shift in the structure of the manufacturing sector. Most of the investments in the 1970s came from multinational corporations, who came to control an estimated one-third of all manufacturing jobs and nearly one-half of all industrial assets. While the older industrial plants in Wallonia stagnated, most of the new ones were under non-Belgian control. This shift also had regional implications. Most of the newer manufactures, especially petrochemicals, were based in Flanders, a region that had been outside the industrial zone until then. For example, between 1981 and 1983, production in chemicals, food and beverage processing, and metalworking increased by 16%, 11% and

8%, respectively, compared with an average of 6.4% for the whole manufacturing sector. Their total share in the gross value-added output in Flanders was 61%, compared with 52% in Wallonia. The relatively greater importance of the declining iron and steel industry in Wallonia thus worked to the disadvantage of the southern region. Industrial production in Wallonia and Brussels has hovered near its 1970 level, but in Flanders it has surged by 50%.

Steel, textiles and clothing, shipbuilding and repair, coal mining and glass were all formally recognized as national sectors in a governmental accord of May 1980 and the Special Law on Institutional Reforms of the same year. As national sectors, they receive government support through the Secretariat for Sectoral Concertation within the Ministry of Economic Affairs. The state has participated in varying degrees in these national sectors through holding companies set up as subsidiaries of NIM/SNI. These subsidiaries are constituted not so much to interefere in internal management as to ensure oversight and control of investment programs. Such participation is limited to limited liability companies, and the terms of intervention are determined by agreement among the parties involved. By 1982 the state's financial obligations in the five national sectors amounted to BF175 billion in Flanders and BF125 billion in Wallonia. In Flanders, over one-third of the amount is allocated to hard coal, about one-quarter to steel and the remainder to shipbuilding and textiles, while in Wallonia 90% of the subsidies are earmarked for steel. The main source of financing is the Fund for National Solidarity, created in 1972. Responding to political pressure, the Martens V government has tied industrial restructuring to regional devolution by turning the five national sectors over to regional councils.

The steel industry is historically the pacesetter of the manufacturing sector. Until 1974 steel production had been expanding rapidly, yielding large trade surpluses. Since 1975, however, the industry has fallen victim to the same problems that afflicted its European and U.S. counterparts: competition from Third World and Japanese steel producers, stagnant domestic demand, outmoded plants and low productivity. Although Belgium was, on a per capita basis, the second-largest steel producer in the world after Luxembourg, it had a very narrow home market. The collapse of steel exports thus led to falling production, employment and corporate profits. Between 1974 and 1982, annual crude steel production decreased nearly 40% and employment by 34%. To counter this decline, the state intervened with massive financial aid to promote consolidation and modernization. State involvement in the steel sector accelerated after 1981, after the merger of the Cockerill and Hainaut-Sambre steel companies, which made the combined company the sixth-largest in the EEC. Controlling 80% of the new company, the government initiated a restructuring plan that involved cutting its capacity to 5 million tons in 1985 (compared with 11.7 million tons in 1980) and firing 26,000 employees, or about 60% of the steel work force. The total cost of restructuring was estimated at BF95 billion, more than one-half of which was met by the EEC. By 1985 the Cockerill-Sambre group had managed to break even.

The textile industry has not been exempt from its share of problems. Competition from low-wage countries prices Belgian clothing and textiles out of the market, particularly in price-sensitive items such as pullovers and stockings. The industry lagged behind France, Italy and West Germany in the design and production of high-fashion garments. Most firms are physically small, employing fewer than 50 persons, and are unable to cope with the increasing concentration in the distribution sector, such as chain stores, which prefer to deal with large suppliers. Reform of the textile industry, which is particularly concentrated in Flanders, began in 1977 with aid from the Commission of the European Communities.

The mechanical engineering and metalworking sector of manufacturing is the most important in terms of employment and output, accounting for 37% of the value added in the industrial sector. Production is highly diversified and oriented toward exports, the share of which was 68% in 1981. On a regional basis, the share of employment is 62%, 28% and 9% in Flanders, Wallonia and Brussels, respectively. Flanders specializes in the lighter branches of engineering, such as electronics and vehicle assembly, while Wallonia is stronger in machine tools and the heavier branches. The three largest heavy engineering firms are in Wallonia. Wallonia firms more generally rely on government contracts than Flemish firms and therefore tend to be more seriously affected by cuts in government spending. While shipbuilding and construction of railroad equipment have declined, motor vehicle assembly and aeronautics have risen sharply. Motor vehicle assembly accounts for a large share of the value added in the metalworking sector. In 1983 more than 1 million vehicles were assembled in Belgium, representing roughly 10% of European production. Some 95% of the production is exported to EEC partners. Five multinationals—Ford, GM, Renault, Volkswagen and Volvo—dominate the industry, and all are located in Flanders.

The food processing sector occupies second place in manufacturing, accounting for 20% of value added in 1981. Milk, fodder, meat and beer are the four leading commodity sectors, together making up more than one-half of the turnover in foodstuffs. Third in manufacturing is the chemical industry, which has escaped the troubles of the other sectors. Belgium's largest corporation is Petrofina, a chemicals company. Almost two-thirds of the output is exported. Heavy chemicals are produced mainly in the Sambre-Meuse Valley and Kempenland but, more recently, Antwerp has become a major chemicals center.

Belgium's high-tech industries include telecommunications, biotechnology, genetic engineering, computer software and robotics. Many of these industries are joint ventures with only a limited domestic input. Flanders particularly has made a determined effort to attract high-tech industries under a program called the Third Industrial Revolution, which has been more successful than the Walloon region's Athena Program.

MANUFACTURING INDICATORS, 1985

Average annual growth rate 1980–85: 1.6%
Share of GDP: 23%
Labor force in industry: 36%
Value added in manufacturing (million 1980 $), 1985: $31,497
    food & agriculture: 19
    textiles: 9
    machinery: 24
    chemicals: 12
Index of Manufacturing Production (1980=100): 105 (1984)

MINING

There is virtually no mining in Belgium, and except for coal (see Energy) and industrial minerals, no revenue from mining. The minerals processing industry, however, is a significant contributor to the GNP. Copper ore comes mainly from Zaire, and zinc and lead ores are imported from a variety of sources, including Zaire, Sweden and Peru.

ENERGY

Belgium is an energy-deficit country despite large but declining coal reserves. The national energy policy supports research in energy conservation, less dependence on oil, diversification of natural gas imports and greater reliance on coal and nuclear energy. Almost three-quarters of government research funds are devoted to nuclear energy and the remainder to solar energy, geothermal energy, biomass energy and the liquefaction and gasification of combustible solids.

Of the total energy consumption in 1983, oil accounted for 43.3%, coal 22.9%, natural gas 20%, nuclear power 13.4% and hydroelectric power 0.4%. Domestic production of primary energy met more than 20% of total domestic energy requirements in 1983. The primary energy trade deficit fell from BF340 billion in 1973 to an estimated BF272 billion in 1984 as a result of both a substantial reduction in oil imports and increased domestic nuclear output. The

share of oil in energy consumption is much smaller in Belgium than in other industrialized countries. At the same time, Belgium has established extensive refining facilities. Antwerp is one of the major refining centers of Europe, with five
refineries having a total capacity of almost 1 million barrels per day. Three-
quarters of the crude oil for these refineries came from the Middle East, some
65% from Saudi Arabia alone.

ENERGY INDICATORS, 1985

Total energy production: 9,267,000 metric tons
Total energy consumption: 48,782,000 metric tons
Annual energy imports: 71,116,000 metric tons
Annual energy exports: 23,771,600 metric tons
Energy consumption per capita (kg of coal equivalent):
4,666
Energy imports as % of merchandise imports: 17
Average annual growth rate (1980–85) of
  Energy production: 14.5%
  Energy consumption: -1.3%
Public utilities' share of GDP: 3.7

Electricity
  Installed capacity: 12.309 million kw.
  Production: 53.7 billion kw.-hr.
    % fossil fuel: 47.7
    % hydro: 0.7
    % nuclear: 51.7
  Consumption per capita: 5,468 kw.-hr.

Natural gas
  Proved reserves: 0
  Production: 46 billion cu. m. (35 billion cu. yd.)
  Consumption: 8.759 billion cu. m. (6.696 cu. yd.)

Petroleum
  Proved reserves: 0
  Years to exhaust proved reserves: 0
  Production: 0
  Consumption: 153 million bl.
  Refining capacity: 652,000 bl. per day

Coal
  Reserves: 440 billion tons
  Production: 6,298,000 tons
  Consumption: 14,956,000 tons

Coal, once the basis of Belgium's industrial wealth, is being fast depleted.
Compared to a peak output of 25.1 million tons in 1927, production had fallen
to 6 million tons in 1983. Most of the coal mined in 1983 was produced by the
Kempenland Coal Mining Company. Wallonia's last coal mine was closed in
1983. Reserves at the Flanders mines are estimated at 423 million tons.

Natural gas in one of the bright features of the energy situation, although Belgium is dependent on imports for four-fifths of its supplies. Gas is brought largely by pipeline from Slochteren in the Netherlands and from the Ekofish field in the Norwegian section of the North Sea. Distrigaz, Belgium's largest natural gas distributor, has also attempted to spread its supply sources by buying gas from Algeria and the Soviet Union.

Nuclear power is responsible for 55 to 57% of electric power generation in Belgium, one of the highest percentages in the world. There are six nuclear power stations in operation—one at Mol, one at Tihange and four at Doel, with a total capacity of 2,700 megawatts. The nuclear power station at Chooz in France also supplies electricity to the Belgian grid. Hydroelectric stations produce 0.6% of electric power and thermal power stations the balance. Some 92% of commercial electric energy is produced by three private companies: Ebes, Intercom and Unerg. All power stations are interconnected and linked to systems in France, West Germany, the Netherlands and Luxembourg.

The fall in energy prices in 1986 is a major factor in Belgium's economic turnaround. BLEU's energy deficit is higher than the EEC average: 8% of the GDP in 1984 and 7½% in 1985. Taking oil products alone, net imports were close to 5% of the GDP in 1984 and 4.3% in 1985 (as against an EEC average of 3%). If energy prices continue to fall for the rest of the 1980s, Belgium could cut its overall energy bill by $1 billion annually.

Given its leadership in nuclear technology, Belgium has exported its knowhow to Third World countries and also participated in the construction of reactors in France, West Germany and the United States.

LABOR

The national labor force is estimated at 4 million, of whom 36% are women. As in many other developed countries, the bulk of the labor force is in service occupations. The proportion of self-employed workers has steadily declined since the war and reached 13% in 1985, while public sector employment has steadily risen, to 31% by the same year. The regional implications of these shifts in employment have not been uniform. The demise of coal mining, steel and heavy manufacturing has affected Wallonia more severly than other areas. The employment belt remains in Brabant Province, particularly the Antwerp–Brussels axis, which accounts for 43% of tertiary employment and 36% of manufacturing labor.

The basic workday is eight hours and the basic workweek is 40 hours, although many branches of industry have negotiated for shorter work hours. Night work is subject to special conditions. Overtime is paid at the rate of 1¼ times the basic rate for the first two hours above 40 and 1½ times thereafter, with double time for Sundays and holidays. Certain service industries and professions are excluded from these regulations.

The hourly and minimum wage rates are fixed by collective agreements of the regional Joint Labor-Management Councils (Commissions Paritaires/Paritaire Commissies) or for the entire country by each trade or industry. Wages are linked by an escalator clause to the cost of living index. Comprehensive legislation covers health conditions in the workplace and the employment of women and minors. Regulations make dismissal of both white- and blue-collar staff extremely difficult for management.

Belgium is one of the most unionized countries in the world, with 70% of its labor forced organized, even though the closed-shop system is illegal. The degree of unionization varies with the sector, from 80% for blue-collar workers to 37% for white-collar ones. The largest trade unions are organized by industrial sectors, not by professions or crafts. The influence of labor on national politics is also high because of strong links with the major political parties, and prolabor pressure groups have succeeded in enacting legislation covering work conditions and Social Security.

It is still rare for employees to be represented on company boards, but worker representation exists at the plant level. These include the union delegation (the equivalent of the shop steward's committee); the works council; and the committee for safety, health and improvement of the workplace. The competence of these bodies is largely advisory. At the national level, employers are represented by the Federation of Belgian Enterprises, composed of sectored associations representing about 35,000 enterprises but excluding agriculture, retail trade, handicrafts and state-controlled enterprises.

Bodies for collective bargaining are set up at the national level. At the industry level, trade unions and employer associations are represented on a parity basis on plant committees, which were first established in 1919. There are 98 such committees, covering all workers in private industry. Bargaining is conducted separately for white-collar and blue-collar workers, and cooperation between the two is rare. At the national level, the so-called social partners are represented on the National Labor Council, which was granted bargaining powers in 1968. Its role in keeping industrial peace has earned the council the title of "Social Parliament." In keeping with the new realities of regionalization, collective bargaining since 1984 has been more often on the regional level. Collective bargaining thus takes place at four levels: national, industrywide, regional and local. Higher-level negotiations set broad standards, while lower-level bargaining gets down to the nuts and bolts.

The economic shocks beginning in 1973 have muted industrial relations and particularly disadvantaged labor negotiators. The loss of productivity and competitiveness on the one hand and the specter of unemployment on the other have made both management and unions wary of the wage-price spiral. The government, with its austerity program and incomes policy (including a wage freeze and partial suspension of wage indexation), has put the lid on any further concessions to labor.

Wage restraint as pursued by the government has been based on work-sharing, i.e., a trade-off of lower wages for additional hiring and shorter work hours. The Martens V government has implemented a 5-3-3 program—a 5% reduction in working hours, a 3% increase in employment and a 3% reduction in pay. To companies that agree to this formula, the government offers fiscal incentives such as reductions in Social Security contributions. The proceeds of the wage restraint would be paid into a central employment fund.

In the past, strikes were rare. However, since 1982, in response to rising unemployment and austerity, workers have become more restive. Statistics for 1982 show a decrease in the number of strikes at the enterprise level and an increase in strikes at the sectoral level. Strikes in 1982 tended to be more spontaneous and also focused more than in previous years on employment guarantees and job security and less on wages and benefits. In 1982 about 10 large-scale plant occupations occured to protest layoffs or closures.

Despite the continued sluggishness of the economy, aggregate employment grew slightly in 1985–86, for the first time since 1979. This was due more to active employment-assistance measures, such as work-sharing, work support and part-time work. This increase in numbers employed led to a further slowdown in per capita productivity. Over the period 1983–85 productivity grew by only 1%. Policies to promote employment were supplemented by efforts to reduce the labor supply. Unemployed persons above 55 years were taken off the labor force statistics. Even so, the unemployment rate was one of the highest in Europe after Ireland and the Netherlands: 13.9% at the end of 1983. Throughout the 1970s layoffs were common in Belgian industry, as management's response to higher wages and lower productivity. The average length of unemployment also remained exceptionally long as compared with other EEC countries. More than two-thirds of the unemployed have been out of work for more than 12 months. Further, the unemployment rates for women and youths are much higher than those for men. Women have experienced more than double the rate of male unemployment, and nearly one-third of all youths are among the unemployed. Among foreigners, the unemployment rate was 13%, slightly higher than their share of the economically active population. Wallonia registered higher unemployment than Flanders or Brussels, but sometimes there are large disparities within each region.

The government has used early retirement as a means of creating new jobs. To ensure that early retirement was not used by companies to reduce payrolls, it was made contingent on the replacement of the retiring worker by a new one. One of the most troubling aspects of unemployment has been its cost to the national government. Average annual compensation per unemployed worker was estimated at $3,983 in 1983. Unemployment benefits and employment-creation programs accounted for 8% of the national budget and 4.5% of the GNP. Therefore, unemployment benefits were among the first to be reduced under the government's austerity programs.

The Belgian labor movement is divided into two major national organizations and one minor one. The two major ones are the Confederation of Christian Trade Unions (ACV in Dutch and CSC in French) and the Belgian General Federation of Labor (ABVV in Dutch and FGTB in French). The third national organization is the Belgian General Central of Liberal Trade Union (ACVLB in Dutch and CGSLB in French). The ACV/CSC is Catholic; the ABVV/FGTB is Socialist; and the ACVLB/CGSLB is conservative-, free-enterprise- and free-market-oriented. The ACV/CSC is linked to the Flemish Catholic political party through the Flemish Catholic Workers' Movement but relates more tenuously to the francophone Catholic Party through the francophone Catholic Workers' Movement, currently estranged from the latter. The ABVV/FGTB has close informal ties to the francophone and Flemish Socialist parties. The ACVLB/CGSLB is close to the francophone and Flemish Liberal parties.

The ACV/CSC and the ABVV/FGTB each claim over 1 million members, (the former over 1,300,000 and the latter nearly 1,200,000) and the ACVLB/ CGSLB about 200,000. The ACV/CSC is strongest in Flanders and substantially outnumbers the ABVV/FGTB except in a few places like Antwerp, the Limburg coal mines and some major industrial plants. The ABVV/FGTB is strongest in Wallonia; its preponderance is strongest in the Liège industrial basin, where it claims 80% of support. In the other major Walloon industrial basin, around Charleroi, the ACV/CSC has made substantial inroads and exceeds 40%. The small, middle-class ACVLB/CGSLB is strongest in the liberal bastion of Brussels but ranks a distant third even there.

Social elections (for works committees or enterprise councils) provide a good gauge of membership trends. In the 1983 elections, for example, the ACV/CSC received 52% of the vote in Flanders, 38% in Wallonia and 43% in Brussels The ABVV/FGTB received 39% in Flanders, 58% in Wallonia and 45% in Brussels. The ACVLB/CGSLB won 9% in Flanders, 5% in Wallonia and 12% in Brussels. In the nonprofit sector, the ACV/CSC swept 85% in Flanders,

---

LABOR INDICATORS, 1985

Total economically active population: 4.213 million
As % of working-age population: 60.6
% female: 38.8
Activity rate
  Total: 43.8
  Male: 54.3
  Female: 33.7

Employment status
  Employers & self-employed: 11.7
  Employees: 71.4
  Unpaid family workers: 3.2
  Other: 13.7

Sectoral employment (%)
  Agriculture, forestry, fishing: 2.9
  Mining: 0.7
  Manufacturing, construction: 28.5
  Electricity, gas, water: 0.9
  Trade: 7.3
  Transportation, communications: 18.8
  Finance, real estate: 7.2
  Services: 33.7

Average annual growth rate of labor force, 1980–2000:
0.2

Unemployment %: 14.4
Earnings in manufacturing: BF270.3 per hour

Hours of work
  Manufacturing: 33.5 per wk.
  Nonagricultural work: 33.6 per wk.

48% in Wallonia and 44% in Brussels; the ABVV/FGTB won 48% in Wallonia and 44% in Brussels; and the ACVLB/CGSLB won 19% in Brussels.

FOREIGN COMMERCE

Trade represents more than 60% of the Belgian GNP. The high dependency on trade has made the economy vulnerable to fluctuations in world trade activity. Belgium therefore is one of the staunchest advocates of free trade and European economic integration.

In 1922 Belgium and Luxembourg entered into an economic union known as the Belgium-Luxembourg Economic Union (BLEU). Trade and balance of payments statistics are combined in a joint statement every year. In 1944 the BLEU signed a convention for a special customs union with the Netherlands known as Benelux, which was later overshadowed when the EEC was formed.

Belgium was a founding member of the EEC. The Spaak Report, written by former Belgian foreign minister Paul Henri Spaak, was the basic document for the establishment of the Treaty of Rome. Since the completion of the EEC customs union in 1968, customs duties on trade between Belgium and its EEC partners have been eliminated and nonagricultural imports from countries outside the EEC have been subject to the EEC Common External Tariff (CET). Duty rates are moderate; most raw materials enter duty-free or at low rates, and rates on most manufactured goods fall within a range of 5 to 17%. The 1977 round of Multilateral Trade Negotiations, known as the Tokyo Round and held under GATT auspices, has reduced the average tariff level on industrial goods by approximately 35%. Under EEC agreements and within the framework of UNCTAD, Belgium extends preferential tariff treatment to a large number of developing countries. Exports are generally free except for temporary or voluntary restrictions.

The government takes an active role in trade promotion, provides trade information, administers trade regulations and negotiates trade agreements through the Belgian Foreign Trade Office, financed through the Foreign Trade Fund. This fund, which extends grants, loans and guarantees to traders and conducts market research, is supported by the National Del Credere Office, which insures political and commercial export risks, and Compromex, which advises on applications for interest rate subsidies. The principal financing facility for medium- and long-term credit is Creditexport, whose members include a number of commercial banks, private savings banks and public financial institutions. The National Bank of Belgium certifies export loans, entitling the borrowers to lower rediscount rates.

Government efforts are also directed toward diversification of exports and promotion of joint ventures. To promote exports to less-developed countries, the government created a special export credit fund in 1982, with a capital of BF3.225 billion. Military supply contracts generally include generous offset agreements.

Despite these efforts, Belgium lost many of its foreign markets between 1973 and 1981 while suffering greater import penetration than its EEC partners. Its poor performance was due partly to the antiquated structure of its production, heavily represented by products in low demand, such as iron and steel and textiles, and in areas where the newly industrializing countries offered the most competition. Poor trade performance was accentuated by the impact of wage indexation and a strong currency policy on export prices.

Until 1977 the trade deficit was offset by an increase in the surplus on services, spending by Brussels-based international organizations and income from overseas investments. Interest charges on foreign borrowing by the public sec-

FOREIGN TRADE INDICATORS (Belgium-Luxembourg Economic Union, 1985)

Exports: $53.3 billion
Imports: $55.8 billion
Balance of trade: -$2.5 billion
Annual growth rate 1980–85 exports: 3.4%
Annual growth rate 1980–85 imports: 1.1%
Ratio of international reserves to imports (in months): 2.4
Value of manufactured exports: $40.86 billion
Commodity concentration: N.A.
Terms of trade (1980=100): 95
Ratio of exports to imports: 96.3
Imports per capita: $5,245
Exports per capita: $5,051
Ratio of exports to GDP: 58.2

Direction of trade (%)

	Imports	Exports
EEC	69.8	70.4
U.S.A.	5.7	6.3
East European economies	3.0	2.0
Developing economies	13.0	20.5

Composition of trade (%)

	Imports	Exports
Food }	14.4	12.0
Agricultural raw materials }		
Fuels	16.6	6.6
Ores and minerals	8.7	6.9
Manufactured goods	67.3	74.5
of which chemicals	10.2	12.8
of which machinery	23.1	23.2

tor caused a reversal of this trend after 1977. The BLEU current account deficit worsened steadily until 1981, when it was equal to 4% of the GNP. Because Luxembourg's current account position remained in surplus because of the strength of its financial sector, the Belgian current account deficit was larger than that reported for BLEU as a whole. This deterioration was halted in 1982 when Belgium adopted a recovery program based on export growth and domestic austerity. These policies coupled with the devaluation of the Belgian franc brought the trade deficit down to BF150 billion from BF280 billion in one year. Improvement in the trade balance, however, was erratic. Much of it was due to an improvement in the energy balance and lower oil imports, while export growth was limited to products that were not export leaders, such as automobiles, plastics, wood and furniture, rubber, food and beverages and carpets. The exports of Belgium's traditional products still sagged.

The momentum of export growth also served to intensify regional disparities. In the early 1980s Flanders accounted for almost 70% of Belgian industrial deliveries abroad, Wallonia for 25% and Brussels for a mere 5%.

Over four-fifths of Belgian trade is with industrialized countries, primarily EEC partners. In 1982 some 63% of the imports came from EEC countries, and 70% of the exports went to the EEC. These proportions are the highest for any EEC country except Ireland. In 1970 West Germany overtook Netherlands as leading supplier and buyer. Since 1983 there have been substantial increases in trade with the Soviet Union and Eastern Europe. Trade relations with the United States have not been significant, although the latter is the sixth-largest importer of Belgian goods. Outside Belgium's former African colonies, trade with developing countries also has been negligible. Of its forays into Asian markets, that into China has been the most successful.

TRANSPORTATION & COMMUNICATIONS

Because of its strategic position and its small size, Belgium has one of the most efficient transportation systems in Europe. It is also one of the densest and most balanced. The three major seaports are the linchpins of the system. The largest is Antwerp, lying 64 km. (40 mi.) inland in the Schelde River estuary. It is the fourth-largest port in Europe and one of the world's busiest. It handles 71% of all Belgian maritime cargo and about three-fifths of the export and import traffic of the BLEU. The port complex covers nearly 110 sq. km. (11,000 ha.) and contains entire industrial plants. The port can accommodate ships up to 90,000 tons. The second-largest port is Ghent, which is accessible to the sea via the Ghent-Terneuzen Canal. Ghent handles about 17% of the country's oceangoing traffic. The port also serves as a focal point for inland river traffic, especially toward the Rhine. The third-largest port is Zeebrugge, at the eastern end of the coast. It can accommodate cargo ships up to 80,000 tons and oil tankers weighing 260,000 tons. It handles a good deal of the passenger traffic between the Continent and the United Kingdom. In 1985 a liquefied natural-gas terminal opened in Zeebrugge, with storage facilities for 400,000 cu. (306,000 cu. yd.). The port of Osten is mainly a passenger terminal for cross-Channel ferries.

Belgium has a very dense rail system, which follows the waterways to a great extent. With Brussels as its hub, the rail system also provides access to the Ardennes. Under government control since 1834, the system comprises some 3,741 km. (2,325 mi.) of which 435 km. (270 mi.) are standard-gauge, 2,563 km. (1,593 mi.) are double track and 1,969 km. (1,224 mi.) are electrified. Transeurope express trains service Brussels, Antwerp and the major cities of the Sambre-Meuse Valley. A planned high-speed rail line based on the French *train à grande vitesse* is expected to link France, the Low Countries and West Germany, reducing the traveling time from Paris to Brussels to 1½ hours. In the capital itself, over 200,000 commuters rely on rail transportation. A complementary system of 539 bus lines covering 25,265 km. (15,702 mi.) of bus routes is operated by the semiofficial Auxiliary Railroads.

COMMUNICATION INDICATORS, 1986

Telephones
  Total: 4.22 million
  per 100: 42.8
  Phone traffic
    Local: 1.5 billion
    Long distance: 1.9 billion
    International: 69,516,000

Post office
  Number of post offices: 1,858
  Domestic mail: 2.9 billion

Telegraph
  Total traffic: 1,353,000
  National: 1,073,000
  International: 280,000

Telex
  Subscriber lines: 23,970
  Traffic (000 minutes): 110,385

Telecommunications
  6 submarine cables
  2 INTELSAT stalins
  2 EUTELSAT antennas

TOURISM AND TRAVEL INDICATORS, 1984

Total tourist receipts: $1.7 billion
Expenditures by nationals abroad: $1.953 billion
Number of hotel beds: 83,200
Average length of stay: 1.3
Tourist nights: 8,386,000
Number of tourists: 6,451,000
  of whom from (000):
  United Kingdom: 12.5
  West Germany: 15.4
  Netherlands: 32.2
  France: 9.0

TRANSPORTATION INDICATORS

Roads
  Length km: 127,688 (79,342 mi.)
  Paved %: 95

```
┌────────────────────────────────────────────────────┐
│        TRANSPORTATION INDICATORS (continued)        │
│                                                      │
│  Motor vehicles                                      │
│    Automobiles: 3,300,248                            │
│    Trucks: 310,685                                   │
│    Persons per vehicle: 2.7                          │
│    Road freight ton-km.: 19.396 billion (12.055 billion ton-
│  mi.)                                                │
│                                                      │
│  Railroads                                           │
│    Track km.: 3,741 (2,325 mi.)                      │
│    Passenger km.: 6,552 billion (4.071 billion mi.) │
│    Freight ton-km.: 8,256 (5,131 ton-mi.)           │
│                                                      │
│  Merchant marine                                     │
│    Vessels: 344                                      │
│    Total dead weight tonnage: 3,853,600             │
│    Oil tankers: 141,000                              │
│                                                      │
│  Ports                                               │
│    Cargo loaded: 47.052 million tons                │
│    Cargo unloaded: 72.096 million tons              │
│                                                      │
│  Air                                                 │
│    Km. flown: 49.6 million (30.83 million mi.) (domestic)
│    Passengers: 2,032 (domestic)                     │
│    Passenger-km.: 5,664 million (3,520 billion passenger-
│  mi.)                                                │
│    Freight ton-km.: 583.4 million (362.6 million ton-mi.)
│    Mailton-km.: 1,035                                │
│    Airports: 2,440–3,659 m. (8,006–12,005 ft.): 14 │
│                                                      │
│  Pipelines                                           │
│    Refined: 1,115 km. (693 mi.)                     │
│    Natural gas: 3,300 km. (2051 mi.)                │
│    Crude: 161 km. (100 mi.)                         │
│                                                      │
│  Inland waterways                                    │
│    Length km.: 1,956 (1,215 mi.)                    │
│    Cargo ton-km.: 5.242 million (3.258 million ton-mi.)
└────────────────────────────────────────────────────┘
```

The waterways of Belgium link all the internal industrial centers with the major seaports and also with Rotterdam and Dunkerque. One-fifth of the imports and one-fourth of the exports are moved by barge. More than 80% of the trade with the Netherlands, more than two-thirds of the trade with West Germany and one-fifth of the trade with France move by canal. The Meuse and Schelde rivers are the main arteries of the system, which also includes the Albert Canal, the Schelde Basin and the Antwerp–Brussels–Charleroi loop. A modernization program undertaken in 1984 has made the canals accessible to the standard 1,350-ton European barges.

The road network consists of 103,096 km. (64,261 mi.) of roads, of which 1,017 km. (632 mi.) are limited-access, divided autoroutes; 11,717 km. (7,282 mi.) are national highways; 1.362 km. (846 mi.) are provincial roads; 38,000 km. (23,617 mi.) are other paved roads; and 51,000 km. (31,697 mi.) are unpaved roads. To deal with the rapid growth of road traffic, ongoing development projects include the extension of three international highways through the southeastern section of the country and the moving of trams underground.

Because of the country's small size, internal air traffic is negligible.

The national-flag airline is SABENA, founded in 1923 as a private company and now 90% government-owned. It regularly flies to 50 countries. Belgium's principal international airport is Zaventen, about 20 miles from the capital. Deurne, Antwerp's airport, is the second-largest airport for international flights. Middlekerke, near Ostend, and Gosselies, near Charleroi, are smaller international airports.

Belgium has three main tourist regions: the seacoast, the old Flemish cities, and the Ardennes in the southeast. Ostend, Blankenberge and Knokke are the main seacoast resorts. Among Flemish cities, Bruges, Ghent and Ypres stand out, while both Antwerp and Brussels have many sightseeing attractions. Louvain, the seat of a renowned university; Malines, the seat of Belgium's primate; and Liège have many old buildings. Tournai is famous for its Romanesque cathedral. Spa, in the Ardennes, is Europe's oldest spa. No visa is required for citizens of OECD countries.

DEFENSE

The armed forces of Belgium are fully integrated into the Western alliance. A founding member of NATO, Belgium has consistently supported the organization, and Brussels has been its headquarters since De Gaulle expelled it in 1967. There are no foreign military bases in Belgium.

The king is technically the commander in chief of the armed forces and in that role is not subject to parliamentary control. However, the operational control of the forces rests with the Ministry of National Defense and a joint ministerial committee composed of the ministers of national defense, foreign affairs, interior and public office, justice and institutional reform and communications.

Approximately two-thirds of the armed forces are volunteers or career military personnel. The army draws about 50% of its personnel from the draft. Eighteen- and nineteen-year olds are subject to conscription, but an all-volunteer force is being evolved. National service is six months at present, part of which is served with NATO forces. Individual basic training of soldiers takes two to three months, depending on arm and function, followed by continuation training in schools or units. Officer cadets undergo two categories of training:

an "all-weapons" course of four years or a "polytechnic" course for five years. Later they attend the École de Guerre, where they must pass an examination in their second language—French or Flemish—and each language is allotted a 50% quota in the corps. There are other training requirements for reserve officers, NCOs and others who may be recalled to the colors if an emergency should arise.

The two main suborganizations of the Ministry of National Defense are the Central Administration and the General Staff. The chief of the General Staff is the head of the operational units in the field. Under him there is a joint staff responsible for the coordination of policy, planning, programs, personnel and logistics, while the army, air force and naval chiefs of staff are responsible for their own services. The Medical Branch is an interservice unit.

The Belgian armed forces operate under two NATO commands: the army and the air force under NATO supreme Allied commander, Europe, and the navy under the commander in chief, Channel. Part of the army remains under Belgian authority as the Forces of the Interior.

The Belgian Army consists of two major components: the I Belgian Corps, which is assigned to NATO; and the Forces of the Interior. The former is deployed operationally, with most of its units in West Germany. It is composed of two active divisions, each having three mechanized brigades, each brigade including two armored infantry battalions, one antitank battalion, one or two tank battalions, one artillery battalion, an engineer company and logistical support units. The I Belgian Corps has an active strength of 34,000 in peacetime. Since 1973 two of its brigades have been reassigned to Belgium, one to the northern Leopoldsburg area and the other to the southern Bastogne/Marche-en-Famenne area.

The Forces of the Interior are made up of army units that could be supplemented by the local gendarmerie in time of war. The Regiment of the Paracommandos is an elite, highly trained unit with three battalions—two airborne infantry units and one commando unit. The paracommando unit is the most battle-experienced unit in the Belgian armed forces.

The Belgian Air Force, part of the NATO Command, Europe, has three major divisions: the Tactical Air Command, the Training Command and the Logistics Command. The majority of flying and technical personnel are volunteers. In 1984 six squadrons of surface-to-air Nike Hercules missiles were assigned to the NATO Second Tactical Air Force by Belgium. Belgium also is responsible for the operation of two NATO Air Defense Ground Environment (NADGE) radar stations.

The shallowness of Belgian waters makes Belgian ports vulnerable to mine and submarine attacks. The Belgian Navy has three different missions: antisubmarine warfare, antimine operations and defense of coastal posts and shipping. Naval ships are stationed in the ports of Oostende, Zeebrugge and Kallo. About 25% of naval personnel are conscripts.

Civil defense has received little emphasis, though such a system exists.

MILITARY BUDGET, PERSONNEL & WEAPONRY

Defense budget: $1.702 billion (1985)

Total armed forces: 91,750 (including 3,580 women and 30,500 conscripts)

Total reserves: 178,500

Army: 67,200

Units: 1 Corps HQ; 2 Divisional HQ; 1 armed brigade (2 rank, 2 mechanized infantry, 1 support artillery battalion; 2 support units); 3 mechanized infantry brigades; 1 para-commando regiment; 3 reconnaissance battalions; 1 tank battalion; 2 motorized infantry battalions; 4 artillery battalions; 1 SSM battalion; 4 AD battalions; 2 SAM with 36 improved HAWK; 2 AA 5 engineer battalions; 4 light aviation squadrons

Equipment: 334 Leopard tanks; 116 Scorpion light tanks; 154 armored fighting vehicles; 10 mechanized infantry combat vehicles; 1,425 armored personnel carriers; 90 howitzers; 80 antitank guns; 40 antitank guided weapons; 5 surface-to-surface missiles; 36 air defense guns; 61 helicopters

Navy: 4,550

Bases: Kallo, Ostend, Zeebrugge

Frigates: 3 mine countermeasures vessels; 6 patrol craft; 10 auxiliaries; 3 helicopters

Air Force: 19,820

Aircraft: 5 fighter squadrons; 2 air defense squadrons; 1 reconnaissance squadron; 2 transport squadrons; 1 liaison fleet; 3 training squadrons; 1 SAR squadron for a total of 181 combat aircraft

---

Military service is not exempt from the language conflict. The basic law of 1938 as amended in 1955, 1961, 1963 and 1970 establishes the right of Belgians to use their mother tongue while satisfying their national military obligations. Basic military training is given to the recruit in his native language, after which the soldier joins a monolingual unit. All official communications and commands are to be exclusively in the language of the unit concerned. Officers and NCOs have to have a working knowledge of both French and Flemish for both entry into the Royal Military College and the War College and for promotion to all the senior ranks above captain. Personnel in the services reflect the national population in a ratio of 60% Flemish and 40% French.

The army and the air force each have a total of 17 ranks, five for enlisted personnel, two for warrant officers and 10 officer grades. In the officer group there are three general, three field-grade and four company-grade ranks. In a departure from typical rank structures in a majority of the world's armed forces, Belgium has a rank of captain commandant between the ranks of captain and major and also limits general officers to three instead of four or five grades.

Warrant officers are referred to as adjutants and chief adjutants. Below them are the three sergeant grades of NCOs. At the lowest end of the scale are corporals and privates.

The navy and the gendarmerie have similar rank structures. Both services have the same number of ranks as the army and air force below that of general officer. The navy has two admiral ranks, two degrees of ensign and two degrees of lieutenant. However, instead of the usual commander ranks, three degrees of captain are used. Petty officer and seaman grades are similar to those of other navies.

The army uses rank insignia primarily on the collars and caps of its uniforms. Sleeve and shoulder board stripes on navy and air force uniforms follow universal patterns. The army service uniform consists of olive-khaki coats and trousers. The navy uniform is navy blue and the air force uniform also dark blue but of a slightly lighter shade. The summer uniforms of all services are identical in color but lighter in weight.

The major military decorations, in decreasing order of importance, are the Order of Leopold with and without collars, the Order of the Crown, the Order of Leopold II, the Iron Cross, the Military Cross and the Croix de Guerre.

Military courts have jurisdiction over military personnel only. They do not ordinarily try civilians, even those who commit crimes on military installations. They also waive jurisdiction for petty offenses committed off the bases. Minor infractions are dealt with by administrative punishments and more serious ones by company punishments. At the appeal level, the civilian Court of Cassation rules on military cases.

Historically, Belgium is one of Europe's major arms manufacturers and traders. In the 15th century, for example, Charles the Bold of Burgundy forbade Liège—then as now the center of the Belgian armaments industry—from producing weaponry, and when the city ignored his order, he had the city razed and its inhabitants slaughtered. Liège supplied arms to both friends and enemies; when the duke of Alba invaded the Low Countries in 1596, both the defenders and the invaders were armed with weapons made in Liège. Liège is the headquarters of the Fabrique Nationale d'Armes de Guerre (FN), one of the world's most aggressive manufacturers and exporters of small arms such as rifles, machine guns and Browning pistols. More than 90% of total Belgian small-arms production is exported each year and finds its way into all regions of conflict in the Middle East, Africa and Central America.

EDUCATION

Education is a major political issue in Belgium, especially because of a number of rival school systems: Flemish and Walloon, Catholic and secular, official and "free." According to Vernon Mallinson, the Belgian system is based on the notion of *suum cuique* (to each his own) rather than *idem uique* (the same for everybody).

The Catholic Church had almost exclusive control over state education prior to 1794, but this power was whittled away during the First School Conflict (1879–84) between the Catholics and the Liberals and effectively challenged during the Second School Conflict (1950–58). The First School Conflict was sparked by an 1879 law removing primary schools from commune control. The church retaliated by fobidding Catholic participation in public schools. Then in 1884 a Catholic government rescinded the 1879 law, and the laws of 1894 and 1895 set the basic framework for an educational system under commune control, especially in budget, the number of schools, the qualifications of teachers and standards. In 1895 religious instruction was made obligatory for Catholics, Protestants and Jews. Under Loi Poullet, education became compulsory in 1914, eventually from ages six to 14.

The Second School Conflict began over subsidies for education beyond the compulsory age. This conflict was solved by the School Pact of 1958, which affirmed freedom of choice between religious and moral instruction and between private Catholic schools and secular state-sponsored ones. It abolished school fees for both kinds and extended subsidies for salaries, equipment and facilities on a per capita enrollment basis. At a cost of massive state subsidization, both sides gained what they wanted. The pact neutralized but did not depoliticize the church's role in education. A majority of Belgian children attend Catholic schools; between 1957 and 1976 the Catholic school share of secondary enrollment increased by 236%. The vast majority of Catholics and Flemings send their children to Catholic schools, while most children of Walloon, Liberal and Socialist families enroll in state schools. In addition to the parallel state and "free" (Catholic) educational systems, there are Dutch and French school systems. The right to choose between Catholic and secular schools, however, does not extend to the two linguistic systems.

Thus the schools are battlegrounds in the historic conflict between the two national languages. After independence, French was the official language while

Flemish (standardized as Dutch in 1864) was the language of the hoi polloi. Further, illiteracy rates tended to be higher in Flanders than in the South. The right to speak Dutch in primary schools was not granted until 1842. In 1850 Dutch was introduced as a second language in Flemish secondary schools. French remained the language of instruction until 1926 for lower secondary schools and until 1932 for upper secondary schools and until 1930 in the University of Ghent. The introduction of universal male suffrage in 1893 and the rise in compulsory education enrollments strengthened the Flemish bloc in their demands for parity in the educational system. The trend, however, was not toward bilingual but toward monolingual education in segregated schools. Bilingualism is perceived as a subtle threat to the status of the historically disadvantaged Dutch language. Only in Brussels is there linguistic coexistence.

The transition to monolingualism was even more traumatic in universities. The Roman Catholic University of Louvain (founded in 1425), where one could study either in Dutch or French, was to some extent a French-speaking island in Flanders. Soon after the passage of the 1963 Act delimiting linguistic areas and requiring the medium of instruction to be only in the mother tongue of the pupil, Flemish faculty members and students proposed splitting up the university and moving the French-speaking half to Wallonia. The Catholic bishops opposed the bifurcation, as a result of which violence erupted on the campus and the government of Belgium was forced to resign in 1968. The new coalition government split the university by legislative decree into two: the Dutch-speaking half remained at Louvain while the French-speaking one moved to Louvain-la-Neuve. The Free University of Brussels was also split up into two on linguistic lines.

A new stage in educational politics began in 1982 following The Reform of the State and the devolution of educational functions to the regions. However, community councils do not have complete control over education; Article 59 of the Constitution defines education as a national matter. Yet, the councils have responsibility for such matters as curriculum, timetables, educational innovations, inspection, scholarships, the open university and distance education. Thus Belgium has virtually five ministers of education: two at the center, one Dutch-speaking and one French-speaking; and three in the regions.

The Law of July 29, 1983, makes full-time education compulsory for a period of nine years (from ages six to 15) and part-time education compulsory for three years, from ages 15 to 18. This means that each student receives the full seven years of primary education, at least two years of secondary education and a further three years' training of his or her choice.

All state schools are mixed, but Roman Catholic schools are generally segregated by sex. With a large migrant presence, the education of aliens has become a major concern. At the primary level, 14% of the enrollment is non-Belgian, with higher percentages in large cities: Brussels 24%, Seraing 24%, Genk 34% and La Louveière 28%.

The school year usually starts on September 1 and lasts until the end of the following June. In addition to a two-month summer vacation, there is a two-week break at Christmas and New Year and a two-week break at Easter. Recently a seven-day midterm vacation was added in the beginning of November and in February. Institutions of higher education have a slightly different schedule, beginning in October and ending in mid-July. The schoolweek is five days long. On Wednesdays, though, students get the afternoon off for school sports and extracurricular activities.

Until 1970 the passage from one grade to the next was based on tests. Since that time continuous evaluation has become the preferred means of evaluation. Moreover, class councils have come to play an increasingly important role in this process. Class councils are composed of all teachers teaching a given grade in addition to a psychologist or counselor.

Much of primary curriculum is based on the ideas of renowned Belgian child psychologist Ovide Decroly. The production of textbooks, audiovisual materials and software is almost exclusively in the hands of private firms.

More than 90% of children from 2½ years to five years are enrolled in kindergarten. There are also day-care centers for babies as young as two to 18 months and nursery schools for those between 18 months and 2½ years. Until kindergarten, however, the services are not free.

Preschool classes are attached to primary schools and employ Decroly, Froebel and Montessori principles.

Primary schools consist of three cycles, each of two years, with one teacher for each cycle. A fourth cycle enrolls those who do not progress to secondary school. The curriculum includes religious instruction, a second language, the mother tongue, natural sciences, geography, music, art, physical education and hygiene. Primary education holds rather rigidly to the year-grade system. As a result, the number of repeaters is rather high, particularly in the first grade and also in the fifth and sixth grades. There are more repeaters in the French-speaking community (32 to 37%) than in the Dutch-speaking community (12 to 16%). The reason lies in the greater number of migrant workers' children in the southern part of country. After successful complation of the sixth grade, the child receives a certificate.

The structure and organization of secondary education was thoroughly changed by the Secondary Education Act of 1971. There are various options at this stage: lower-level, technical, vocational and artistic school; general middle school; and six-year academic high school in the state system *atheneum/*

athenée for boys and *lyceum/lycée* for girls; in the Catholic system *collège* for boys and *institute* for girls. The general middle school parallels the first cycle of the academic high schools by offering a general section of Greek and Latin studies and a preprofessional section with secretarial, commercial and handcraft courses. The student is aided in the choice of programs by a system of counseling and testing at 13 psychomedical centers across the country.

The traditional secondary system consists of two cycles of three years each. Students who do not go to a six-year academic high school could transfer to one after the first cycle of a middle school. Academic high schools having the highest standards offer a special core of Greek and Latin studies but otherwise parallel the middle and technical schools during the first cycle. Other sections include a core of classical or modern humanities, economics, science and modern languages. The second cycle at the academic high schools presents specialized fields of study, the choice of which depends upon the pupil's anticipated university discipline.

In 1969 the government inaugurated a reform of secondary education *(vernieuwd secundair onderwijs; enseignement secondaire rénové)*. The new system established three cycles of two years each. The first was directed toward an observation of a student's capabilities; the second toward orientation and specialization; and the third toward determination of a specialty. There are four areas of secondary education under this program: general, technical, artistic and vocational. The new program postpones career decisions and makes it easier to switch from one area to another until the third year. Technical and artistic programs prepare students for both university study and employment. Students are assigned to a program on the basis of aptitude as well as grades. Promotion is based on diagnostic tests rather than final examinations, and evaluation is based on effort and determination as well as scholastic ability.

The extension of the age of compulsory education in 1983 has benefited technical education. New part-time options to combine with part-time education or "social promotion" include apprenticeships. Secondary schools are encouraged to direct the more motivated and abler students away from technical training during the first cycle, after which they could receive three years of such training and qualify as full technicians. Less able students might qualify as semiskilled vocational workers at about age 16. Students could study for three or four additional years after age 18 in nonuniversity programs to graduate as nongraduate technologists. Vocational training is similar but offers fewer options.

On completing secondary school, students receive one of four diplomas: a lower secondary school certificate, attainable after three years of general, artistic or technical studies; a higher secondary school certificate, attainable after six years of general, artistic or technical studies; a diploma of aptitude for higher education as proven by a "maturity" examination; or a certificate of qualification as proven by an examination at the end of the fourth, fifth, sixth or seventh year of technical or professional studies. To receive a humanities diploma a student has to pass oral and written "maturity" examinations in the three fields he or she plans.

University education consists of three cycles. The first culminates in the degree of candidate, awarded after at least two years of study and two annual examinations (three years for medicine). The second cycle leads to the degree of licentiate after two years of study and two annual examinations (three years for law, education, psychology, engineering and pharmacy and four years for medicine). Concurrent with the licentiate, the degree of *agrégé*, which is a qualification to teach, may be obtained after a separate examination. The third cycle consists of postgraduate specialization or work toward a doctoral degree. Nonuniversity education consists of long and short professionally oriented programs at colleges of technology, economics, art, teaching, social work, agriculture and paramedical professions. Long programs include engineering, commerce and architecture. There are short, specialized two- or three-year courses in subjects such as hotel management, secretarial studies, nursing, marketing and social work. Art and music are offered at municipal academies, music schools, royal conservatories and royal academies of fine arts. Teachers attend normal schools at nursery school, primary school and lower secondary school levels. Teachers in upper secondary schools require a university degree in their subjects as well as a teaching certificate that usually is earned in coursework and training during the last year of university study.

Belgium has six full-fledged universities, each including at least the five traditional faculties of philosophy, law, medicine, science and applied science engineering. The doyen is the Catholic University of Louvain, one of the oldest and foremost Catholic universities in the world. The Free University of Brussels was founded by Freemasons and Liberals in 1834, and the state Universities of Ghent and Liège were established in the following year. There are 11 additional university-level institutions, including university centers, of which those at Antwerp for Dutch-speaking students and at Mons for French-speaking students are the most outstanding.

Although all universities receive some government funds per capita, the state controls only the admissions and syllabi at state schools. There is no restriction—*numerus clausus*—on university admissions. This results in a costly 50% dropout rate. Only 11% of the age-appropriate cohort enter a university, and only 6 to 7% complete their studies. Tuition is charged at universities, but more than one-third of the students receive grants and loans, and tuition is generally affordable. Foreign students make up about 12% of university enrollment, and about 39% of the total number of students are women. The worldwide reputation of the Catholic University of Louvain attracts students from all continents. Some 52% of university students are Dutch-speaking, and 40% French-speaking. In spite of several official efforts to democratize the universities, the enrollment of working-class children has increased only slightly during the past 20 years.

EDUCATION INDICATORS

Literacy
  Total %: 100
  Male %: 100
  Female %: 100

First level
  Schools: 2,261
  Students: 814,089
  Teachers: 24,106
  Student-teacher ratio: 1:33
  Net enrollment %: 94
  Female %: 49

Second level
  Schools: 759
  Students: 848,590
  Teachers: 56,719
  Student-teacher ratio: 1:15
  Net enrollment ratio %: 84
  Female %: 49

Vocational
  Schools: 209
  Students: 218,717
  Teachers: 6,364
  Student-teacher ratio: 31.9
  Vocational enrollment %: 45

Third level
  Institutions: 19
  Students: 245,762
  Teachers: N.A.
  Student-teacher ratio: N.A.
  Gross enrollment %: 28.2
  Graduates per 10,000, ages 20–24: 2,285
  % of population over 25 with postsecondary education: 7.5
  Female %: 45

Foreign study
  Foreign students in national universities: 21,188
  Students abroad: 2,037
    of whom in
      U.S.A.: 634

EDUCATION INDICATORS *(continued)*

France: N.A.
West Germany: 541
United Kingdom: 51

Public expenditures
  Total: BF261.038 billion (1984)
  % of GNP: 6
  % of national budget: 13.8
  % current: 94.8

Graduates, 1982

Total: 18,135
Education: 1,050
Humanities & religion: 4,058
Fine and applied arts: N.A.

Law: 1,777
Social and behavioral sciences: 1,343
Commerce and business: 1,213

Mass communication: N.A.
Home economics: N.A.
Service trades: N.A.

Natural science: 2,268
Mathematics and computer science: N.A.
Medicine: 3,160

Engineering: 1,312
Architecture: N.A.
Industrial programs: N.A.

Transportation and communications: N.A.
Agriculture, forestry and fisheries: 997
Other: 1,157

Teaching styles in Belgian universities tend to be traditional. Owing to the large number of students in the first cycle, or undergraduate level, lecturing dominates classwork. Seminars, groupwork and discussions are used more during the second cycle.

Administration of education is somewhat complex. According to the new Constitution, the community councils are responsible for education except for items defined as national. The two national Ministries of Education are responsible for state schools and for subsidies to the schools in their respective areas. Because of persisting ethnolinguistic rivalries, the two ministries often are the foci of bitter criticism. Roman Catholic schools are coordinated by the National Secretariat for Catholic Education, which also conducts educational research.

Nonformal education consists of evening schools that enable students to work for a higher diploma or attend short courses in professional subjects, correspondence courses organized by the Ministry of Education, and folk high schools (some of them residential). Belgium has no open university.

Kindergarten, primary school and lower secondary school teachers are required to hold diplomas from their respective training colleges after a three-year course. Upper secondary school teachers receive their training (*agrégation*) at the universities. A new kind of training for upper secondary school teachers was announced in 1985.

LEGAL SYSTEM

Belgium has a codified civil law system based on the Napoleonic Code. The judiciary is patterned on the French model. Judges are appointed for life and may not be removed except through due process. The Constitution permits judicial review of administrative acts to determine their compliance with the law but not their constitutionality. Acts or decrees issued by the government or decisions of local authorities but not the laws of Parliament are subject to court judgments. Courts and tribunals may issue rulings only on the particular issues brought before them.

For judicial purposes the country is divided into nine provinces, 26 districts and 222 cantons. At the base of the four-tier system are 222 justices of the peace and 20 police tribunals, which hear minor civil and criminal cases. In cantons where there no police tribunals, the justices of the peace assume criminal jurisdiction. Each of the 26 districts has one tribunal of first instance that handles more serious criminal and civil cases as well as juvenile offenses. When hearing criminal cases, these district tribunals sometimes are called correctional courts.

Assize courts meet in each of the nine provincial capitals. These are the only courts in the country that have a jury trial. In cases where the court does not agree with the majority of the jury, it may write a minority opinion and acquit the defendant. On the same level as the assize courts are five courts of appeals— one in Brussels, two in Flanders (Ghent and Antwerp) and two in Wallonia (Liège and Mons). These courts hear appeals on points of law from lower courts and also serve as courts of first instance for offenses involving senior public officials.

The highest court of the land is the Court of Cassation in Brussels. It hears appeals from all lower courts on all matters. It may overturn verdicts of lower courts only on points of law and has no authority to consider the facts of the case. If it sets aside a verdict, the case is returned to the original court for retrial. The sole original jurisdiction of the Court of Cassation deals with the removal of judges and the trial of cabinet members upon indictment by the House of Representatives.

Aside from these civil courts, there are several special courts, such as tribunals of commerce and labor courts, both at the district level. The tribunals of commerce arbitrate commercial disputes, and their judges are chosen by the business community.

Administrative disputes are under the purview of the Council of State, whose rulings are final. Its responsibilities include rendering advisory opinions on bills referred to it by the legislature of executive; drafting texts of bills and regulations at the instance of the prime minister; ruling, upon appeal, on the legality of administrative acts and decisions; settlement of commune-level electoral dispute; and resolving conflicts of authority involving provincial and communal authorities.

No information is available on the criminal justice system or the legal system.

LAW ENFORCEMENT

Public order is maintained by three types of police organizations: the commune police, descended from the municipal police forces of the 14th and 15th centuries; the gendarmerie, created during the French occupation of the country, and the Judiciary Police.

The gendarmerie is part of the Belgian armed forces and reports to the Ministry of National Defense on military matters, to the Ministry of the Interior and Public Office on police matters and to the Ministry of Justice on matters relating to internal security. Below the general headquarters in Brussels it is organized into territorial groups, mobile groups and criminal investigation detachments. Its main functions include investigation of crimes, escorting prisoners, preventive police work, maintenance of public order, enforcement of traffic laws and military policing. Although the gendarmerie has jurisdiction over the entire country, it normally operates only in those areas outside the jurisdiction of commune police forces. For operational purposes the country is divided into five regions, each of which covers two provinces, and is commanded by a colonel. Within each region are two territorial groups (one in Brussels) and a mobile group commanded by a major or lieutenant colonel. Each of the nine territorial groups covers a province and is divided into a number of districts. There also is a traffic police section attached to each territorial group. Each district is divided into brigades, each composed of a warrant officer and at least six other officers. These brigades are scattered over the whole country, each covering one or more rural communities. A surveillance and investigation detachment also is assigned to each district. Its members work in civilian clothes.

The mobile gendarmerie's main unit is based in Brussels, but there are groups in each region. Their main mission is to suppress civil disturbances and to support the armed forces as required. Their equipment includes artillery, armored vehicles and helicopters. The gendarmerie also is responsible for the security of the royal palaces and maintains a special unit for that purpose.

The standard gendarmerie uniform is blue with red piping on the trouser legs, cuffs and caps. Red collar tabs bear the gendarmerie insignia and, in the case of officers, insignia of rank. To this uniform is added a Sam Browne belt, which carries the standard 9mm automatic pistol as well as a billy club. This uniform is similar to that worn by the commune police, except that the latter have silver, not red, embellishments.

The commune police have primary jurisdiction over all important towns, of which there are 345. They have both criminal and general police duties. On criminal matters they are under the direction of the royal procurator, but in the discharge of their regular duties they are answerable to the mayor. They are authorized to carry either a 7.65mm automatic pistol or a .38-caliber revolver.

Small country towns and villages are patrolled by the rural police. Each village has one or more constables. One parish constable may look after several communities if their total population does not exceed 5,000.

The Judiciary Police (also known as the Criminal Police) is a centralized force under the direction of the Ministry of Justice and the procurator general. It is commanded by a commissioner of police. Its agents are civil servants who carry out investigation of criminal offenses and prepare evidence for trials. They work in plain clothes. One Judiciary Police brigade, under the command of the commissioner of the courts, is attached to each main court. The Judiciary Police also maintain the Central Criminal Police Records Office and the Scientific Police Laboratory.

HEALTH

Each city or town has a public assistance committee that is elected by the city or town council and that is in charge of health and hospital services in the community. These committees organize clinics and visiting nurse services, run public hospitals and pay for poor patients in private hospitals. A school health program provides annual free medical examinations for all schoolchildren. Health organizations receive government subsidies.

Mortality and morbidity rates have decreased substantially since the war. The major causes of death are, in descending order of frequency, circulatory diseases, cancer, vascular lesions affecting the central nervous system, respiratory diseases, accidents and suicides. The most frequent communicable diseases, which are obligatorily reported, include salmonellosis, gonorrhea, infectious hepatitis, scarlet fever, syphilis, meningitis and tuberculosis. Poliomyelitis has virtually disappeared.

As a result of virtually universal health insurance, Belgians enjoy exceptionally high health standards.

```
HEALTH INDICATORS, 1985

Health personnel
  Physicians: 28,365
    Per capita: 1 per 347
  Dentists: 5,911
  Nurses: 91,253
  Pharmacists: 10,608
  Midwives: 4,920

Hospitals
  Number: 531
  Number of beds: 92,138
    Per capita: 94
  Admissions/discharges per 10,000: 1,552
  Bed occupancy %: 85.3
  Average length of stay: 19 days

Type of hospitals
  Government: 36.3
  Private nonprofit: ⎱
  Private profit:    ⎰ 63.7

Public health expenditures
  As % of national budget: 1.7
  Per capita: BF80.20

Vital statistics
  Crude death rate per 1,000: 11
  Decline in death rate, 1965–85: -7.4
  Life expectancy at birth
    Males: 72
    Females: 78
  Infant mortality rate per 1,000 live births: 9.4
  Child mortality rate ages 1–4 per 1,000: insignificant
  Maternal mortality rate per 100,000 live births: 13.1
```

FOOD & NUTRITION

The per capita daily food supply for Belgium and Luxembourg is 3,679 calories and 103.3 g. (3.64 oz.) of protein.

MEDIA & CULTURE

The Belgian press is one of the oldest in Europe, dating back to 1649, when Jean Mommaert II published *Courrier véritable des Pays Bas*, Brussels' only newspaper until 1791. In 1666 the *Gensche Postijdinghen* appeared in Ghent and

PER CAPITA CONSUMPTION OF FOODS

Potatoes: 103.6 kg. (228.4 lb.)
Wheat: 70.0 kg. (154.3 lb.)
Rice: 6.0 kg. (13.2 lb.)
Fresh vegetables: 76.2 kg. (168.0 lb.)
Fruits (total): 48.8 kg. (107.6 lb.)
 Citrus: 22.0 kg. (48.5 lb.)
 Noncitrus: 26.8 kg. (59.1 lb.)
Eggs: 14.0 kg. (30.9 lb.)
Honey: 0.5 kg. (1.1 lb.)
Fish: 2.6 kg. (5.8 lb.)
Milk: 100.0 kg. (220.5 lb.)
Butter: 9.4 kg. (20.7 lb.)
Cream: 2.9 kg. (6.4 lb.)
Cheese: 13.0 kg. (28.7 lb.)
Yogurt: 4.8 kg. (10.6 lb.)
Meat (total): 86.4 kg. (190.5 lb.)
 Beef and veal: 24.8 kg. (54.7 lb.)
 Pig meat: 45.4 kg. (100.1 lb.)
 Poultry: 14.6 kg. (32.2 lb.)
 Mutton, lamb and goat: 1.6 kg. (3.5 lb.)
Sugar: 37.0 kg. (81.6 lb.)
Chocolate: 5.6 kg. (12.3 lb.)
Ice cream: 8.4 l. (8.9 qt.)
Margarine: 13.3 kg. (29.3 lb.)
Biscuits: 10.7 (23.6 lb.)
Breakfast cereals: 1.4 kg. (3.1 lb.)
Pasta: 4.4 kg. (9.7 lb.)
Frozen foods: 12.7 kg. (28.0 lb.)
Canned foods: 11.5 kg. (25.4 lb.)
Beer 133.8 l. (141.4 qt.)
Wine 22.7 l. (24.0 qt.)
Alcoholic liquors: 2.2 l. (2.3 qt.)
Soft drinks 65 l. (68.7 qt.)
Mineral waters 52.8 l. (55.8 qt.)
Fruit juices 12.7 l. (13.4 qt.)
Tea: 0.1 kg. (0.2 lb.)
Coffee: 8.3 kg. (18.3 lb.)
Cocoa: 3.6 kg. (7.9 lb.)

during the same period *Den Ordinarien Posten* appeared in Antwerp. Two other papers were founded at this time in Bruges and Liège. During the Austrian and Dutch rule, the press began to experience the sting of censorship, from which it emerged only with independence in 1830. The Constitution stipulated that the press is free to publish without fear of censorship. For the next half century the press proliferated, especially representing political parties. The daily press was entirely French until 1844, when the first Flemish paper, *Het Handelsblad*, was founded. By 1874 Belgium had 68 daily newspapers with 175,000 subscribers. The two world wars were periods of shakeout for the press, and hundreds of papers died during the process. At the end of hostilities in 1945 there were 42 French-language and 19 Flemish-language papers published by 42 ownership groups. After World War II there were numerous attempts to start up new papers, of which six dailies have survived.

In the mid-1980s there are 40 dailies being published in Belgium—26 in French, 13 in Dutch and one in German—as well as four financial papers, one official gazette and a French-language newspaper in Flanders. The total circulation of 2,242,000 copies in 1982 is shared almost equally by Flemish and French dailies. About 58% of the circulation is accounted for by the country's top 10 dailies, but one-third have circulations of less than 35,000 each. The main cleavage in the daily press is between Catholic and secular. The Catholic press includes the French editions of *L'Avenir du Luxembourg, Le Courrier de Verviers, Le Courrier, La Libre Belgique* and *Gazette de Liège,* the Dutch editions of *Het Volk-De Nieuwe Gids, De Staandaard, Het Nieuwsblad, De Gentenaar* and *Het Handelsblad,* and the German edition of *Grenz Echo.* Many papers are officially affiliated with political parties. The Christian Democrat papers include *Gazet Van Antwerpen, La Cité, Gazet Van Mechelen* and *Vers l'Avenir;* Social Christian papers include *Le Rappel, La Journal de Mons, Echo du Centre, Het Belang van Limburg* and *Le Courrier de l'Escaat;* Socialist papers include *Da Volksgazet* of Antwerp and *Voorhuit* of Brussels.

Belgian dailies appear both in standard broadsheet and tabloid page sizes. The former typically runs from 16 to 24 pages in a seven- or eight-column format. Seven Belgian cities have competing newspapers. Twelve dailies are published in Brussels, six in Antwerp, three in Ghent and two each in Charleroi, Liège, Tournai and Verviers.

There are also 14 specialized dailies published in Belgium in addition to 506 weeklies, 345 semimonthlies, 1,133 bimonthlies and 1,884 quarterlies and biannuals. Some of the weeklies report high circulations, including Antwerp's *Libelle/Rosita, TV Ekspress* and *TV Strip* and Brussels' *Bonne Soirée, Kwik/ Zondag Nieuws* and *Humo,* all of which have circulations over 225,000. Because there is no compulsory auditing of circulation figures, Belgian newspapers do not generally make their circulation figures public. Thus accurate data are not available on circulation of individual dailies, but by unofficial figures the largest 10 dailies are as follows:

The Belgian press, like the economy as a whole, is beset by critical problems, leading to the closure of many publications in the 1970s and 1980s. The decreasing number of titles has resulted in growing concentration of ownership. Together there are 19 press groups or consortiums and six associated companies,

Daily	Language	Circulation (daily)
Het Laatste Nieuws	Flemish	331,068
Le Soir	French	224,394
Hert Volk	Flemish	204,636
Gazet van Antwerpen	Flemish	185,448

Daily	Language	Circulation (daily)
La Dernière Heure	French	110,000
Het Belang van Limburg	Flemish	100,000
La Libre Belgique	French	100,000
The Staandaard Group: De Staandaard Het Nieuwsblad De Gentenaar Het Handelsblad	Flemish	78,000
Vers l'Avenir	French	63,427
L'Avenir du Luxembourg	French	34,932

of which the largest are the Rossel Group, the Vers l'Avenir Company and Édi-tions de la Libre Belgique on the French side and the Staandaard Group, the Hoste Group and the Het Volk Group on the Dutch side.

Belgium produces about half the newsprint is uses. Newspaper advertising is on the rise, and its share of all advertising expenditures is close to one-third. The amount of advertising varies from paper to paper; in the top two dailies, *Het Laatste Nieuws* and *Le Soir*, it is as high as 50%.

The long tradition of press freedom in Belgium is rooted in Articles 14 and 18 of the Constitution. Article 14 guarantees freedom of expression of opinion on all subjects. Article 18 refers specifically to the press: "The press is free. Censor-ship may never be established; no deposit in earnest of good faith may be de-manded from writers, editors or printers. When the author is known and is resi-dent in Belgium, the publisher, printer or distributor may not be prosecuted."

Restraints on the abuse of this freedom are found in the Penal Code and the Civil Code. For example, Article 1832 of the Civil Code calls for prosecution of a journalist who has "caused material or moral damage to another." Article 253 prohibits publication of divorce court proceedings. The code also prohibits the advertising of illegal lotteries, maneuvers to influence stock and currency prices, illustrations that offend public decency, and publication of materials abusive of the Belgian King, royal family and foreign heads of state. Such abuses are called press misdemeanors. They are usually settled in lower courts. The Belgian citizen is further protected by the so-called right to reply to any published item that is factually in error about him or her. Newspapers and journalists are not licensed, but the Association des Journalistes Professionnels de Belgique was instrumental in passing legislation in 1963 that created the rank and title of professional journalist. All freedoms of the press may be suspended and censorship imposed during times of war.

Since 1972 the Belgian government has provided financial aid to ailing newspapers to keep them solvent. This aid is apportioned according to a complicated financial formula that ensures that French- and Dutch-language newspapers of all types of political persuasion receive an equitable share.

The national news agency is the Agence Belga (Agence Télégraphique Belge de Presse), located in Brussels. It has branch offices in Antwerp, Kinshasa and Cotonou (in Benin). Founded in 1920, it is largely owned by Belgian dailies. About half of its news dispatches cover foreign news.

MEDIA INDICATORS, 1985

Newspapers
    Number of dailies: 26
    Circulation (000): 2,209
    Per capita: 223

    Number of nondailies per 1,000: 2
    Circulation (000): 22
    Per capita: 2 per 1,000

    Number of periodicals: 11,256,000
    Circulation: N.A.

    Newsprint consumption
    Total: 190,600 Tons
    Per 1,000: 19,306 kg (42,562 lb.)

Book publishing
    Number of titles: 8,065

Broadcasting
    Annual expenditures: BF10.487 million
    Number of employees: 5,308

Radio
    Number of transmitters: 41
    Number of radio receivers: 4,617,000
      Per capita: 468 per 1,000
    Total program hours: 49,175

Television
    Television transmitters: 31
    Number of TV receivers: 2,981,000
      Per capita: 303
    Total program hours: 8,756

```
┌─────────────────────────────────────────────────┐
│          MEDIA INDICATORS, 1985 (continued)      │
│  Cinema                                          │
│     Number of fixed cinemas: 472                 │
│     Seating capacity: N.A.                       │
│        Seats per 1,000: N.A.                     │
│     Annual attendance (million): 20.5            │
│     Gross box office receipts: BF2.289 billion   │
│  Films                                           │
│     Production of long films: 14                 │
│     Import of long films: N.A.                   │
└─────────────────────────────────────────────────┘
```

Broadcasting began in the 1920s. In 1930 Parliament set up a semi-independent public broadcasting service, the Institut National de Radiodiffusion. For a while some private radio stations also were allowed to operate. During World War II the Belgian government set up, in Condon, the Office de Radiodiffusion Nationale Belge, which merged with the Institut Nationale Radiodiffusion after the war. Shortly thereafter, TV commenced.

A new law in 1960 established two national broadcasting organizations: the Flemish-language Belgische Radio en Televisie (BRT) and the French-speaking Radio-Télévision Belge de la Communauté Culturelle Française (RTBF). Although subject to government supervision and financial controls, the two organizations are autonomous in terms of programming and policies. Article 28 of the law calls for "rigorous objectivity in the sphere of news and information." Article 28 allows political parties, trade unions, religious and other special-interest groups to utilize radio and television services according to equality rulings established by statute. The institutes were required to broadcast 10 hours of official announcements each month, but this provision was invalidated in 1977. There are no commercials on radio or television.

Belgian broadcasting has been increasingly buffeted by competition from foreign stations and cable TV. The 1970s also witnessed the rise of "free" or pirate radio stations. Such stations usually broadcast clandestinely with low power.

The Belgian proclivity for associations extends to the media. The most powerful press body is the Association des Journalistes Professionnels de Belgique/Algemene Vereniging van de Beroeps-journalisten in Belgie, founded in 1979 through the merger of two older associations. Education in mass communications is provided at the Universities of Ghent and Liège.

SOCIAL WELFARE

Virtually all Belgians are covered by national health insurance. Made compulsory as part of social legislation passed in 1945, health insurance is administered by about 1,745 mutual aid societies, allied to trade unions and grouped as Cath-

```
┌─────────────────────────────────────────────┐
│        CULTURAL & ENVIRONMENTAL INDICATORS    │
│  Libraries                                    │
│     Number: 2,351                             │
│     Volumes: 24.14 million                    │
│     Registered borrowers: 1,731,000           │
│     Loans per 1,000: 4,300                    │
│                                               │
│  Museums: 132                                 │
│     Annual attendance: 3,454,000              │
│     Attendance per 1,000: 350                 │
│                                               │
│  Performing arts                              │
│     Number of performances: N.A.              │
│     Annual attendance: N.A.                   │
│     Attendance per 1,000: N.A.                │
│                                               │
│  Ecological sites                             │
│     Number of facilities: 4                   │
│     Annual attendance: N.A.                   │
└─────────────────────────────────────────────┘
```

olic (45% of the insured population), Socialist (29%), Liberal (5%), professional (10%) or neutral (10%). Health insurance covers both medical and dental care, hospital stays, part of the costs of drugs and prostheses, treatment of mental illness, tuberculosis, cancer and congenital problems. The cost is underwritten by payroll contributions by the employer and the employee. By contast, benefits for the self-employed cover only catastrophic illness and are paid out of income.

Nearly 15.6% of the GNP is spent on various kinds of medical care, and 10% of the work force participates directly or indirectly in the health sector. Health insurance costs have tended to rise faster than the economy as a whole, partly due to the aging of the population, high costs of medical technology and personnel, and the growing proportion of migrant children with more health problems.

Social Security programs are administered by the National Office of Social Security, established in 1944. These programs include disability and retirement pensions, survivors' benefits, unemployment and family allowances. Retirement pension is based upon 60% of average annual income adjusted to the Consumer Price Index and the marital status of the pensioners. Survivors' benefits are paid to widows and widowers, while children receive family allowances. Unemployment benefits are calculated at 60% of earnings payable indefinitely, and disability benefits continue at the same rate for one year. Workmen's compensation is provided by public and private insurance.

Social Security benefits are financed on a pay-as-you-go basis from government subsidies and payroll deductions from employers and employees, having ceilings and floors on the range of earnings taxed. In 1984 workers contributed

12.2% on full wages and salaries and employers contributed 37.7% (43.7% for manual workers). In 1982 there were 1,354,262 persons receiving retirement and survivors' persions.

Social Security is both a political and an economic issue. It grew by 437% during the 1970–82 period—the most rapid growth in the EEC. Government transfers to Social Security grew far more rapidly than the GNP. An aging population has meant that there are more dependents on fewer contributors. With fewer younger workers and more unemployed, the ratio of contributors to pensioners fell from 4:1 in 1954 to 1:8 in 1979. In 1979 and 1980 the government spent more on Social Security than it collected and there were more recipients of Social Security than active workers in the private sector. Even with 80% of expenditures coming from payroll taxes, the government spent 30% of its 1984 budget on Social Security. Unemployment, indexation and an aging population are long-term problems that are expected to intensify during the rest of this century.

Efforts to get the Social Security system back on track include reduced benefits, increased contributions, medical cost containment and raising the retirement age of women to 65.

CHRONOLOGY (FROM 1945)

1946—Royal decree establishes Social Security system. . . . Benelux Convention signed.

1947—Language census marks the start of linguistic conflict between French-speakers and Dutch-speakers. . . . Paul Spaak become prime minister in place of A. van Acker.

1948—Women are given right to vote.

1949—NATO is founded, with Belgium as a founding member. . . . G. Eyskens is named prime minister.

1950—Second School Conflict begins. . . . J. Duvieusart is elected prime minister but resigns after two months in favor of J. Pholen.

1951—Leopold III abdicates in favor of his son Baudouin.

1952—J. van Houtte is sworn in as prime minister.

1954—A. van Acker returns as prime minister.

1958—School Pact ends Second School Conflict. . . . EEC is established. . . . G. Eyskens returns as prime minister.

1960—Austerity budget is announced following general strike in Wallonia.

1961—T. Lefevre takes office as prime minister.

1962—Belgium's African colonies, Congo, Rwanda and Burundi, become independent. . . . Linguistic boundaries are delimited.

1965—P. Harmel is sworn in as prime minister.

1966—P. van den Boeynants is named prime minister.

1968—G. Eyskens begins new term as prime minister. . . . Violence erupts at the Catholic University of Louvain as angry Flemish students call for the removal of French as medium of instruction. . . . Social Christians split into French and Flemish sections.

1971—Third reform of the Constitution establishes four linguistic regions and three cultural communities.

1972—Liberals split into Flemish, Walloon and Brussels wings.

1973—Oil crisis threatens Belgian economy. . . . E. Le Burton is sworn in as prime minister.

1974—Leo Tindemans is elected prime minister.

1977—The Egmont Pact is signed by Social Christians, Socialists and Liberals but collapses following persisting party differences.

1978—P. van den Boeynants returns as prime minister. . . . Socialists split into Flemish and Walloon wings.

1979—Wilfried Martens forms his first cabinet as prime minister.

1980—The Reform of State is adopted through a revised Constitution; regionalization takes effect as major national powers are devolved to regional and communal councils.

1981—M. Eyskens is prime minister for nine months, but Wilfried Martens returns to office as head of a coalition government following general elections.

1982—Martens coalition government is granted special power to establish an austerity regime.

1985—In new elections, the Martens center-right coalition retains majority; Martens VI is installed in office.

1986—Former prime minister Boeynants is convicted of tax evasion and fraud.

BIBLIOGRAPHY

BOOKS

Cowie, Donald. *Belgium: The Land and the People*. Cranbury, N.J., 1977.

Fitzmaurice, John. *The Politics of Belgium*. New York, 1983.

Flynn, Gregory. *NATO's Northern Allies: The National Security Policies of Belgium, Netherlands, Norway and Denmark*. Totowa, N.J., 1985.

Goris, Jean-Albert. *Belgium*. Berkeley, Calif., 1945.

Helmreich, Jonathan E. *Belgium and Europe: A Study in Small-Power Diplomacy*. The Hague, 1976.

Huggett, Frank E. *Modern Belgium*. London, 1969.

Lipjhart, Arend. *Conflict and Coexistence in Belgium: The Politics of a Culturally Divided Society*. Berkeley, Calif., 1981.

Mallinson, V. *Belgium*. London, 1969.

Riley, Raymond. *Belgium*. Boulder, Colo., 1976.

OFFICIAL PUBLICATIONS

GENERAL

Annuaire de la Statistique de la Belgique
Bulletin du Commerce Extérieur
Bulletin de Statistique (monthly)
Chiffres Officiels de la Population Droit par Commune (annual)
Recensement Général de l'Agriculture
Recensement de la Population et des Logements au 1er Mars 1981
Statistiques Démographiques

MINISTRY OF FINANCE

Communiqué Mensuel du Ministre des Finances (Monthly Report of the Minister of Finance)
Rapport Annuel de la Caisse de Dépôts et de Consignations (Annual Report of the Deposit and Consignment Fund)
Rapport de la Caisse d'Amortissement (Report of the Amortization Fund)
Situation Mensuelle de Caisse (Monthly Cash Statement) (statement on the execution of the budget)
Situation Mensuelle du Trésor (Monthly Treasury Statement)

OTHER UNITS OF THE CENTRAL GOVERNMENT

Annuaire Statistique de la Sécurité Sociale (Social Security Statistical Yearbook)
Bulletin de Statistiques (Bulletin of Statistics), Institut National de Statistique (National Institute of Statistics) (monthly)
Cahier de la Cour des Comptes (Report of the Court of Accounts)
Exposé Général du Budget et Budgets des Différents Départements (General Report on the Budget and Budgets of the Different Departments)
Rapport Annuel du Fonds des Rentes (Annual Report of the Open Market Operations Fund)
Rapport Annuel de l'Institut National d'Assurance Maladie-Invalidité (Annual Report of the National Sickness-Disability Insurance Institute)
Rapport Annuel de l'Office National de l'Emploi (Annual Report of the National Employment Office)
Rapport Annuel de l'Office National de Sécurité Sociale (Annual Report of the National Social Security Office)
Rapport Annuel de l'Office de la Sécurité Sociale d'Outre-Mer (Annual Report of the Overseas Social Security Office)

Rapport du Fonds de Logement de la Ligne des Familles Nombreuses de Belgique (Report of the Housing Fund of the Belgian League of Large Families)

Rapport Général sur la Sécurité Sociale (General Report for Social Security), Ministère de la Prévoyance Sociale (Ministry of Social Security)

BANQUE NATIONALE DE BELGIQUE

Bulletin (monthly)

Rapport

Situation Hebdomadaire (Weekly Statement)

LOCAL GOVERNMENT

Bulletin Périodique du Crédit Communal de Belgique (Periodic Bulletin of Municipal Credit of Belgium) (monthly)

Rapport Annuel du Crédit Communal de Belgique (Annual Report of Municipal Credit of Belgium)

All sources are in French or Dutch only and annual except as indicated.

LUXEMBOURG

LUXEMBOURG

BASIC FACT SHEET

OFFICIAL NAME: Grand Duchy of Luxembourg (Grand-Duché de Luxembourg; Grossherzogtum Luxemburg)

ABBREVIATION: LU

CAPITAL: Luxembourg-Ville

HEAD OF STATE: Grand Duke John (from 1964)

HEAD OF GOVERNMENT: Prime Minister Jacques Santer (from 1984)

NATURE OF GOVERNMENT: Constitutional monarchy

POPULATION: 366,127 (1987)

AREA: 2,586 sq. km. (998 sq. mi.)

ETHNIC MAJORITY: Celtic base with French and German blend

LANGUAGES: French, German, Letzeburgesche

RELIGION: Roman Catholicism

UNIT OF CURRENCY: Luxembourg franc

NATIONAL FLAG: A tricolor of red, white and blue horizontal stripes

NATIONAL EMBLEM: A gold-crowned red lion on a shield of alternate white and blue stripes, topped by a ducal gold coronet in the center; around the shield is the gold and green Grand Collar of the Order of the Oaken Crown, from which is suspended the cross of the order. Red-tongued and crowned gold heraldic lions guard the emblem. When the emblem is displayed, the background is a gold and red pavilion crested with a massive gold crown.

NATIONAL ANTHEM: "Ons Hemecht" (Our Homeland)

NATIONAL HOLIDAYS: June 23 (Grand Duke's Birthday); all major Catholic festivals

NATIONAL CALENDAR: Gregorian

PHYSICAL QUALITY OF LIFE INDEX: 96 (on an ascending scale with 100 as the maximum)

DATE OF INDEPENDENCE: 963

DATE OF CONSTITUTION: 1868 (as revised in 1919, 1946 and 1956)

WEIGHTS & MEASURES: Metric

GEOGRAPHICAL FEATURES

A landlocked country in Western Europe, Luxembourg has an area of 2,586 sq. km. (998 sq. mi.) extending 82 km. (51 mi.) north to south and 57 km. (35 mi.) east to west. Its boundary with the Federal Republic of Germany, formed by the Our, Sauer and Moselle rivers, is 135 km. (34 mi.) long; that with France on the south is 73 km. (45 mi.) long; and that with Belgium on the west and north is 142 km. (92 mi.) long. The total boundary length is 356 km. (221 mi.). The eastern boundaries of Luxembourg were fixed by the demarcation treaty at

Aachen on June 28, 1816, between the Netherlands and Prussia. Article 27 of the treaty establishes a condominium over natural or man-made features serving as the border. The boundary between France and Luxembourg was fixed by the Treaty of Courtrai on March 28, 1820, between France and the Netherlands. The border is a rigid one, with no condominium. The boundary between Belgium and Luxembourg was drawn up on April 19, 1839, at the Treaty of London, also known as the Treaty of 24 Articles.

The capital is Luxembourg-Ville, with a 1983 population of 89,000. The other major towns are Esch-sur-Alzette (25,100), Differdange (16,700), Dudelange (14,100) and Petange (12,100).

Luxembourg consists of two distinct geographical regions: the rugged uplands of the Ardennes in the North, with elevations ranging from 396 to 549 km. (1,300 to 1,800 ft.) above sea level; and the fertile lowlands of the South called Bon Pays, with a mean altitude of 229 km. (750 ft.) above sea level. Crisscrossing the area are deep valleys. Most rivers drain into the Sauer, which, in turn, flows into the Moselle on the eastern border. The northern region, comprising one-third of the country, is heavily forested. Along the Moselle is a very fertile wine-growing region. The soil is generally sandy, with sandstone and limestone prevalent.

CLIMATE & WEATHER

Luxembourg has a temperate and mild climate, with generally cool summers and mild winters. Mean summer temperatures are about 16.6°C (62°F), while winter temperatures rarely drop below the freezing point. The high peaks of the Ardennes in the North shelter the country from the rigorous north winds, while the prevailing northwesterly winds have a cooling effect. The Southwest receives more rainfall. The average annual precipitation is about 762 mm. (30 in.).

POPULATION

The population of the Grand Duchy was estimated in 1987 at 366,127 on the basis of the last census held in 1981, when the population was 364,606. The population is projected to reach 375,000 in 1990 and 400,000 in 2000. About one-fourth of the population lives in the capital and about half in other urban areas. The annual growth rate is close to zero. The average density is much higher than that of France but lower than that of Belgium and of West Germany.

There are no barriers to immigration from EEC countries, except for Greece, Spain and Portugal. Until these countries become full EEC members, their citizens must obtain work permits to reside in Luxembourg. Such work permits are readily granted. Since 1970 Luxembourg has had a large Portuguese population. Large numbers of Vietnamese also have been admitted as refugees, although Luxembourg is not a country of first application for asylum.

Although discrimination based on sex is prohibited by law, women occupy a less prominent position in public life than in neighboring countries. There are very few women in senior positions either in business or in politics.

ETHNIC COMPOSITION

Luxembourgers consider themselves a distinct ethnic group, based, however, more on political than on racial tradition. The desire to be regarded as separate from their neighbors is expressed in the national motto: We Want to Remain What We Are. Native Luxembourgers are of French, Belgian and German ancestry. Nearly 22% of the population is of foreign origin. The majority of foreigners are of Italian descent.

LANGUAGES

French is the official language used extensively in the media and for administrative purposes. German is the written language used in commerce and the press. Letzeburgesch is native dialect of the country, and it competes with French and German as the language of instruction in primary schools. Letzeburgesch is a Germanic dialect related to the Moselle Frankish language once spoken in Western Germany. French is the most common medium of instruction in secondary schools.

RELIGIONS

The population is overwhelmingly Roman Catholic. Catholicism was introduced into Luxembourg by the French missionary Willibrord, who built the monastery at Echternach in 698. Although the proportion of professing Catholics has decreased slightly since World War II, the church is still institutionally strong, as witnessed by the influence of the Christian labor unions; the Christian Social People's Party (which has been in power for more than 50 years); and the pro-church newspaper *Luxemburger Wort*, the largest daily in the country.

Most Protestants are foreigners. Mennonites form a large congregation, aided by Mennonite missionaries from the United States.

Church-state relations are smooth. The Napoleon Concordat of 1801 has never been expressly abolished with the exception of a few articles that have

```
┌─────────────────────────────────────────────────────┐
│                DEMOGRAPHIC INDICATORS                 │
│ Population: 1987 (000): 366,127                        │
│ Year of last census: 1981                             │
│   Males (000): 179        Females (000): 183          │
│   Sex ratio: 48.67 (males): 51.33 (females)           │
│ Population trends (000)                                │
│   1930: 297     1960: 314      1990: 366              │
│   1940: 296     1970: 339      2000: 367              │
│   1950: 296     1980: 364      2020: N.A.             │
│ Population doubling time in years at current rate:     │
│   3,465                                                │
│ Hypothetical size of stationary population (million):  │
│   N.A.                                                 │
│ Assumed year of reaching net reproduction rate of 1:   │
│   N.A.                                                 │
│ Age profile (%)                                        │
│   0–14: 18.5     30–44: 21.2     60–74: 12.8          │
│   15–29: 23.7    45–59: 18.8     Over 75: 5.00        │
│ Median age (years): 36.4                               │
│ Density per sq. km.: 141.5                             │
│ Annual growth rate (%)                                 │
│   1950–55: 0.60 1970–75: 1.32 1990–95: 0.08           │
│   1955–60: N.A. 1975–80: 0.14 1995–2000: 0.06         │
│   1960–65: 1.11 1980–85: 0.12                          │
│   1965–70: 0.43 1985–90: 0.11                          │
│ Vital statistics                                       │
│   Crude birth rate 1/1000: 10.1                        │
│   Crude death rate 1/1000: 11.9                        │
│   Dependency (total): 44.8                             │
│   Infant mortality rate 1/1000: 11                     │
│   Maternal mortality rate: 1/100,000: N.A.            │
│   Natural increase 1/1000: -1.8                        │
│   Total fertility rate: 1.38                           │
│   General fertility rate: 41                           │
│   Gross reproduction rate: 0.67                        │
│   Marriage rate 1/1000: 5.3                            │
│   Divorce rate 1/1000: 1.8                             │
│   Life expectancy males (years): 66.9                  │
│   Life expectancy females (years): 73.5                │
│   Average household size: 2.8                          │
│   % illegitimate births: 8.2                           │
│ Youth                                                  │
│   Youth population 15–24 (000): 100                    │
│   Youth population in 2020 (000): 30                   │
└─────────────────────────────────────────────────────┘
```

been expressly superseded by subsequent laws. The legal status of the church is found in the Constitution of 1868 (Articles 19, 20, 21 and 26) and follows essentially the provisions of the Belgian Constitution. The only difference is the law of April 30, 1873, which requires the Catholic bishops to pledge an oath of allegiance to the crown. All religious organizations are required to be authorized by law. In primary education, a course in Catholic theology is obligatory except where parents specifically request that their children be excused. Beyond a school for the secondary education of girls, the Catholic Church has not established schools. The curators who supervise public education represent the interests of the Catholic Church as well.

HISTORICAL BACKGROUND

Luxembourg was founded in 963 by Count Sigefroid, who rebuilt a small ruined fortress called Lucilinburhuc (Little Burg) on site of the present city of Luxembourg. The dynasty became powerful under the blind John, count of Luxembourg and king of Bohemia (1310–46), who is the national hero. His son Charles IV (1346–78) was the second of four Luxembourg princes to become Holy Roman emperor.

In 1443 Luxembourg came under Burgundian rule and for the succeeding 400 years was under foreign control: Spain from 1506 to 1714 (except for 13 years from 1784 to 1797, when it was ruled by France); Austria (1714–95); and France (1795–1815). The Congress of Vienna, which redrew European frontiers in 1815, made Luxembourg a grand duchy and allotted it to the king of the Netherlands after forcing it to cede to Prussia its territory east of the Moselle, Sure and Our. Luxembourg lost more than half its territory to Belgium in 1839. By the 1867 Treaty of London, Luxembourg was proclaimed an independent state under the protection of the Great Powers but was required to dismantle its fortress. In 1890 Adolphe of the House of Nassau-Weilbourg became the grand duke. After the end of World War I, Grand Duchess Charlotte succeeded to the throne. The Grand Duchy was under German rule from 1940 to 1944. In 1960 it joined an economic union with Belgium and the Netherlands. In April 1963 Luxembourg celebrated its millennium as an independent state. In the following year, Grand Duchess Charlotte abdicated in favor of her son Jean.

CONSTITUTION & GOVERNMENT

Luxembourg is a constitutional monarchy governed by the Constitution of 1868 as amended in 1919, 1948 and 1950. Legislative power is vested in the Chamber of Deputies. The Constitution also provides for an advisory Council of State.

Executive power is vested jointly in the sovereign, who may initiate legislation, and a prime minister (technically, president of government) appointed by the monarch. The separation of powers between the executive and the legislature is not clear-cut and permits free interaction. The grand duke's competence in legislative matters is limited by Article 36 of the Constitution, which permits him to issue regulations and orders necessary for carrying laws into effect but debars him from suspending the laws themselves and from dispensing with their enforcement. The responsibility of the ministers to the Chamber of Deputies, the annual vote on the budget, and review of administrative orders by the courts are all constitutional trammels on the executive.

However, the preponderance of the executive over the legislature was clearly established in the 1868 Constitution, and although appreciably reduced through the 1919 revision, has not entirely disappeared. This is because the executive power is exercised by the grand duke and the prime minister, but they also have a substantial legislative role.

The Constitution may be amended only through the revision procedures laid down in Article 114. When the Chamber of Deputies calls for any amendment, it is automatically dissolved, and new elections are to be held within three months. Revision must be confined to articles expressly specified by the dissolved Chamber. A two-thirds majority is required for adoption of the amendment.

Since World War II, power has been exercised by a series of coalition governments in which the Christian Social People's Party has traditionally been the dominant partner. The pattern was broken only from 1974 to 1979, when the Socialist Workers and Democratic parties formed a coalition government under Gaston Thorn. The Christian Social People's Party returned to office in 1979 in partnership with the Democratic Party. In 1984 Pierre Werner, the Christian Social People's Party leader who had led his party since 1949, stepped down in favor of Jacques Santer.

Grand Duke Jean, the head of state, succeeded his mother, Grand Duchess Charlotte, in 1964. The crown of the Grand Duchy is hereditary in the House of Nassau. The spouse of the grand duke is Grand Duchess Josephine-Charlotte, sister of King Baudouin, king of the Belgians.

Constitutionally, the grand duke is inviolate and legally irresponsible. He cannot be accused or prosecuted by anyone, cannot be called upon to account for his acts and is not subject to the jurisdiction of any court. The political irresponsibility of the grand duke has its counterpart in ministerial responsibility. Any law or decree signed by the grand duke must be countersigned by a councillor of the crown, who then assumes full responsibility for that measure.

The sessions of the Chamber of Deputies are opened and closed by the grand duke in person or in his name by an authorized person. He may summon the Chamber in an extraordinary session and is obliged to do so if requested by one-third of its membership. He may adjourn the Chamber but not for a period exceeding one month, and the adjournment cannot be repeated during the same session without the Chamber's consent. Finally, the grand duke may dissolve the Chamber provided new elections are held within three months. In legislation, the grand duke participates on an equal footing with the Chamber. He may initiate any bill, and no bill can be enacted without his consent. The Constitution allows the grand duke three months to sign a bill after its passage in the Chamber; in the event of his failing to do so, the bill becomes null and void.

The grand duke appoints the president of the government, as the prime minister is known, and he, in turn, names the cabinet members, who are also known as secretaries of state or ministers. When no party has an absolute majority in the Chamber, government formation can be a long, drawn-out affair in which the grand duke plays a pivotal role as matchmaker. Ministers are individually and collectively responsible for their actions, and the consequences for illegal acts can be political as well as judicial. A written or oral order from the grand duke does not absolve a minister of his responsibility, and a minister may *not* receive a pardon from the grand duke for his illegal acts without the approval of the Chamber of Deputies.

RULERS OF LUXEMBOURG

Grand Dukes/Duchesses

March 1815–Oct. 1840	Guillaume I (Willem I of the Netherlands) (abdicated)
Oct. 1840–March 1849	Guillaume II (Willem II of the Netherlands) (*son*)
March 1849–Nov. 1890	Guillaume III (Willem III of the Netherlands) (*son*)
Nov. 1890–Nov. 1905	Adolphe (*f* Adolf, Duke of Nassau)
Nov. 1905–Feb. 1912	Guillaume IV (*son*)
Feb. 1912–Jan. 1919	Marie Adelaide (*daughter*) (abdicated)
Jan. 1919–May 1940	Charlotte (*daughter*) (1st) (exiled)
(May 1940–Sept. 1944	German occupation)
Sept. 1944–Nov. 1964	Charlotte (2nd) (abdicated)
Nov. 1964–	Jean (*son*)

Prime Ministers

Aug.–Dec. 1848	J.-T.-I. de la Fontaine
Dec. 1848–Sept. 1853	Jean-Jacques Willmar
Sept. 1853–Sept. 1860	Mathias Simons
Sept. 1860–Dec. 1867	Victor de Tornaco
Dec. 1867–Dec. 1874	Emmanuel Servais
Dec. 1874–Feb. 1885	Félix de Blochausen
Feb. 1885–Sept. 1888	Edouard Thilges
Sept. 1888–Oct. 1915	Paul Eyschen (†)

RULERS OF LUXEMBOURG *(continued)*

Oct.–Nov. 1915	Mathias Mongenast
Nov. 1915–Feb. 1916	Hubert Loutsch
Feb. 1916–June 1917	Victor Thorn
June 1917–Sept. 1918	Léon Kauffmann
Sept. 1918–March 1925	Émile Reuter (Right P.)
March 1925–July 1926	Pierre Prum (Nat. Indep. P.)
July 1926–Nov. 1937	Joseph Bech (1st) (Right P.)
Nov. 1937–May 1940	Pierre Dupong (1st) (Right P.)
(May 1940–Sept. 1944	German occupation)
Sept. 1944–Dec. 1953	Pierre Dupong (2nd) (†) (Chr. Soc. P.)
Dec. 1953–March 1958	Joseph Bech (2nd) (Chr. Soc. P.)
March 1958–March 1959	Pierre Frieden (Chr. Soc. P.)
March 1959–June 1974	Pierre Werner (1st) (Chr.Soc. P.)
June 1974–June 1979	Gaston Thorn (later president of the EEC Commission) (Lib. P.)
June 1979–July 1984	Pierre Werner (2nd) (Chr. Soc. P.)
July 1984–	Jacques Santer (Chr. Soc. P.)

Organization of Government

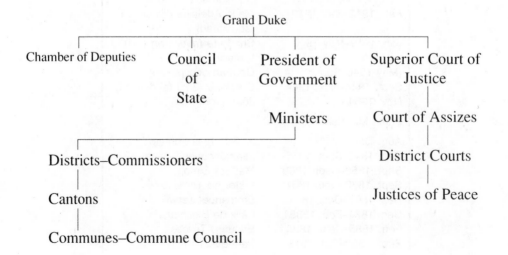

```
┌─────────────────────────────────────────────┐
│                 CABINET LIST                  │
│ Grand Duke                   Jean             │
│ Prime Minister               Jacques Santer   │
│ Vice Prime Minister          Jacques Poos     │
│ Min. of Agriculture          Marc Fischbach   │
│ Min. of Budget               Jean-Claude Juncker │
│ Min. of Civil Service        Marc Fischbach   │
│ Min. of Communications       Jacques Santer   │
│ Min. of Cultural Affairs     Robert Krieps    │
│ Min. of Defense              Marc Fischbach   │
│ Min. of Education            Fernand Boden    │
│ Min. of Energy               Marcel Schlechter │
│ Min. of Environment          Robert Krieps    │
│ Min. for Family, Housing and                  │
│   Social Affairs             Jean Spautz      │
│ Min. of Finance              Jacques Santer   │
│ Min. of Foreign Affairs      Jacques Poos     │
│ Min. of Foreign Trade and                     │
│   Cooperation                Jacques Poos     │
│ Min. of Interior             Jean Spautz      │
│ Min. of Justice              Krieps Robert    │
│ Min. of Labor                Jean-Claude Juncker │
│ Min. of Middle-Class Affairs Jacques Poos     │
│ Min. of National Economy     Jacques Poos     │
└─────────────────────────────────────────────┘
```

FREEDOM & HUMAN RIGHTS

Individual human rights are provided for by the Constitution and protected in practice. Human rights are protected at home and actively promoted abroad. The relatively large foreign population is treated fairly. Although not a country of first application for refugees, large numbers of refugees have been admitted in recent years. Nationals enjoy a fair and efficient judicial and penal system.

CIVIL SERVICE

No information is available on the Luxembourg civil service

LOCAL GOVERNMENT

For purposes of local administration, Luxembourg is divided into three districts (Luxembourg, Diekirch and Grevenmacher) comprising 12 cantons, which in turn make up 126 communes. The districts are headed by commissioners who are part of the national civil service.

The communes are the only constitutional units of local self-government. Each commune has its own elected communal council. Communal elections are held on the second Sunday of October preceding the expiration of the term of the sitting council Members, whose numbers vary with the population, are elected for a term of six years. In some communes elections are held under the simple majority system. In others, with over 3,000 inhabitants, several candidates are voted for on the party-list system with proportional representation, as in the legislative elections. The grand duke has the right to dissolve the communal councils; when he does so, new elections are held within a month.

The executive of the communal council is the corporate body of burgomasters and aldermen. The competence of the communal council is unlimited with regard to internal administration, communal property, budget and education. The council also draws up local regulations as long as they do not conflict with the general regulations of the state, and maintains law and order.

The burgomasters, who preside over the communal councils, are appointed and dismissed by the grand duke, as are the town aldermen. Aldermen of non-town communes are appointed by the minister of the interior. The burgomaster is responsible for enforcing laws and regulations under the supervision of the district commissioner. One of the principal duties of the burgomaster is issuance of birth, marriage and death certificates and the keeping public registers for such purposes. The burgomaster and aldermen are responsible for implementing the communal council's resolutions, administration of the communal budget and the conduct of judicial proceedings. The communes cover their expenditures from revenues derived from their own property and from the proceeds of communal taxes and duties.

Central government authority over communes is exercised through the district commissioner appointed by the grand duke. District commissioners are civil servants who reside in the chief town of the district. Certain decisions of the communal council — for example, those relating to the sale of property or the determination of taxes and dues — must be approved by the grand duke or by the minister of the interior.

FOREIGN POLICY

Luxembourg's former neutral status was abandoned after World War II, and the Grand Duchy has taken a leading role in the formation of European regional organizations such as Benelux and the EEC. Luxembourg is the headquarters of the Secretariat of the European Parliament. Relations with Belgium are particularly close, cemented by the fact that the ducal consort is the sister of King Baudouin.

| Districts and Cantons | Area | | Population |
	Sq. Mi.	Sq. Km.	1984 Est.
Diekirch	447	1,157	55,600
Clervaux	128	332	9,800
Diekirch	92	239	24,200
Redange	103	267	10,300
Vianden	21	54	2,600
Wiltz	102	265	8,700
Grevenmacher	203	525	39,700
Echternach	72	186	10,900
Grevenmacher	82	211	16,700
Remich	49	128	12,100
Luxembourg	349	904	278,700
Capellen	77	199	28,900
Esch	94	243	114,300
Luxembourg (Ville et Campagne)	92	238	118,100
Mersch	86	224	17,400
TOTAL	999	2,586	374,000

Source: Official government figures.

PARLIAMENT

The national legislature is the Chamber of Deputies, with the appointed Council of State exercising some vestigial legislative functions.

The Chamber of Deputies consists of 64 deputies elected for five-year terms by direct universal suffrage on a proportional representation system. The Chamber of Deputies can be dissolved.

The Grand Duchy is divided into four electoral districts: the South, comprising the cantons of Esch and Capellen; the East, comprising the cantons of Grevenmacher, Remich and Echternach; the Center, comprising the cantons of Luxembourg and Mersch; and the North, comprising the cantons of Diekirch, Redange, Wiltz, Clervaux and Vianden. The number of deputies is determined by the size of the population on the ratio of one deputy per 5,500 inhabitants. This number is revised every five years by ministerial order. Voting is compulsory, and electors cannot vote by proxy. Those unable to vote must notify a justice of the peace of the reason for their absence. Abstention without such notification entails a fine, which becomes more severe on each subsequent failure to vote.

Elections are carried out under the party-list system. Independents are treated as a single list. Seats are allocated according to proportional representation and the principle of the smallest electoral quota. Voting is compulsory for all citizens 18 years and older.

ELECTIONS TO THE CHAMBER OF DEPUTIES, 1984		
	% of Votes	Seats
CSV	34.9	25
LSAP	35.9	21
DP	18.7	14
KPL	5.0	2
SDP	2.5	0
Others	5.4	2

The status of electors is established by an entry in the register of voters, which is drawn up by communal authorities annually in April. To be eligible, voters must be Luxembourg citizens over 21 years of age and normally resident in the Grand Duchy. Civil servants are not permitted to run for office. Deputies may not be related either by blood or marriage to each other up to the second degree. Should two related persons be elected simultaneously, the husband or the elder of the two is chosen. Elections are supervised by electoral officers. Each elector has as many votes as there are deputies to be elected in the constituency. The vote can be cast either under the party-list system or on a nominal basis. Under the latter, they may select their candidates from the same list or from different lists.

The Chamber of Deputies begins its ordinary sessions on the second Tuesday in October at 3:00 P.M. Sessions are opened and closed by the grand duke in person or by his representative. After consideration of the credentials, the Chamber appoints a permanent bureau consisting of a president, three vice presidents and five secretaries. Much of the Chamber's work is done in three types of committees: a working committee, standing committees and special committees. The working committee conducts much of the parliamentary business between the president of the Chamber and the parliamentary groups and determines the time to be allotted to each bill and for taking a vote. Examples of the standing committees are the Petitions Committee, the Accounts Committee, the Foreign Affairs Committee, the Social Affairs Committee, and the Finance and Budget Committee. The standing committees consist of at least five and not more than 11 members in proportion to the party strength in the Chamber. Special Committees are appointed to examine specific bills or proposals; they are disbanded after their work is done. The standing and special committees may set up subcommittees.

Legislation may be initiated either by the grand duke or by any member of the Chamber of Deputies. In either case, a bill must be submitted first to the Council of State for its review. Amendments to a bill also undergo this procedure. However, in extraordinary and urgent cases, the prior opinion of the Council of State may be dispensed with. After the opinion of the Council of State is received, the bill is referred to a standing committee or a special committee and then presented on the floor of the Chamber along with the committee's report. Parliamentary discussion includes general discussion and discussion of the articles. The Chamber votes at least four times on any bill. No bill may be adopted until it has been voted upon article by article. The Chamber then proceeds to what is known as the second mandatory vote. At this stage there is a procedure that is unique to Luxembourg: the second constitutional vote, with a three month interval between the first and second votes. Although the Constitution permits the Chamber to dispense with the second vote, it can do so only with the approval of the Council of State.

In addition to its control over the budget, the Chamber of Deputies enjoys a broad range of prerogatives. Each deputy has the right to put forward a motion, which is then debated and voted on if supported by at least five deputies. Such motions may ask the government to take certain steps' or express confidence or lack of confidence in the government. The Chamber also has the right to hold inquiries and call witnesses. Certain grand ducal appointments are made on the basis of the Chamber's recommendations. These include the two judges and the two deputy judges of the Audit Office and councillors of state. Finally, the Chamber has the right to make accusations against members of the government and to have them brought before the Superior Court of Justice in plenary assembly.

The Council of State is a deliberative body required to review all legislative proposals and their amendments and settle any questions relating to administrative disputes. Its ambit covers the legislative, administrative and judicial fields. In the exercise of these duties, it sits either as the General Assembly or as the Disputes Committee.

The Council of State consists of 21 councillors, 11 of whom make up the Disputes Committee. This number does not include members of the royal family who belong to the body. The councillors must be citizens between 30 and 72 years of age; members of the Disputes Committee also must have a doctor of laws degree. Of the 21 councillors, seven are appointed directly by the grand duke, seven are chosen by the grand duke from a list of 10 candidates submitted by the Chamber of Duties and seven are chosen by the grand duke from a list of 10 candidates chosen by the previous Council of State. Vacancies are also filled in this order, the Duke directly filling the first vacancy but choosing from a list of names submitted by the Chamber and the Council of State for the second and third vacancies. The General Assembly performs the consultative duties of the Council of State — that is, review of legislation. The Disputes Committee performs the judicial and administrative functions of the Council of State, has supreme jurisdiction over all administrative disputes and acts both as a court of appeal and as a court of annulment.

POLITICAL PARTIES

There are three major political parties who among them control 60 of the Chamber of Deputies' 64 seats and who garnered 87% of the votes in the 1984 elections. The three parties are Christian Social People's Party, the Democratic Party and the Luxembourg Social Workers' Party.

The Christian Social People's Party (Chreschtlich-Sozial Vollekspartei, CSV), originally founded as the Party of the Right, took its present name in 1944. It has been represented in every government from 1919 to 1974 and from 1979 and has supplied every prime minister but one since 1945. In an overwhelmingly Catholic country, the CSV enjoys wide support fairly evenly distributed among all ages, classes and regions. The party's faithful number about 8,000. The CSV has close ties to the Catholic Church and to the Christian trade union movement. From 1959 to 1974 and from 1979 to 1984 the party was led by the veteran statesman, Pierre Werner.

The Democratic Party (Demokratesch Partei, DP) was founded in 1945 on the remains of the prewar Liberal Party, from which it inherited a strong anticlerical bias. From 1974 to 1979 it was a junior partner in a coalition government with the Socialists but switched sides to join the CSV in the same role. The party favors free enterprise and has a strong electoral base in the middle classes and the white-collar employees in the urban areas of Luxembourg-Ville.

Luxembourg Socialist Workers' Party (Letzeburger Sozialistisch Arbrechterpartei, LSAP) is the oldest political party, having been founded in 1902. A militant working-class party with strong trade union ties, the LSAP has never able to achieve a strong electoral majority, although it won a slight plurality in 1974. Nevertheless, it has been in and out of coalitions with the CSV. Party membership is estimated at about 6,000. Despite its hard-shell ideological stance, it has lacked charismatic leaders in recent years.

Minor parties include the Communist Party (KPL); the Social Democratic Party (SDP); and the Alternative List, a loose coalition of antinuclear and environmental concerns similar to the West German Green Party.

ECONOMY

Luxembourg has a developed free-market economy in which the private sector is dominant. Luxembourg is one of the most prosperous countries in the OECD area, with a per capita GNP estimated at $14,340, exceeded in this respect only by Switzerland among the industrialized nations. The per capita GNP grew by an average of 4% per year between 1960 and 1982, one of the highest rates in Western Europe.

However, the economy experienced some turbulence during the early 1980s, and the GDP fell by 1% in 1984. In 1982 the government introduced a freeze on wages and prices in its efforts to cushion the devaluation of the franc. The government also suspended automatic wage indexation as part of its austerity program. This led to a 24-hour general strike, the first industrial stoppage in Luxembourg in 60 years. Unemployment rose to 2% of the work force by 1984. The average annual inflation rate was 9.5% in 1982 and 8.7% in 1983, but it fell to 4.9% in 1984. Despite a restraint on public expenditure and an increase in tax revenues, the heavy expenditure required for the restructuring of the steel industry led to budget deficits from 1980 to 1984.

By 1985 the Luxembourg economy had bounced back, with the GDP climbing at a rate comparable to the West European average. The unemployment rate had dipped to 1½% and the CPI fell as a result of lower import costs. There also was a substantial surplus on the current account made possible by earnings from banking. As the heavy expenditures on the restructuring of the steel industry are now complete, budgets have begun to show large surpluses. Tax rates were cut in 1986, and a further tax reform was instituted in 1987.

PRINCIPAL ECONOMIC INDICATORS

Gross National Product (1985): 4.98 billion
GNP per capita (1985): $13,610
GNP average annual growth rate: 2.8%
GNP per capita average annual growth rate: N.A.

PUBLIC FINANCE

The fiscal year is the calendar year. The annual budget is drawn up in the form of a finance bill. Each year the government submits to the Chamber of Deputies a general account of revenues and expenditures accompanied by an opinion prepared by the Audit Office. All taxes and increases in taxes require the consent of the legislature.

GROSS DOMESTIC PRODUCT

GDP nominal (national currency): 195.3 billion
GDP real (national currency): 142.4 billion
GDP per capita ($): 9,431

Average Annual Growth Rate of GDP, 1973–84: 3.8%

GDP by type of expenditure (%)
Consumption
   Private: 59
   Government: 15
Gross domestic investment: 26
Gross domestic saving: N.A.
Foreign trade
   Exports: 93
   Imports: -93

Cost components of GDP (%)
Net indirect taxes: 12
Consumption of fixed capital: 11
Compensation of employees: 58
Net operating surplus: 19

Sectoral origin of GDP (%)
Primary
   Agriculture: 3
   Mining: N.A.

Secondary
   Manufacturing: 30
   Construction: 6
   Public utilities: 3
Tertiary
Transportation and Communications: 6
   Trade: 17
   Finance:
   Other services: } 36
   Government:

Average annual sectoral growth rates: N.A.
Agriculture: N.A.
Industry: N.A.
Manufacturing: N.A.
Services: N.A.

The early 1980s presented severe strains on the public finance of the Grand Duchy because of the steel crisis. Initially, support for the restructuring program was provided without additional borrowing or taxes, by drawing on surpluses of previous years. The general government transactions account moved from a surplus of 2% of the GNP in the 1970s to a deficit averaging 1½% in 1980–83, and the budget reserve was virtually depleted. In 1983 it was decided to increase direct and indirect taxes steeply so that the central government take as a percentage of the GNP rose by 1¾%. In addition, ordinary central government expenditure was substantially curbed, reducing its share of the GNP from 25% in 1981 to 23% in 1984 and to 22½% in 1985. As a result, the restructuring of the steel industry was financed without any marked acceleration of borrowing, except temporarily in 1983. Moreover, tax revenues in 1984 and 1985 were higher than forecast, so that budget outturns were better than expected and it was possible to replenish the budget reserves and make substantial block grants to the Investment Fund.

Luxembourg's quick recovery from financial doldrums was also helped by its small public debt and an interest service burden that is lower than those of other OECD countries. Although rising fast (by 80% between 1980 and 1985) the gross central government debt still represented only 6% of the GNP in 1985. Moreover, these central government liabilities were offset by considerable financial assets of other public sector components, such as the Investment Fund and the Social Security Fund, leaving aggregate government as a net creditor.

Because of the soundness of its financial position, the government relaxed its fiscal controls once the steel crisis was over. In 1986, budget expenditures rose quite steeply, by 6%. The new measures included civil service pay increases; higher family allowances; and increased investment, especially in telecommunications. At the same time, taxation was eased by about 1% of the GNP, and the tax burden was lowered on the financial sector to make it more competitive. A proposal to introduce a minimum guaranteed income is currently under study. It will replace the various allowances now available. The tax system also will be reformed to achieve a better balance between direct and indirect taxes. While the total tax pressure is close to the West European average, the relative share of direct taxes is significantly larger than in other EEC countries.

BUDGET

(million Luxembourg francs, 1986; provisional accounts)

Revenues: income tax, 37,879.0; other direct taxes, 3,669.7; turnover tax, 11,534.8; customs duties, 9,078.3; other indirect taxes, 7,060.7; other ordinary receipts, 12,971.9; other extraordinary receipts, 157.2; total, 82,351.6. *Expenditures:* administration, 6,524.8; defense, 2,245.6; public order and foreign affairs, 2,232.7; education and arts, 11,007.0; social security, 21,262.4; health, sport and housing, 4,332.8; transportation and power, 16,319.2; agriculture and economic affairs, 7,208.5; war damage and national disasters, 341.0; public debt, subsidies, etc., 9,370.5; miscellaneous, 1,170.8; total, 82,015.3. Source: Ministère des Finances.

CURRENCY & BANKING

The Luxembourg monetary unit is the Luxembourg franc, which is par with the Belgian franc. Belgian currency also is legal tender in the country. Coins are issued in denominations of 25 and 50 centimes and 1, 5, 10 and 20 Luxembourg francs, and notes in denominations of 20, 50 and 100 Luxembourg francs and 20, 50, 100, 500, 1,000 and 5,000 Belgian francs.

In 1973 Luxembourg was one of the eight original countries that established a joint currency float that in 1979 was converted into the European Monetary System (EMS). Initially, the strength of the currency and the low inflation rates of the main trading partners — Belgium, France and West Germany — aided Luxembourg's trade position. However, the deficit on trade in goods and services increased from 926 million francs in 1976 to 23 billion francs in 1983. Revenues from banking and tourism compensated for this deficit, and there was an overall current account surplus of 40 billion francs in 1981.

FINANCIAL INDICATORS, 1986

International reserves minus gold: N.A.
   SDRs: $21.45 million
   Reserve position in IMF: 14.96
   Foreign exchange: N.A.
Gold (million fine troy oz.): 0.29

Money supply
Stock in billion national currency: 51.6
M^1 per capita: 141,000

Private banks
Assets:
   Loans to government: N.A.
   Loans to private sector: 2.2
   Reserves: N.A.
   Foreign assets: 97.8%

Liabilities: Deposits of which: 6.769 trillion francs
   Demand deposits: 1.0%
   Savings deposits: 5.0%
   Government deposits: N.A.
   Foreign liabilities: 86.9%

In 1982 Belgium devalued the two countries' linked currencies by 8.5% without prior consultation with Luxembourg. This led to demands by the Grand Duchy for separate valuation of each country's reserves and for exchange rate guarantees for assets held in Belgian francs. The Institut Monetaire Luxembourgeois was established in 1983 to centralize monetary functions vis-à-vis Belgium and the EMS.

In recent years the focus of the economy has shifted from industry to banking. The development of Luxembourg as a financial market has been facilitated by specific features such as complete freedom of capital movements, absence of a central bank and monetary policy constraints, little prudential regulation, flexible banking supervision and an equally flexible tax system. There are at present 117 banking institutions (plus 22 nonbank financial institutions) with combined assets in excess of 7.2 trillion francs in 1984 and a GNP/bank assets ratio of 1:30 (compared with 1:2 in most industrialized countries). The share of the credit and insurance sector has grown from 4.6% of the total value added in 1970 to 14% in 1982 and from 4.3% to 9.2% of dependent employment. Since the mid-1970s, tax revenues from financial institutions has accounted for 10 to 15% of total tax revenues. Finally, the investment income item of the balance of payments showed a surplus of 62.5 billion francs in 1984, equivalent to nearly 24% of the GNP.

During the 1970s the financial market expanded mainly as a result of the growth of the Eurobond and subsequently Eurocurrency markets. During this period, bank assets increased by nearly 30% per year. Since 1979 the increasing risk of default by some debtors and the shrinking interest margins resulting from increased competition among banks have led financial institutions to reduce their lending, to diversify the sources of refinancing and to step up their off-balance-sheet commission-earning activities. Thus the Luxembourg banks' share of total Eurocurrency assets fell from 12½% in 1979 to 9½% in 1985, although, if adjustments were made for the individual composition of Luxembourg assets, Luxembourg has roughly maintained its market share. The policy of diversification into cash and portfolio management security and precious metal dealing, and the development of investment funds have resulted in a major change in the sources of financing. Thus the private/interbank liabilities ratio rose from 1:8 in 1979 to 1:4 in 1984. Off-balance-sheet liabilities also increased considerably, with fiduciary accounts for half of deposits in 1984 and 70% in 1985. Profits have improved rapidly as a result of these changes, to 27% in 1985.

Paralleling these developments are legislative measures designed to reduce the cost of certain transactions (such as the abolition of VAT on investment gold transactions and stamp duty on certificates of deposit). To strengthen the credibility of banking institutions, bank deposits (but not bank assets) were granted secrecy by an act of 1981, and bank supervision was strengthened by the creation of the Luxembourg Monetary Institute. In addition to its watchdog functions, the Institute has been given the status of a bank of issue. Its first note issue, made possible by a revision in 1984 of the rules of the Belgian-Luxembourg Monetary Union, was made in 1985.

AGRICULTURE

About 1.3 billion sq. m. (132,680 ha.) or about 51% of the land are devoted to agriculture and grazing. Of this area, 47.45% are cultivated, with the rest meadows and pastures. Farms are generally small, although the trend is toward larger holdings. Agriculture and forestry employed 5% of the work force in 1981 but provided only 2.2% of the GDP. Mixed farming is practiced in most areas because of the variability of climate and soil. The major agricultural exports are wine, grown in the Moselle Valley, clover; and rosebushes. Barley, oats and potatoes are grown in the North.

Agriculture employs 6,900 workers, or 4.2% of the labor force.

Livestock raising is an important activity, and Luxembourg exports both hogs and dairy products. Most fishing is for sport.

There are some 840 million sq. m. (84,000 ha.) of woodland, of which about 60% are publicly owned. Forest reserves have been severely depleted since 1800, when three-fourths of the country was forested. Commercial stands are spruce and oak. essential for the country's tanning industry.

AGRICULTURAL INDICATORS

Average size of holding (ha.): 29
Size class %:
  Below 1 ha. – 5 ha.: 26.3
  5–10 ha.: 9.0
  10–20 ha.: 11.8
  20–50 ha.: 30.5
  50–over 200 ha.: 22.3

Tenure %
  Owner-operated: 52.2
  Rented: 47.1
  Other: 0.7

Farms as % of total land area: 48.8

Land use %
Permanent crops: 2.7
Temporary crops: 96.7
Fallow: 0.7
Meadows and pastures: 55.6
Woodland: N.A.
Other: N.A.

MANUFACTURING

Luxembourg is one of the largest steel producers in the world on a per-capita basis. Steel production is entirely in the hands of ARBED, the giant steel combine. Most of ARBED's blast furnaces and steel mills are in Bassin Minière, in the Southwest.

Deposits of iron ore found in the Southwest supplied the steel mills until 1981, when mining ceased. Iron ore now is imported, as is much of the coal. Since 1974 the steel industry, in common with the steel industries in the rest of Western Europe, has been in a slump, with production declining from 5.469 million tons in 1974 to 2.3 million tons in 1983 for pig iron and from 4.519 million tons in 1980 to 3.294 million tons in 1983 for crude steel. Despite these cuts, ARBED contributed 20% of the GNP in 1981.

Prior to the first oil shock, the steel industry was one of the mainstays of the economy, with the value of the output rising by over 15% annually between 1966 and 1974. During this period the steel industry accounted for 60% of the value added in industry and 25.6% of total value added, two-thirds of exports and one-third of employment. Although the crisis in the steel sector has been broadly comparable with the EEC average, its impact has been on the whole much greater on the Luxembourg economy. In response to the steep drop in demand, restructuring was started as early as 1974, as a result of which production capacity was cut by 15% between 1974 and 1980. Until the 1980s, restructuring was carried out almost entirely by the private sector. But as the financial position of ARBED deteriorated, large-scale government intervention became necessary from 1983. Capacity has been cut to a little less than 4 million tons or by 30%, and the steel labor force to 11,000. The work-force cuts have been achieved virtually without redundancies by introducing early retirement and diversion of labor to community programs. Financial restructuring has involved liquidation of the steel companies' shareholdings, subscription of convertible bonds by the bank shareholders, special loans by the Société Nationale de Credit et d'Investissement (SNCI) authorized and backed by the government, and government aid. Aid over the period 1983–85 was nearly 20 billion francs, or 10% of the GDP in 1984, of which slightly more than a quarter was in the form of investment subsidies. However, the government has sought to adjust the legal mix of its contributions to avoid a de facto nationalization of the sector. In addition, there were expenditures estimated at 6 billion francs between 1976 and 1982. Simultaneously, wage earners in the industry suffered wage reductions ranging from 6 to 25%.

The financial restructuring of the steel industry has been a particularly heavy budget liability, particularly in order not to contravene EEC regulations, which virtually prohibit assistance other than interest relief. The plan, and the general pickup in the steel market in 1984 and 1985, produced significant improvements. By 1984 the industry began to show a substantial surplus and also a reduction in debt.

On account of the crisis in the steel industry, the government has begun to follow a policy of diversification, initially focused on industry and later extended to services. About 60 new production units have been created, concentrated in the chemicals, metalworking, glass and aluminum industries. With an annual investment of 2.5 billion francs, the program has created 5,000 new jobs.

MINING

With the depletion of its iron ore reserves in 1981, Luxembourg has no mineral reserves of commercial value.

ENERGY

Much of Luxembourg's electric power is produced and consumed by the steel industry. As fuel, thermal plants use gas released during the smelting of iron ore. Luxembourg is a net importer of electric power. Virtually all of the country's hydroelectric potential has now been put to use. Total production of electric power in 1985 was 956 million kwh, or 2,605 kwh per capita.

LABOR

The total labor force in 1985 was 161,000, up from 140,200 in 1970. Unemployment is virtually nonexistent. Foreigners make up about one-third of the labor force, employed mostly in the steel industry.

The labor movement is strong in Luxembourg. The two major unions are the Socialist-dominated General Confederation of Labor and the Confederation of Christian Trade Unions. Strikes are virtually unknown.

Luxembourg has extremely progressive labor legislation. The right to work is guaranteed by the Constitution. The normal workweek is 40 hours, spread over five days. Work on Sundays is generally prohibited except in continuous-process industries. Also prohibited is the employment of children under 16 years. Worker representatives are required in all businesses employing 15 or more persons. In businesses over 150 employees, 50% of the joint works councils are elected by the employees. In businesses with over 1,500 employees, one-third of the boards of directors must consist of employees or their representatives.

Wage agreements are generally concluded by industrywide bargaining between management and labor. Workers may strike only after their dispute has been submitted to the National Conciliation Office and all mediation efforts have failed.

```
┌──────────────────────────────────────────────────┐
│                ENERGY INDICATORS                   │
│                                                    │
│ Total energy consumption: 4.4 million tons of coal equiva- │
│ lent                                               │
│ Average annual energy growth rate (1974–81): N.A. │
│ Public utilities' share of GDP: N.A.              │
│ Energy consumption per capita (000 kg. oil equivalent): │
│ N.A.                                               │
│ Energy imports as % of merchandise imports: N.A.  │
│ Average annual growth rate of energy consumption: N.A. │
│                                                    │
│ Electricity                                        │
│    Installed capacity: 1,238,000 kw.              │
│    Production: 502 million kw.-hr.                │
│       % fossil fuel: 86.1                          │
│       % hydro: 13.9                                │
│       % nuclear: N.A.                              │
│    Consumption per capita: 11,088 kw.-hr.         │
│                                                    │
│ Natural gas                                        │
│    Proved reserves: N.A.                           │
│    Production: N.A.                                 │
│    Consumption: 373 million cu. m. (285 million cu. yd.) │
│                                                    │
│ Petroleum                                          │
│    Proved reserves: N.A.                           │
│    Years to exhaust proved reserves: N.A.         │
│    Production: N.A.                                 │
│    Consumption: 1.5 million tons of coal equivalent │
│    Refining capacity: N.A.                         │
│                                                    │
│ Coal                                               │
│    Reserves: N.A.                                  │
│    Production: N.A.                                 │
│    Consumption: 2.1 million tons of coal equivalent │
└──────────────────────────────────────────────────┘
```

FOREIGN COMMERCE

The foreign trade accounts of Belgium and Luxembourg are treated jointly by the Belgium-Luxembourg Economic Union (Bleu), which has an administrative commission to determine export and import policy and an institute to administer exchange regulations. Although Luxembourg is generally committed to free enterprise and liberal trade policies, it participates in Common Market trade restrictions. Intra-EEC trade is essentially duty-free, as is trade in manufactured products with EFTA.

LABOR INDICATORS

Total economically active population: 161,000

As % of working-age population: 61.3
Female: participation %: 34.1
Activity (%)
　Total: 42.2
　Male: 57.7
　Female: 27.4

Employment status (%)
　Employers & self-employed: 9.4
　Employees: 85.1
　Unpaid family workers: 3.5
　Other: 2.0

Sectoral employment (%)
　Agriculture, forestry, fishing: 4.2
　Mining: N.A.
　Manufacturing, construction: 31.8
　Electricity, gas, water: 0.9
　Trade: 33.7
　Transportation, communications: 6.5
　Finance, real estate: 6.7
　Services: 2.7
　Public administration & defense: 11.9
Average annual growth rate of labor force, 1980–2000:
N.A.

Unemployment %: 1.6
Labor under 20 years: 9.2
Earnings in manufacturing: N.A.

Hours of work
　Manufacturing: 41.0 per week

TRANSPORTATION & COMMUNICATIONS

Some 436 km. (271 mi.) of railway track provide direct links with Belgium via Arlon; with France via Metz and Longwy; and with West Germany via Trier. The government owns 51% of the Société Nationale des Chemins, with the remaining 49% divided equally between France and Belgium. Direct roads connect all important towns. The only river suitable for commercial transportation is the Moselle, which permits navigation of barges of up to 1,500 tons. The country's only airport is Findel, near Luxembourg-Ville. Regular flights to other European cities are operated by Luxair.

COMMUNICATION INDICATORS

Telephones
  Total: 210,000
  Per 100: 55
  Phone traffic
    Local: ⎫
    Long distance: ⎬ 127,393
    International: 2,779

Post office
Number of post offices: 105
Domestic mail: ⎫
Foreign mail received: ⎬ 128,404
Foreign mail sent: ⎭

Telegraph
  Total traffic: 46
  National: 13
  International: 33

Telex
  Subscriber lines: 1,952
  Traffic (000 minutes): 9,035

Telecommunications

TOURISM AND TRAVEL INDICATORS

Total tourist receipts: N.A.
Expenditures by nationals abroad: N.A.
Number of hotel beds: 2,266
Average length of stay: 3.5 days
Tourist nights: 2,266,000
Number of Tourists: 616,000
  of whom from:
    United States: 39,900
    Netherlands: 60,800
    United Kingdom: 24,400
    West Germany: 55,700
    Belgium: 123,700

DEFENSE

Compulsory military service, introduced in 1944, was abolished in 1967. Luxembourg maintains an army of 720 volunteers as part of NATO. The 1984 defense budget was 2.0 billion francs.

EDUCATION

The earliest schools in Luxembourg were the monastic schools founded at Echternach in 698 and at Luxembourg-Ville in 1083. The Jesuits founded the coun-

```
┌─────────────────────────────────────────────────────┐
│              TRANSPORTATION INDICATORS               │
│ Roads                                                │
│    Length km.: 5,164 (3,209 mi.)                     │
│    Paved %: 99                                       │
│ Motor vehicles                                       │
│    Automobiles: 156,048                              │
│    Trucks: 14,108                                    │
│    Persons per vehicle: 2.1                          │
│    Road freight ton-km.: 219 million (136 million ton-mi.) │
│ Railroads                                            │
│    Track km.: 270 (168 mi.)                          │
│    Passenger km.: 276 million (171 million mi.)      │
│    Freight ton-km.: 600 million (373 million ton-mi.) │
│ Merchant marine                                      │
│    Vessels: N.A.                                     │
│    Total dead weight tonnage: N.A.                   │
│    Oil tankers: N.A.                                 │
│ Ports                                                │
│    Cargo loaded: N.A.                                │
│    Cargo unloaded: N.A.                              │
│ Air                                                  │
│    Km. flown: 2.6 million (1.6 million mi.)          │
│    Passengers: 234,000                               │
│    Passenger-km.: 109 million (68 million mi.)       │
│    Freight-km.: 0.3 million (0.2 million mi.)        │
│    Mail—ton-km.: 0.2 million                         │
│    Airport with scheduled flights: 1                 │
│ Pipelines                                            │
│    Refined: N.A.                                     │
│    Natural gas: N.A.                                 │
│    Total: N.A.                                       │
│ Inland waterways: data N.A.                          │
└─────────────────────────────────────────────────────┘
```

try's first college, in Luxembourg-Ville, in 1603, but with the suppression of that order 170 years later, the college was transformed into the Athénée Grand-Ducal. The first education law, of July 26, 1843, authorized the opening of the first normal school to train teachers. Article 23 of the 1868 Constitution declares that the state is responsible for primary education that is both free and compulsory. The duration of compulsory education has grown longer over the years and now stands at nine years. Private schools are permitted but not subsidized by the state.

A number of laws passed during the 1960s affected every branch of education. The law of August 5, 1963, reformed preprimary and primary education; the law of August 16, 1965, instituted a five-year intermediate school (*collège d'enseignement moyen*) to replace the upper primary course; the law of May 10, 1968, reorganized secondary education; and the law of June 18, 1968, reformed postsecondary education.

Luxembourg's educational system has adapted some of the more prominent features of its neighbors, Belgium, France and West Germany. Because of the country's trilingual status, it is necessary to teach children more than one language. As a result, a large portion of the class load is devoted to the teaching of languages to the exclusion of other subjects.

The rapid growth of the number of postprimary pupils between 1960 and 1970, known as the *explosion scolaire*, created a number of problems, including shortage of buildings, teachers and equipment. As a result, intermediate schools were established in 1965 to provide vocational instruction more or less on the model of the German *Realschulen*. At the second stage, specialization is delayed to make it easier for students to transfer from one type of school to another. This has been done by instituting *classes d'orientation* in the *lycée* course.

Pupils in the northern areas of the Grand Duchy have traditionally received fewer educational opportunities and facilities. As a result, private schools in these areas had to shoulder much of the burden. To remedy the imbalance, the state has permitted boys' schools in these areas to admit girls.

The academic year runs from September 1 through July 16 and is divided into two terms. There are two-week vacations at Christmas and Easter.

Attendance at preprimary schools is compulsory for five-year-olds and voluntary for children under five. Communes are required to set up kindergartens with financial support from the state if there are at least 20 children in the preprimary age group.

Primary education runs for six years, from ages six through 12, and is divided into three cycles of two years each. Generally, primary schools are coed in rural areas and unisex in urban areas. The curriculum includes religious instruction, Letzeburgesch, German, French, arithmetic, history, environment, geography, natural history, arts, crafts, music, writing, physical education and traffic education. By the second year, the medium of instruction shifts to German. French remains a foreign language throughout. The average class size is 20.

Pupils who complete six years of primary schooling but who do not wish to pursue secondary studies spend the last three years of compulsory education either in *classes complémentaires* or in the *école primaire supérieure*, both of which are considered part of the primary cycle.

Higher intermediate schools, established in 1965, provide a general course lasting five years on a less theoretical basis than in secondary schools. The five-year course is divided into two cycles: a lower cycle of three years and an upper cycle of two years. During the former, the curriculum is the same for all pupils, and during the latter, the pupils choose one of three elective groups: biological and social; commercial; and technical.

Secondary education lasts for six years. The law of 1968 abolished the distinction between the classical boys' and girls' *lycées* and established a common *lycée* that may be compared to the German *Gymnasium*. Secondary education is completely free, and poorer children receive grants. Private schools are mostly girls' schools run by the Catholic Church.

The *lycée* lasts seven years and is divided into a lower cycle of three years and an upper cycle of four years. Pupils pass from the lower to the upper cycle by passing an *examen de passage*. In the first year, the *classe d'orientation*, the curriculum is identical for all pupils. Beginning in the second year, pupils must choose between the classical branch (with Latin) and the modern branch (with English); if the former is chosen, English is added to the timetable from the third year. From the fourth year, the degree of specialization increases. The classical branch and the modern branch split into two sections each, one concentrating on language and the other on sciences. At the end of the final class, pupils take the *examen de fin d'études secondaires*, conducted by the Ministry of National Education in either French or German. Pupils who fail are allowed to take the examination twice, while those who pass receive the *diplôme de fin d'études secondaires*, which gives them access to higher education.

Technical schools provide a five-year postprimary course consisting of a two-year orientation cycle followed by a three-year specialization cycle. The diploma awarded at the end of the course is equivalent to the French *certificat d'aptitude professionnel* (CAP). Students may stay at a technical school for two additional years to obtain a *diplôme de technicien*. Pupils wishing to study commercial subjects take a four-year course followed by one year of practical training.

Luxembourg has no national university. Until 1969 students who went to foreign countries and obtained degrees had to take supplementary examinations before nationally appointed examining bodies. The law of 1969 abolished these examinations with effect from 1974 and extended automatic recognition to all foreign degrees.

The Centre Universitaire offers two types of university-level courses in Luxembourg: *cours universitaires* for first-year courses and *cours complémentaires* for postgraduate courses. The year is divided into two semesters, with oral and written examinations at the end of each. On the bases of these examinations and the classwork, the student is awarded the *certificat d'études* in the appropriate subject. The Centre Universitaire is governed by an administrative council headed by a president. In practice, most third-level students go to France, West

Germany, Belgium, Switzerland, Austria, the United States or the United Kingdom, in roughly that order.

Luxembourg has a highly centralized educational administration directed and financed by the Ministry of National Education. At the primary level, the ministry shares some responsibilities with the local communes, the latter having the right to appoint teachers and supply school buildings and equipment. A corps of primary-school inspectors assists the ministry in its supervision of all aspects of first-level education, except curricula and textbooks. The curricula are prescribed and the textbooks prepared by the ministry in direct consultation with the teachers. The ministry also exercises control over education.

Since 1972 courses for nursery-school teachers and primary-school teachers have been integrated at the Institut Pédagogique at Walferdang. Primary-school teachers take a two-year course and receive the *brevet d'aptitude pédagogique*. Teachers for the lower cycle of the intermediate school are required to possess a *brevet d'enseignement moyen* and to attend a foreign university for two years followed by a two-year program in Luxembourg. Secondary-school teachers, known as *professeurs-docteurs*, must hold a university degree. In addition, these teachers must take a two-year professional course, at the end of which they receive the *certificate d'aptitude aux fonctions de professeur d'enseignement secondaire.*

EDUCATION INDICATORS

Literacy
    Total %: 100
    Male %: 100
    Female %: 100

First level
    Schools: 541
    Students: 21,979
    Teachers: 1,685
    Student-teacher ratio: 16:1
    Net enrollment %: 88
    Female %: 49

Second level
    Schools: 53
    Students: 8,705
    Teachers: 2,407
    Student-teacher ratio: N.A.
    Net enrollment %: 58
    Female %: 48

Vocational
    Schools: N.A.
    Students: 16,571
    Teachers: N.A.

EDUCATION INDICATORS *(continued)*

Student-teacher ratio: N.A.
Vocational enrollment ratio: N.A.

Third level
Institutions: 2
Students: 785
Teachers: 181
Student-teacher ratio: N.A.
Gross enrollment %: N.A.
Graduates per 10,000, ages 20–24: 270
% of population over 25 with postsecondary education:
N.A.
Female %: 36

Foreign study
Foreign students in national universities: 83
Students abroad: 2,421
of whom in
    U.S.A.: 30
    West Germany: 825
    Belgium: 1,021
    Switzerland: 356

Public expenditures
Total: 13.114 billion
% of GNP: 6.4
% of national budget: 14.1
% current: 93.9

LEGAL SYSTEM

The legal system is based on the Napoleonic Code, except for the commercial and penal sections, which are similar to their Belgian counterparts.

The court structure comprises 13 justices of the peace, at the bottom level; two district courts, one in Luxembourg-Ville and one in Diekirch; and the Superior Court of Justice as the court of appeal. Crimes are judged by the court of assizes. There is no jury system.

The justices of the peace preside over the police and conciliation courts. There are three such courts, one at Luxembourg-Ville, one in Esch-sur-Aizette and one in Diekirch. Administrative conflicts are within the jurisdiction of the administrative courts, such as the Disputes Committee of the Council of State, the Audit Office, the Pensions Committee, the Social Insurance Higher Council and the Arbitration Board. The High Court of Justice comprises a court of appeal and a supreme court of appeal. The court of appeal is subdivided into four chambers, each sitting with three justices. It deals with judgments passed in the district courts. The supreme court of appeal consists of one chamber with five justices. It may review decisions made by the court of appeal or the assize court. All judges are appointed by the grand duke for life terms.

LAW ENFORCEMENT

The small corps de police, with a personnel strength of about 600, is responsible for the maintenance of law and order. The former small regional commands were replaced by a centralized national command in 1930. The chief of police reports to the Ministry of Armed Forces for administrative matters and to the Ministry of the Interior for all other purposes.

The Corps de Police is organized into brigades, allocated to towns and divided into borough *commissariats*. The *commissaires* are subject to military penal and disciplinary regulations but, to some extent, are answerable to the local mayor. Villages have village police posts.

The gendarmerie has its headquarters in Luxembourg-Ville, with various regional brigades. Its commander is a serving army officer of lieutenant colonel rank. Its commissioned officers are army officers of lesser rank, and its NCOs and men are recruited from army sergeants and corporals. The brigades are allocated to three gendarmerie districts: North, Central and South. The gendarmerie also is in charge of traffic control and of criminal investigation. The latter duties are handled by the Public Security Branch. Candidates for both forces are trained at the National Gendarmerie And Police School.

Offenses reported to police are 3.9 per 100 inhabitants. There is one policeman for every 730 inhabitants, which is about the West European average. Public expenditure for police protection is $15 per inhabitant, compared to $87 per inhabitant in the United States.

The uniform is based on the French model with a dark blue jacket and trousers worn with a blue kepi. On ceremonial occasions a shako cap is worn with aiguillettes from the left shoulder. The gendarmerie grenade symbol is worn on the lapels of all ranks.

HEALTH

Luxembourg has no national health service, although medical facilities are highly advanced. Private hospitals are operated by the Roman Catholic Church.

```
HEALTH INDICATORS
Health personnel
Physicians: 663
  Population per physician: 553
Dentists: 168
```

```
┌─────────────────────────────────────────────────────┐
│              HEALTH INDICATORS (continued)            │
│  Nurses: 93                                           │
│  Pharmacists: 250                                     │
│  Midwives: 102                                        │
│                                                       │
│  Hospitals                                            │
│  Number: 33                                           │
│  Number of beds: 4,587                                │
│    Per 10,000: 125                                    │
│  Admissions/discharges per 10,000: 1,878              │
│  Bed occupancy rate: 80.9%                            │
│  Average length of stay: 14                           │
│                                                       │
│  Type of hospitals                                    │
│    Government: 60.6                                    │
│    Private nonprofit: 39.4                            │
│    Private profit: N.A.                               │
│                                                       │
│  Public health expenditures                           │
│  As % of national budget: 2.2                         │
│  Per Capita: 106.0                                    │
│                                                       │
│  Vital statistics                                     │
│  Crude death rate per 1,000: 11                       │
│  Decline in death rate, 1960–82:                      │
│  Life expectancy at birth                             │
│    Males: 70.0                                        │
│    Females: 76.7                                      │
│  Infant mortality rate per 1,000 live births: 9       │
│  Child mortality rate ages 1-4 per 1,000: N.A.        │
│  Maternal mortality rate per 100,000 live births: 24.5│
└─────────────────────────────────────────────────────┘
```

FOOD & NUTRITION

The daily per capita food intake for Belgium and Luxembourg is 3,679 calories and 103.3 g. (3.64 oz.) of protein.

```
┌─────────────────────────────────────────────────────┐
│            PER CAPITA CONSUMPTION OF FOODS            │
│         (included in Belgium for items not shown)     │
│  Potatoes: 102.5 kg. (226.0 lb.)                      │
│  Wheat: 69.0 kg. (152.1 lb.)                          │
│  Rice: 6.0 kg. (13.2 lb.)                             │
│  Eggs: 14.0 kg. (30.9 lb.)                            │
│  Butter: 8.8 kg. (19.4 lb.)                           │
│  Cheese: 7.5 kg. (16.5 lb.)                           │
│  Meat (total): 71.1 kg. (156.7 lb.)                   │
│    Beef and veal: 24.6 kg. (54.2 lb.)                 │
│    Pig meat: 44.9 kg. (99.0 lb.)                      │
│    Mutton, lamb and goat: 1.6 kg. (3.5 lb.)           │
│  Sugar: 36.7 kg. (80.9 lb.)                           │
│  Chocolate: 3.8 kg. (8.4 lb.)                         │
└─────────────────────────────────────────────────────┘
```

MEDIA & CULTURE

Luxembourg has two of the oldest dailies in Europe: The venerable *Luxembourger Vort/La Voix du Luxembourg*, founded in 1848, is one of the most distinguished Christian Democratic and Catholic newspapers on the Continent; the liberal *Letzberger Journal* is also over 100 years old, having been founded in 1880. Three other dailies are published in the country: *Le Républicain Lorraine, Tageblatt/Le Journal d'Esch* and *Zeitung vum Letzberger Vollek*. The latter two are affiliated to political parties. However, the most widely read dailies in the Grand Duchy are Belgian: *Le Soir* and *Het Laatste Nieuws*. Along the domestic dailies, the *Luxemburger Vort* has the highest circulation (77,000), followed by *Tageblatt* (32,500) and *Le Républicain Lorraine* (24,000).

The periodical press consists of 16 titles. The largest circulation is reported by the illustrated weekly *Revue*, which sells over 30,000 copies. Luxembourg has no national news agency.

Luxembourg is one of the few countries where all radio and television services are operated by a private commercial company. French financial interests have a majority shareholding in this company, known as Compagnie Luxembourgeoise de Télédiffusion, or Radio Tele-Luxembourg for short. Its finances are entirely drawn from advertising revenues.

MEDIA INDICATORS

Newspapers
  Number of dailies: 4
  Circulation (000): 130
  Per capita: 358 per 1,000
  Number of nondailies: 4
  Circulation (000): N.A.
  Per capita: N.A.
  Number of periodicals: 427
  Circulation: N.A.
  Newsprint consumption: N.A.
  Total: N.A.
  Per capita: N.A.

Book publishing
  Number of titles: 341

Broadcasting
  Annual expenditures: N.A.
  Number of employees: N.A.

Radio
  Number of transmitters: N.A.

```
┌─────────────────────────────────────────────┐
│          MEDIA INDICATORS (continued)         │
│  Number of radio receivers: 235,000           │
│      Per capita: 644 per 1,000                │
│  Total program hours: N.A.                    │
│                                               │
│  Television                                   │
│    Television transmitters: N.A.              │
│    Number of TV receivers: 94,000             │
│      Per capita: 256 per 1,000                │
│    Total program hours: N.A.                  │
│                                               │
│  Cinema                                       │
│    Number of fixed cinemas: N.A.              │
│    Seating capacity: N.A.                     │
│      seats per 1,000: N.A.                    │
│    Annual attendance (million): N.A.          │
│    Gross box office receipts: N.A.            │
│                                               │
│  Films                                        │
│    Production of long films: N.A.             │
│    Import of long films: N.A.                 │
└─────────────────────────────────────────────┘
```

```
┌─────────────────────────────────────────────┐
│     CULTURAL & ENVIRONMENTAL INDICATORS       │
│  Libraries                                    │
│    Number: N.A.                               │
│    Volumes: N.A.                              │
│    Registered borrowers: N.A.                 │
│    Loans per 1,000: N.A.                      │
│                                               │
│  Museums: 14                                  │
│    Annual attendance: 225,000                 │
│    Attendance per 1,000: 630                  │
│                                               │
│  Performing arts                              │
│    Number of performances: 303,000            │
│    Annual attendance: 212,000                 │
│    Attendance per 1,000: 580                  │
│                                               │
│  Ecological sites                             │
│    Number of facilities: 4                    │
│    Annual attendance: N.A.                    │
└─────────────────────────────────────────────┘
```

SOCIAL WELFARE

An extensive system of unofficial social welfare has been built up over the years and now includes health insurance, accident insurance, pensions insurance, unemployment insurance, maternity benefits, old-age benefits, disability benefits and family allowances.

CHRONOLOGY

1948 — The first phase of the Benelux Union (Belgium, the Netherlands, Luxembourg) takes effect.

1953 — Prime Minister P. Dupong resigns and J. Beck is named as head of government.

1958 — Prime Minister J. Beck resigns and is replaced by P. Frieden.

1959 — Pierre Werner succeeds P. Frieden as prime minister.

1963 — Luxembourg celebrates the 1,000th anniversary of its founding as an independent state.

1964 — Grand Duchess Charlotte abdicates in favor of her son Jean.

1974 — Pierre Werner is ousted by a coalition cabinet headed by Democratic Party leader G. Thorn.

1979 — Pierre Werner returns to office following electoral success for the Christian Social People's Party.

1983 — Luxembourg Monetary Institute is founded.

1984 — Pierre Werner steps down and Jacques Santer is named head of government.

BIBLIOGRAPHY

BOOKS

Hemmer, Carlo, and Schroeder, Marcel. *Luxembourg.* Luxembourg-Ville, 1956.

Margue, Paul. *A Short History of Luxembourg.* Luxembourg-Ville, 1974.

Wolseley, Ronald. *The Low Countries: Gateways to Europe.* Camden, N.J., 1969.

THE NETHERLANDS

THE NETHERLANDS

BASIC FACT SHEET

OFFICIAL NAME: Kingdom of Netherlands (Koninkrijk der Nederlanden)

ABBREVIATION: NE

CAPITAL: Amsterdam

HEAD OF STATE: Queen Beatrix Wilhelmina Armgard (from 1980)

HEAD OF GOVERNMENT: Prime Minister Rudolphus (Ruud) Lubbers (from 1982)

NATURE OF GOVERNMENT: Parliamentary democracy; constitutional monarchy

POPULATION: 14,641,554 (1987)

AREA: 40,844 sq. km. (15,892 sq. mi.)

ETHNIC MAJORITY: Dutch

LANGUAGE: Dutch

RELIGIONS: Roman Catholicism and Protestantism

UNIT OF CURRENCY: Guilder (1.956/U.S. dollar, 1987)

NATIONAL FLAG: Tricolor of red, white and cobalt blue horizontal stripes

NATIONAL EMBLEM: A central shield, the arms of the House of Orange-Nassau, in azure blue dotted with gold billets or small rectangles as the background for a gold-crowned lion with red tongue and claws brandishing in its right forepaw a naked silver sword and in its left a bundle of gold-tipped arrows. Larger gold lions flank the shield, which is topped by a rendition of the crown used by William I on his seal. The device is backed with a red, gold-fringed, ermine-lined pavilion and crested with a royal crown. The emblem rests on a blue ribbon scroll bearing the motto *Je Maintiendrai.*

NATIONAL ANTHEM: "Wilhelmus van Nassouwen"

NATIONAL HOLIDAYS: April 30 (queen's birthday); January 1 (New Year's Day); all major Christian holidays

NATIONAL CALENDAR: Gregorian

PHYSICAL QUALITY OF LIFE INDEX: 98 (on an ascending scale with 100 as the maximum)

DATE OF INDEPENDENCE: 1648

DATE OF CONSTITUTION: 1848

WEIGHTS & MEASURES: Metric

GEOGRAPHICAL FEATURES

The Netherlands forms part of the Northwest European Plain and is bounded on the east by West Germany, on the south by Belgium and on the north and west by the North Sea. It is crossed almost at its central point by latitude 52° North and longitude 5° East. The total official area is 41,548 sq. km. (16,038 sq. mi.), including more than 4,243 sq. km. (1,638 sq. mi.) of territorial waters and inlets. The actual area is slightly larger than Belgium and slightly smaller than

Denmark or Switzerland. The official name is Netherlands (Low Lands), but the country is commonly referred to as Holland, which, strictly speaking, applies only to the western coastal provinces of North and South Holland. It extends 312 km. (194 mi.) north–south and 264 km. (164 mi.) east–west. Its total boundary length of 1,605 km. (998 mi.) is shared with West Germany (556 km. [246 mi.]) and Belgium (407 km. [253 mil.]). The North Sea coastline is 642 km. (399 mi.) long.

The highest point is in the extreme Southeast, 321 m. (1,053 ft.) above sea level. The areas in the North and West that lie below sea level account for nearly half of the total land area. The lowest area is a reclaimed polder northeast of Rotterdam and is 6.7 m. (22.0 ft.) below sea level. By the end of the present century, when the reclamation of the Zuyder Zee will be completed, an area roughly equivalent to the area relinquished to the sea in past centuries will have been reclaimed.

The Hague ('s Gravenhage), the seat of government and the capital of the province of South Holland, is between the mouths of the Oude Rijn and Nieuwe Maas rivers, about three miles from the North Sea, northwest of Rotterdam. Although The Hague is the seat of government, Amsterdam is considered to be the capital and also is the nation's most populous city. The other major cities are Rotterdam and Utrecht. The 1985 populations of the major cities were as follows:

Amsterdam (capital)	676,439	Nijmegen	147,102
Rotterdam	555,349	Enschede	144,938
's Gravenhage (The Hague)	445,213	Apeldoorn	144,108
		Arnhem	128,431
Utrecht	230,414	Zaanstad	128,413
Eindhoven	192,854	Breda	118,662
Groningen	167,866	Maastricht	113,277
Tilburg	154,094	Dordrecht	107,475
Haarlem	152,511	Leiden	104,261

Despite its small size, the Netherlands has a varied topography as a result of its complex geological history. The country is divided into two main regions, one comprising areas below sea level (Low Netherlands) and the other those above sea level (High Netherlands). Although primarily based on elevation, this classification coincides with the broad division of the country according to its geological formation. The High Netherlands was formed mainly in the Pleistocene Age (which began about 2 million years ago and ended about 10,000 years ago) and is composed chiefly of sand and gravel. On the other hand, the Low Netherlands is relatively younger, having been formed in the Holocene Age (less than 10,000 years ago) and consists mainly of clay and peat. There are other differences. The High Netherlands is undulating and even hilly in places, with farms alternating with woodland and heath. The Low Netherlands is predominantly flat and is intersected by natural and man-made waterways.

The Netherlands has nine distinct topographical regions:

1. The South Limburg Plateau is the only part of the country not classed as lowland. The hills, which rise to over 300 m. (984 ft.), are the foothills of the Central European Plateau. This is also virtually the only area of the country where rocks can be found at or near surface levels.

2. The ground moraine region of Drenthe and East Friesland covers the northern part of the country approximately from Haarlem to Nijmegen.

3. The terminal moraine region covers the central part of the High Netherlands. There are parallel ranges of hills up to 100 m. (328 ft.) high in the provinces of Utrecht, Gelderland and Overyssel, dissected by the valley of the Yssel River.

4. The sandy region of North Brabant and Limburg.

5. The raised bog region, a transitional region between the High and Low Netherlands where marshy conditions were conducive to peat formation.

6. The peat regions of Holland and Utrecht, Friesland and Overyssel, an area historically subject to erosion by the sea. The polders are more than 4 m. (13 ft.) below sea level.

7. The young marine clay regions in the south western and northern coastal districts, including areas reclaimed from the Zuyder Zee.

8. The alluvial clay regions.

9. The dunes created by the action of wind and water. The new dunes are at least 30 m. (98 ft.) high in places and several kilometers wide.

Much of the Low Netherlands has been wrested from the sea over the course of some eight centuries. Before the rise in the sea level after the last great ice age, large parts of the North Sea were dry, and Great Britain was joined to the Continent. Rivers such as the Rhine, the Thames and the Elbe flowed on well to the north of their present courses and did not empty into the sea until what is now the Dogger Bank. After the sea level had reached approximately the present coastline, the rise became slower and more irregular. At times of rapid rise, extensive coastal areas were swallowed by the sea, and only islands remained in the southwestern and northern Netherlands. The former Zuyder Zee reached its greatest extent in about A.D. 1250. The struggle waged by the inhabitants against the encroachments of the sea was purely defensive. They first built homes or villages on artificial mounds known as "terps," which later were linked by dikes. In the 17th century some of the lakes in North Holland were drained with the use of windmills. The 180-million-sq.-mi. (18,000-ha.) Haarlemmermeer, southwest of Amsterdam, and the area north of Rotterdam were drained in this fashion. In the archipelago of the Southwest and in the coastal areas of the North, reclamation took place in a different manner. The sea flowed in twice a day at high tide and left sand and silt behind as it retreated. When this process continued long enough, these areas came to be above sea level and were then surrounded by a dike. In the areas north of Groningen and in Friesland, low dams were built out into the sea and behind which sand and silt could quietly settle.

After 1900, land reclamation was undertaken on a larger scale. An ambitious plan was drawn up for reclaiming part of the Zuyder Zee. The firt polder, Weiringermeer, was drained in 1930. In 1932, the Zuyder Zee—now called IJsselmeer or Lake IJssel—was sealed off from the Wadden Zee by a 30-km. (19-mi.) barrier dam. Since then, other areas reclaimed from the sea include Lauwers Zee on the northern coast between Groningen and Friesland, and the Maasvlakte, south of the entrance to the new waterway. Environmental objections have delayed the reclamation of the Wadden Zee.

Dunes and dikes protect the Low Netherlands against flooding. Almost all the area to the west and north consists of polders where the water level is mechanically controlled at about 1 m. (3 ft.) below ground level, thus permitting cultivation. However, the more marshy soils of the older polders, reclaimed before 1850, can be used only for grazing. Polders do not necessarily lie below sea level, although this is the case with the IJsselmeer polder, which are 3.5 m. (11.5 ft.) below sea level and with polders created by draining lakes, which lie often below 6.7 m. (22.0 ft.). In areas of young marine clay and along the rivers, many polders lie above the average sea level, which means that it is not always necessary to pump the water out. The total number of polders is about 5,000; the older ones small.

As early as the Middle Ages, the inhabitants of the polders were faced with the task of safeguarding their area by joint effort once it had been wrested from the sea. At that time, the first *waterschappen* (water control boards) were created. Numbering 200, they are public bodies under the provincial authorities but elected by th *ingelanden* (landowners). The executives of these bodies are appointed by the crown. The boards have authority over water quality, environmental quality and recreation in the polder areas. Their duties are funded by a water control tax supplemented by central government funds.

In January 1986 the Northeast Polder and the two Flavoland polders were constituted as the Province of Flavoland. Nearly half the province will be set apart for agriculture, while Lelystad in eastern Flavoland and Almere in southern Flavoland are expected to have populations of 100,000 and 250,000, respectively, by the end of this century. The reclamation of the final Zuyder Zee polder, the Markerwaard, has been delayed because of political and environmental reasons.

The southwestern part of the Netherlands consists of an area of islands and peninsulas among which the Rhine, Maas and Scheldt rivers and their tributaries find their way to the sea. Much of the area was reclaimed as a result of accretion and embanking, and small islands grew to become larger areas. Sometimes these gains were lost through fresh flooding. In 1953 a great storm inundated 648 sq. km. (160,000 ac.) and caused 1,800 deaths in the low-lying polders. Following this disaster the Delta Project was launched to reduce danger of floods through construction of a number of dams. A movable water surge barrier was built in Hollandse IJssel east of Rotterdam. Thirteen other dams, sluices, bridges and canals were built before the project was completed in 1987. Strong tidal currents necessitated development of new techniques for sealing the estuaries. The project has not only eliminated the danger of floods in this region but also has opened up the previously isolated archipelago by roads built over the dams. The project has had serious drawbacks, the most important being damage to fisheries.

The Randstad, the western and most urbanized section of the Netherlands, is formed by the provinces of North Holland, South Holland and Utrecht and more specifically by the urban regions of Amsterdam, Rotterdam and Utrecht, forming a nearly complete ring of towns. The term Randstad is used to designated this area, although this term has no official status. Literally, the term is translated as "Rim City." The term "Greenheart City" also is used. However, the English term conurbation expresses the idea more clearly. Official reports refer to it as an urban zone.

The principal agglomerations of the Randstad cover 1,712 sq. km. (661 sq. mi.), roughly comparable to Greater Los Angeles or Greater London. But unlike them, the Randstad remains a congeries of cities, each with its own function; for example, The Hague is the seat of government; Amsterdam, the capital; Rotterdam, the chief port; and Utrecht, the transportation hub.

The Randstad is commonly subdivided into 21 functional regions:

1. Amsterdam, the capital region, at the confluence of the Amstel and the IJ rivers.

2. and 3. Het Gooi and South Kennemerland. Het Gooi is on the gently undulating land of the low hills and includes Hilversum and Bussum. The South Kennemerland area west of Amsterdam is centered in Haarlem.

4. The Zaan, an industrial region north of Amsterdam and centered on the town of Zaandam.

5. IJmond, a heavy industrial region located together with a fishing port complex at the seaward end of the North Sea Canal.

6. and 7. The North Kennemerland and South Kennemerland/Rijnland districts in the coastal dune belt and, in the North, the polders behind them.

8. and 9. Bollenstreek and Rijnsburg. Bollenstreek is the chief bulb-growing area, and Rijnsburg, at the mouth of the Old Rhine, west of Leiden, is a vegetable-growing area.

10–13. The Hague Agglomeration, Scheveningen, Wassenaar and Delft, cities on the western end of the southern belt of the Randstad.

14–17. Westland, Berkel, Boskoop and Aalsmeer, horticultural or market gardening areas.

18. Rotterdam, a continuous industrial and residential zone along both banks of the New Waterway and upstream along the Rhine tributaries of the Maas and Waal to Dordrecht and Gorinchem. It also includes the Hook of Holland and Europoort.

19. Utrecht. An old ecclesiastical and university town and transportation center.

20. Utrecht Glacial Ridge, a mainly residential area interspersed with wooded heathlands.

21. The Central Region, the rural "greenheart" of the Randstad.

CLIMATE & WEATHER

The Netherlands lies in the temperate zone of the Northern Hemisphere, with a maritime climate influenced by the North Sea and the Altlantic Ocean. Daily and annual temperature ranges are moderate; the mean January temperature is a little over 1°C (33°F), rising to 17°C (63°F) in July. There have, however, been extreme temperatures: The maximum and minimum temperatures recorded by the Royal Netherlands Meteorological Institute at De Bilt near Utrecht are 37°C (98°F) and (-25°C -13°F).

Since the country is small, there is little variation in climate from region to region, but the influence of the sea is less on inland temperatures. Regional differences are most marked in temperatures. The average number of summer days (with a maximum temperature of 25°C (77°F) or more) ranges from five in the Frisian Islands off the northern coast to more than 35 in the southern province of Limburg.

Changeability is the main feature of the Dutch climate. There is a lower incidence of frost in the coastal areas than inland. Although the mild, damp climate is suited to grassland and to dairy and livestock use, there is too little sunshine in the summer months for many arable crops. In winter the frequent changes in weather cause the roads to be slippery. The Netherlands is not subject to major wind systems.

Although spring is usually drier than autumn, rainfall is fairly even throughout the year, with an annual average of about 30 inches. There is no decrease in rainfall away from the coast, since summer storms are more frequent inland.

POPULATION

The 1987 population of the Netherlands was 14,641,554, with an average annual growth rate of 0.51%. The Netherlands ranks 52nd in the world in population. The population is expected to reach 15,380,000 in the year 2000.

Since 1830, when the first national census was held, the Dutch population has increased more than five times from 2.6 million. Much of this growth took place before this century. Since 1900 the birth rate has fallen from 31.6 per 1,000 to 11.8 per 1,000. The decline is attributable to the fall in the percentage of married women and the number of children per family. The death rate has also declined, from 17.9 per 1,000 in 1900 to 8.2 per 1,000 as a result of a reduction in infant mortality and improvements in medical care and social conditions. Around the two world wars there were sudden spurts in both birth rates and death rates. During the 1960s the deathrate showed a slight rise as a result of a relative growth in the number of people in the highest age brackets. Since that date, the birthrates and deathrates have tended to converge, reflecting a decline in natural increase. In 1960 the Netherlands had a natural increase of 13 per 1,000, one of the highest rates in Western Europe. By 1983 the natural increase had fallen to 3.7 per 1,000. This decline was partly compensated for in the 1960s and 1970s by a substantial net migration gain through the arrival of guest workers and their families and of Surinamese who were granted rights of domicile when Suriname became independent in 1975. This trend reverse a century-old pattern of outmigration to Canada, the United States, South Africa, Australia and New Zealand. The peak year of 1952 showed a net migration loss of 50,000. By 1960 emigration and immigration were approximately in balance. The largest net migration gain, of 72,000 people, was recorded in 1975. In the 1980s the net migration gain has declined, to about 6,000 annually.

Reflecting the population decline, the age pyramid has changed shape.

Age Group	As % of Total Population	
	1900	1983
0–19	44.3	30.3
20–64	49.7	58.0
65 and over	6.0	11.7

The 40 to 45 age group is rather weakly represented in the 1983 age pyramid, while the postwar bulge in the birth rate accounts for the many 35- to 40-year-olds. The increase in average life expectancy has contributed to a broadening of the apex representing the population over 65.

From the 1960s there were significant changes in the nature of marriages and household formation in the Netherlands. Both the number of marriages and the percentage of men and women marrying for the first time declined during the period from 1960 to 1983. The number of divorces also increased, from 5,670 in 1960 to 30,000 in 1982. The remarriage rate of divorced and widowed men and women halved. Marriage itself was being replaced increasingly by cohabitation. Between 1979 and 1983 the percentage of cohabiting women increased from 1 to 3% among the 18–19-year-olds, from 10 to 16% for the 20–24-year-olds and up to 10% for the 25–29-year olds. There also is a larger number of single-person households; these now account for 22% of all households, compared with only 12% in 1960.

An even more significant phenomenon was the increase in voluntary childlessness among married couples. Although the percentage of marriages in which at least one child was born decreased between 1960 and 1982, there was at the same time a steep rise in first births within marriage as a proportion of total births. The most striking feature of this trend was in fourth and later births, the share of which fell from 25% in 1960 to 5.7% in 1983. Considered from the standpoint of the age of the wife, childbearing has declined dramatically among older women: by 90% among women over 40, and by 80% among women from 35 to 40.

There also are equally marked changes in childbearing outside marriage, although of a different nature. From 1975 there was an increase in the number of children born to unmarried, divorced or widowed women, particularly in the 25 to 34 age group. The average age of women who gave birth outside of marriage for the first time rose from 21.4 in 1971 to 24.5 in 1982. This is particularly the case in large cities. For example, in Amsterdam 20% of all children are born to unmarried, divorced or widowed women. Childbearing outside marriage is the predominant social feature among the Surinamese women. The changing nature of marriage and fertility will have far-reaching implications on Dutch demographics well into the 21st century.

With a nationwide density of 428 people per sq. km. (165 people per sq. mi.), the Netherlands has one of the highest population densities in the world, but even within the small land area, there are significant regional differences. Northern and southwestern Netherlands generally have lower than average densities, while the highest concentrations are found in eastern, western and southern Netherlands, particularly in the historic population centers of South Holland, North Holland and Utrecht as well as in the provinces of North Brabant and Limburg. South Holland has the highest regional density, with 1,084 people per sq. km. (418 people per sq. mi.), followed by North Holland with 866 people per sq. km. (334 people per sq. mi.) and Utrecht with 703 people per sq. km. (271 people per sq. mi.). The fastest-growing province is the reclaimed land of S. IJsselmeer Polders, whose population grew by 85% between 1980 and 1985.

Population distribution reflects the dynamics of internal migration, which began to change after the 1960s. Originally there had been considerable movement to the West from all parts of the country except the South, but this was reversed after 1970. As the western provinces and cities became saturated, larger numbers of people began to settle in smaller towns in the neighboring provinces to the east and south. As a result, the western conurbation extended eastward across its boundaries in the direction of Arnhem and Nijmegen and southward in the direction of Breda, Tilburg and Eindhoven. With the completion of the Delta Project, the islands and peninsulas in the Southwest became less isolated. Other shifts in population occurred, as when the coal mines of Limburg were closed between 1966 and 1975. Emigrants from the west are more often from North or South Holland than from Utrecht, while the influx in the East is far more pronounced in Gelderland than in Overijssel.

The internal migration up to about 1960 was largely a flight to the towns as a result of the graying of the countryside. Urban population peaked in the 1960s and then began to decline, while the population of small towns and villages has grown correspondingly. As the more affluent age groups are leaving the cities, their place is being taken by young students and foreign workers, creating in the process inner cities with poorer standards of public housing and facilities. Because of the rapid growth in the number of commuters, there are traffic jams every day on the motorways, especially at bridges and tunnels.

DEMOGRAPHIC INDICATORS

Population: 1987: 14,641,554
Year of last census: 1985
  Males (000): 7,211,000   Females (000):
    7,296,000
Sex ratio: 49.5 males: 50.5 females

DEMOGRAPHIC INDICATORS *(continued)*

Population trends (million)

1930: 7.936	1960: 11.417	1990: 14.783
1940: 8.836	1970: 12.958	2000: 15.380
1950: 10.027	1980: 14.150	2020: 14.000

Population doubling time in years at current rate: 192 years

Hypothetical size of stationary population (million): 14

Assumed year of reaching net reproduction rate of 1: 2020

Age profile (%)

0–14: 19.7	30–44: 22.4	60–74: 11.7
15–29: 25.6	45–59: 15.6	Over 75: 5.0

Median age (years): 33.5 year

Density per sq. km.: 355 (per sq. mi.: 137)

Annual growth rate (%)

1950–55: 1.22	1965–70: 1.17	1980–85: 0.40
	1970–75: 1.14	1985–90: 0.30
1960–65: 1.37	1975–80: 0.61	1990–95: 0.23
		1995–2000: 0.15

Vital statistics

Crude birth rate 1/1,000: 12.1

Crude death rate 1/1,000: 8.5

Change in birth rate 1965–85 %: -40.2

Change in death rate 1965–85 %: Insignificant

Dependency (total): 44.8

Infant mortality rate 1/1,000: 8

Child (0–4 years) mortality rate 1/1,000: Insignificant

Maternal mortality rate 1/100,000: 5.3

Natural increase 1/1,000: 3.6

Total fertility rate: 1.44

General fertility rate: 45

Gross reproduction rate: 0.68

Marriage rate 1/1,000: 5.7

Divorce rate 1/1,000: 2.4

Life expectancy, males (years): 73.0

Life expectancy, females (years): 79.5

Average household size: 2.6

% Illegitimate births: 7.7

Youth

Youth population 15–24 (000): 2,500

Youth population in 2020 (000): 1,500

Women

Of childbearing age 15–49 (000): 3,800

Children per: 1.5

% women using contraception: 70

% women married 15–19: 2

Urban

Urban population (000): 13,416

% urban 1965: 86   1985: 88

Annual urban growth rate (%)

DEMOGRAPHIC INDICATORS *(continued)*

1965–80: 1.5   1980–85: 0.9
% urban population in largest city: 9
% urban population in cities over 500,000: 24
Number of cities over 500,000: 3
Annual rural growth %: -8.3

ETHNIC COMPOSITION

The Dutch are an ethnically homogeneous people descended from Saxon, Frankish and Frisian tribes. However, since the end of World War II, ethnic homogeneity has been considerably diluted by the arrival of both European and non-European immigrants, as a result of which the Netherlands has a pluralist society.

Immigrants are of two types: former colonials and repatriates, and guest workers. The largest group of the former type are repatriates from the Dutch East Indies, who came to the Netherlands between 1945 and the 1960s. This group, estimated at between 250,000 and 300,000, are mostly of mixed Dutch and Indonesian parentage. Since they were officially Dutch citizens, although born overseas, they were rapidly assimilated into Dutch society and experienced little if any prejudice.

A second group from Southeast Asia were Moluccans, mostly ex-soldiers of the Royal Netherlands East Indies Army. When they arrived in 1951, they were expected to stay only for a short while until they could return to their homeland after it achieved independence from Indonesia. They were housed in camps, and no attempt was made to integrate them into Dutch society, indeed, the Moluccans themselves were averse to integration. Yet, as the dream of an independent Moluccas faded, their presence became an embarrassment to the Dutch government. In the mid-1970s young Moluccans tried to demonstrate their plight by hijacking trains and occupying government offices. There are an estimated 35,000 Moluccans in the kingdom, of whom 60% are classified as stateless, 30% are Dutch subjects and 10% are Indonesian citizens.

Suriname entered the picture in about 1965, when an increasing number of Surinamese creole blacks came to the Netherlands as workers. Net migration increased from 2,300 in 1966 to 5,500 in 1970. Then fears of impending immigration control led to a further jump, to 15,000 in 1974 and to 36,000 in 1975. After Suriname's independence, immigration continued under a bilateral agreement, much of it restricted to reunification of families. The agreement expired in 1980, and since then Surinamese have required visas to enter the Netherlands. The Surinamese population in the Netherlands was estimated at about

200,000 in the mid-1980s. Labor migration from the Netherlands Antilles continues at about 2,500 per year.

Import of labor has a curious history in the Netherlands. Officially an overpopulated nation, the Netherlands was an improbable destination for guest workers. However, by the early 1960s the economy was booming and all available labor reserves had been exhausted. The result was a rapid rise in wages and a reduction in working hours. To reduce labor union pressures, employers started recruiting in Mediterranean countries. The government made a series of bilateral recruiting agreements with Italy (1960), Spain (1961), Portugal (1963), Turkey (1964), Greece (1966), Morocco (1969), Yugoslavia (1970) and Tunisia (1970). The number of workers from these countries rose from a few hundred in 1960 to 46,000 in 1966.

The Mediterranean workers were regarded as temporary labor to be used as buffer against economic downturns. However, during the recession of 1967, a total of 39,000 guest workers remained in the country despite high unemployment. Employed in menial jobs that the Dutch themselves were averse to do, the guest workers were proving to be a necessary evil. When the recession ended, recruitment resumed, rising to 90,000 by 1974. Recruitment of workers ceased in 1974, following the recession caused by the oil shocks. Even so, the number of guest workers continued to climb, reaching 105,000 in 1977, excluding 80,000 dependents. By 1984 the number of aliens in the economy reached an all-time high of 316,000.

The foreign presence was reflected in the census figures. In 1947, the 104,000 aliens made up 1.1% of the national population. The relative figure for 1982 was 544,000, or 3.8% of the population, excluding the so-called repatriates. The nationality and size of the alien work force, as shown in the following table, reveals a shift from an initial Western European composition to a Southern European and later to a Muslim Third World composition. This pattern is not dissimilar to that experienced by West Germany, France, the United Kingdom and other receiving countries. There also is a lowering of the skills level of the guest workers, and a lengthening of the cultural and racial distance from the host country.

The Dutch are less tolerant of guest workers than of former colonials. There were anti-Italian riots as early as 1959; racist attacks on Moroccans in 1969; and street riots against Turks in Rotterdam in 1972 and in Schiedam in 1976. The principal reason for such hostility is, of course, economic, because foreign workers tend to depress wages and compete with nationals for manual jobs, housing and regarding other bread-and-butter issues.

In response, the government made belated efforts to push back the tide of immigration, beginning in the mid-1970s. Entry of workers was curtailed, border

GUEST WORKERS, 1971 and 1982				
Nationality	1971			1982
	000	% of Total	000	% of Total
United Kingdom	12	4.9	40	7.4
Belgium	24	9.2	24	4.4
West Germany	37	14.4	43	7.9
Italy	18	6.9	21	3.9
Yugoslavia	8	3.1	14	2.6
Spain	28	11.0	23	4.2
Turkey	30	11.9	148	27.2
Morocco	22	8.5	93	17.1
Other	76	29.8	103	18.9
TOTAL	255	100.0	544	100.0

controls were tightened and illegal aliens were deported. In many cases migrants were denied unemployment benefits. In 1974 the minister of social affairs proposed new legislation: Employers were required to obtain employment permits for each migrant worker, thus increasing the migrant's dependence on the employer and restricting the migrant's job mobility.

In 1981 the government adopted a more realistic policy toward ethnic minorities, recognizing their claim to equal status with nationals in matters of housing, social services and employment. The new policy was aimed at creating a pluralist society in which legal minorities will have a secure place. The new Netherlands Constitution also granted them voting rights in local elections.

However, despite official endorsement of a multi-ethnic society, little has been done to implement the new policy. In fact, the regulations governing entry of migrants' dependents have been tightened. The problem is complicated by the rise of blatantly racial political parties and increased racial tensions. For example, the Centrum Party runs on an openly racist platform.

LANGUAGE

The official language is Dutch or Hollands, and it is also the mother tongue of all inhabitants except the 340,000 Frisians, who speak their ancient language of the same name. Frisian is closely related to Anglo-Saxon, while Dutch belongs to the Germanic language group.

Dutch has six dialects, notably Gelders and Groningen. The general language of communication, or standard Dutch, is called ABN (Algemeen Beschaafd Nederlands, or General Educated Dutch). There are some differences in sound and vocabulary between the language in the South and in the North, roughly comparable to the difference between the German spoken in Hamburg and that spoken in Vienna. The influence of Dutch goes beyond the national borders. Dutch (called Flemish) is the language of the majority in Belgium. An earlier offshoot, known as Afrikaans, is one of the two official languages in South Africa.

Dutch has received less attention from linguists than it deserves because, for them, it is overshadowed by German. The myth persists that the Dutch once spoke German and raised their local dialect to the status of a language only on achieving independence in the 16th century. That is an unfortunate conclusion based upon certain similarities in the two languages. The pronunciation of German is sharper, harder and more precise than that of Dutch. Dutch sounds a little more slovenly and a little softer. The range of verb and noun inflections is also less in Dutch than in German. Dutch has only two forms of the definite article, *de* (German *der* or *die*) and *het*, and it has no noun declension system. Many German and Dutch words look alike but differ radically in meaning. Dutch is more analytical than German. Long compounds and long sentences are considered ugly. Whereas German has a predilection for the abstract, Dutch has countless plastic expressions that form part of everyday educated speech.

Frisian, the second official language of Friesland, is even older than Dutch and has an extensive literature of its own. In Friesland it is the language of instruction for the first three years of primary education, and it is taught well into the secondary grades. There are chairs of Frisian at five Dutch universities, and there are also Frisian libraries and the Frisian Academy.

RELIGIONS

Evangelization of the Netherlands began in the 7th century, when the Franks established a church at Utrecht, but little progress was made before the arrival of the English missionaries Willibrord and Boniface during the first half of the 8th century. German mysticism became dominant in the 14th century through the influence of John of Ruysbroeck, Gerhard Groot and Thomas à Kempis. Many banded themselves together as Brethren of the Common Life, living essentially a monastic life with common rules but without permanent vows. After the Reformation, Holland became a refuge for the followers of Luther, Zwingli and Calvin, the latter ultimately taking precedence. With the attempt of Philip II to force Catholicism, the Dutch Reformation became allied with the struggle for freedom, which lasted from 1568 to 1648. In 1581 the northern provinces under William of Orange began fighting the southern Catholic provinces, persecuting them once Spanish rule ended at the conclusion of the Thirty Years' War. The Dutch Reformed Church became Holland's official religion in 1651. Under the French rule from 1795 to 1815 the Catholic Church once again gained recognition. The Constitution of 1848 affirmed religious liberty for all, and the Catholic hierarchy was reestablished in 1853.

The Roman Catholic population has remained relatively stable since the middle of the 19th century. At that time the Catholics numbered 38% of the total, rising to 40.2% in 1985. From 1955 to 1964 the Catholic birth rate was 2.7% above that of the national average, but by 1970 the difference had been reduced to 0.7%, indicating that Catholics had by and large adopted family planning, like the rest of the population. Apostasy also is becoming as common among the Catholics as it was for a long time with the Reformed Protestants.

The geographic spread of the Catholic population is uneven. The three northern provinces (Groningen, Drente and Friesland), which make up the Diocese of Groningen, are 8% Catholic and form only 2% of the total Catholic population. The central provinces (Utrecht, Haarlem and Rotterdam) are 25 to 30% Catholic, but the percentage is weaker in the strongly urbanized west-central area (including Amsterdam and Rotterdam) than in the eastern area. The southern areas (dioceses of 's Hertogenbosch, Breda and Roermond) are between 85 and 90% Catholic.

Catholic religious practice still is high compared to neighboring countries or to that prevailing in the Dutch Reformed community. The national average of Sunday Mass attendance is estimated at about 30%, compared to 64% in 1966, 56% in 1968, 46% in 1970 and 41% in 1972. The increasing number of mixed marriages, civil marriages and unbaptized children of Catholic parents indicate a weakening of adherence to traditional practices. Another disturbing trend is a steady decline in the number of new priests. More than a third of the parish priests are over 55 years of age.

Dutch Catholicism has experienced recent changes that have radically altered its character. For almost a century after the reestablishment of the Catholic hierarchy in 1853, the Catholic Church remained aloof from the mainstream, dominated by Protestants, Socialists and liberal humanists. In the latter part of this century the Catholics began to reintegrate themselves into the community through the formation of a system of organizations in every sector of national life—Catholic newspapers, radio and television broadcasting, a political party (Katholieke Volkspartij), a trade union and numerous social and professional groups. Thus it was able to achieve social and political equality through a peculiarly Dutch concept known as compartmentalization or pillarization (ver-

zuiling). A similar compartmentalization among Protestants and Socialists has created a vertically pluralist society in which each group exercises reciprocal tolerance.

The insular character of the Catholic Church that compartmentalization fostered was radically altered following the Second Vatican Council. The trend was reinforced by open dissent within the church, calling for a more open Catholicism with room for dialogue and change. Under the guidance of the episcopate, the influential liberal theological journal *Concilium* was founded in 1965. The struggle between the liberals and the conservatives was joined with the publication of the immensely popular *New Catechism* for adults, which was translated into 10 languages. This catechism was opposed by the conservative groups, especially Confrontation, the Legion of St. Michael, and Truth and Life, which succeeded in having the Roman Curia appoint conservative bishops in Rotterdam and Roermond. Perhaps the most important event contributing to Catholic renewal in the Netherlands was the Pastoral Council, held between 1966 and 1970, which called upon the faithful to assume a new form of coresponsibility for the church. Among its starting declarations were calls for a more moderate stand on contraceptives, abolition of priestly celibacy and intercommunion with other Christian denominations. The Council also succeeded in creating the National Pastoral Committee, an example that was followed in Austria, West Germany and Switzerland. Dutch Catholicism also has been in the vanguard of the charismatic movement, with its emphasis on the gifts of the Holy Spirit.

The principal Protestant tradition is the Dutch Reformed Church, which is at present divided into six different major denominations, not including the Moluccan Protestant Church, formed in 1950 by Indonesians. The total affiliated Reformed population is estimated at 4.5 million. The mother church is the Netherlands Reformed Church (Nederlandse Hervormde Kerk, NHK), which retains a confessional balance between liberals and Calvinists. The NHK is divided into 11 church provinces with 2,275 congregations, in addition to 16 Walloon (French-speaking) parishes. Its central administrative body is the general synod assisted by numerous boards and commissions.

Reaction against liberalism and state influence in the NHK has produced a number of neo-Calvinist schisms, beginning in the early part of the 19th century. The first of these, called Afscheiding, or Secession, took place in the village of Ulrum in Groningen in 1834 and led to the formation of over 100 free churches. More schisms followed in the 1840s, and in 1886 another large exodus called Dolcante, or Dissension, took place in Amsterdam. The most recent schism, in 1944, led to the formation of the Liberated Reformed Churches. Some breakaway groups, such as the Christian Reformed Churches (founded in

1834) and the Old Reformed Churches (founded in 1841), still retain their separate identity, but others have coalesced into two major bodies, the Reformed Churches in the Netherlands (founded in 1892) and the Reformed Communities in the Netherlands (founded in 1907). The former is now the second-largest Protestant denomination after the NHK, with 1,400 parishes in 14 synods and with an affiliated body in West Germany and the Free Reformed University in Amsterdam.

The NHK lost its special status as the state church in 1795 under the French occupation, but nevertheless it considers itself to be the national, or folk, church. However, its has steadily lost its numerical strength, which has declined from 60% in the 19th century to a little over 20% in the 1980s. The neo-Calvinists have maintained a more stable membership, at about 7%. The growth of the unchurched has been mainly at the expense of the NHK.

Other Dutch Protestant communities include the Congregationalists (divided into two groups: the Remonstrant Brotherhood, founded in 1618, and the Association of Free Evangelical Congregations, founded in 1834); the Mennonites; the Salvation Army; and 12 Pentecostal bodies, of which the largest is the Apostolic Church. Schismatic Catholic churches include the Old Catholic Church, created in 1724 following the Jansenist controversy; the Old Roman Catholic Church, founded in 1790; and the Catholic Apostolic (Irvingite) Church, which spread to Holland from England in 1867.

Religious freedom was established in several articles of the Constitution of 1814. However, religious processions are permitted only as authorized by laws and regulations and remain a sore issue for Catholics. The Netherlands has no concordat with the Holy See, and there has been no ministry of religious affairs since 1871. However, state approval is required for an expatriate to hold ecclesiastical office. Following the Napoleonic Code, clergy are prohibited from celebrating a religious marriage prior to a civil ceremony.

Although both church and state are constitutionally separate, religious communities receive considerable aid and support from the state. These include laws enforcing Sunday observance, and prosecution of those who offend religious scruples. Religious communities and their autonomous associations have a juridical personality that may not be abridged. The state pays the salaries of prison and military chaplains, and salaries, pensions and other benefits to ministers. For a period, the construction of new churches was eligible for state subsidies of up to 40%. Religious bodies are given free radio and television time in the state-run electronic media. Confessional presence also is strong in Parliament where, of the 14 political parties represented, two are Catholic and four are Protestant. Besides the theological faculties in state-run universities, the theological faculties of the Free Reformed University of Amsterdam and the

Catholic University of Nijmegen also receive public subsidies. Church-run elementary and secondary schools receive partial state subsidies.

Of the non-Christian religions, Islam, with over 100,000 members, is the largest and is almost entirely foreign in origin. Muslims are concentrated in the provinces of North and South Holland. The number of Jews was severely decimated during the Nazi occupation, decreasing from 140,000 before World War II to about 25,000 today. As in other countries of Europe, the nonreligious constitute the fastest-growing group. They make up over 12% of the population in the Netherlands, compared to 1.5% in 1900.

HISTORICAL BACKGROUND

After the death of Charlemagne and the dismemberment of his realm, several duchies were founded in the region called the Low Countries. In the Middle Ages, the province of Holland rose to prominence under Count Floris V (1256–96). As the seat of an ancient bishopric, Utrecht became an important principality, while Amsterdam, Haarlem and Groningen became prosperous trading centers. In the 15th century, most of the Low Countries came under the rule of the Dukes of Burgundy and later, on the marriage of Mary of Burgundy to Archduke (later Emperor) Maximilian I in 1477, under the Austrian House of Habsburg. Mary's son Philip of Habsburg married Joanna of Castile, and their son Charles V became king of Spain in 1516. In 1519 he united the Netherlands and Spain and became the master of the Low Countries. The Spanish hegemony continued under his son Philip II, who directed his energies toward stamping out Protestantism and suppressing the political and religious liberties of the Dutch. The 17 provinces comprising the Low Countries thereupon rose in revolt under the leadership of William the Silent, prince of Orange. Much of the country was freed by 1577, with William as the acknowledged ruler. However, in 1578 the southern provinces, now Belgium, turned against William. In 1579 the northern provinces concluded the Union of Utrecht as the United Provinces. Upon the assassination of William the Silent in 1584, his son Maurice was installed as the stadtholder of the republic. Final recognition of Dutch independence by Spain was not obtained until the Treaty of Westphalia in 1648. Meanwhile, the southern provinces remained loyal to Spain and were thereafter known as the Spanish Netherlands.

In the 17th century, the United Provinces became the leading commerical and martime power in Europe, with settlements and colonies in the East Indies, the crown jewel of its empire, as well as South Africa, the West Indies and South America. For a time the Dutch were also dominant in Ceylon (now Sri Lanka). Alongside trade and commerce, arts, sciences, literature and philosophy flourished. It was the golden age of the great Dutch masters in painting. In terms of religious freedom, it was the most liberal in the world and a haven for refugees from religious persecution. At the peak of their power, the Dutch led several coalitions of European powers to victory over France. From 1688 to 1707, William III, the great-grandson of William the Silent, and his wife, Mary, were monarchs of England.

In the 18th century, the Dutch decline was as swift as its rise. Intense rivalries among the provinces and four naval wars with the rising power of Great Britain sapped its strength. In 1795 a much weakened republic was overrun by the revolutionary French armies. After the fall of Napoleon, the Congress of Vienna (1814–15) set up a new kingdom of the Netherlands composed of the United Provinces and the former Spanish (or Austrian) Netherlands under a prince of the House of Orange, King William I. In 1830 the southern provinces broke away to form the Kingdom of Belgium. Dutch claims to the principality of Luxembourg ended with the death of William III in 1890. Threafter, the Dutch became more insular, concerned mainly with domestic problems, such as electoral reforms and conflict over secular versus religious instruction. The Dutch remained neutral in World War I but succumbed to Nazi forces in 1940. Dutch resistance lasted for only five days, and destruction, particularly in the cities of Rotterdam, Arnhem and Nijmegen, was extensive. The Netherlands was liberated by Allied forces in May 1945. Queen Wilhelmina abdicated in 1948 and was succeeded by her daughter Juliana. The Dutch had lost the East Indies to the Japanese in 1942. After the fall of Japan, a group of Indonesian nationalists proclaimed an independent republic and resisted Dutch reoccupation. After four years of hostilities, Indonesia was granted independence in 1949. Dutch Guiana, a Dutch possession since 1815, became an independent nation as Suriname in 1975.

CONSTITUTION & GOVERNMENT

The Netherlands is a constitutional monarchy. It has had three constitutions since the establishment of the monarchy: that of 1814–15; that of 1848; and the present one, which came into force on February 17, 1983. In addition, the relationship between the Netherlands and Netherlands Antilles is defined in the Charter of the Kingdom of the Netherlands signed by Queen Juliana in 1954.

The Constitution regulates the royal succession and regency in great detail. Article 10 states that "The crown of the Netherlands is and shall remain vested in the House of Nassau-Orange" and in the legitimate descendants of William Frederick. A successor to the throne may be appointed by an act of Parliament if there is no heir apparent. In other cases, the sovereign is succeeded by his or her oldest child. The age of majority for a sovereign is 18 years. Until a sovereign attains that age, royal powers are exercised by a regent. Since 1890, when

William III died, the Netherlands has been ruled by queens: Queen Wilhelmina from 1898 to 1948 (regency from 1890 to 1898); Queen Juliana from 1948 to 1980; and Queen Beatrix from 1980.

Executive authority is vested in the Council of Ministers (Ministerraad), which is appointed by the monarch but is responsible to the States General, the parliament. The ministerial responsibility to the States General is twofold: under criminal law and under civil law, both specified in the Constitution. There is also a political responsibility, of which the electorate is the ultimate judge.

General elections are held every four years to the Lower House, and on that day ministers of the outgoing government submit their resignations en bloc. Immediately after the election, results are known, the queen seeks advice on the formation of a new government. Usually she consults the vice president of the Council of State, the speakers of both houses of parliament and the leaders of all major political parties. Their initial verbal recommendations are followed by written reports. If no party commands a clear majority in the Lower House, the queen invites someone to act as a special adviser, called *informateur*, who then acts as a mediator. When he has succeeded in this work, he withdraws to make way for the *formateur*, who proceeds to form a cabinet, although not necessarily as a prime minister. On the prime minister's advice the queen appoints the members of the new government.

RULERS OF THE NETHERLANDS

Stadhouders

Jan. 1579–July 1584	Willem I (assassinated)
July 1584–April 1625	Maurits (*son*)
April 1625–March 1647	Frederick Hendrik (*half brother*)
March 1647–Nov. 1650	Willem II (*son*)
(Nov. 1650–July 1672	post vacant)
July 1672–March 1702	Willem III (William III of England) (*son*)
(March 1702–May 1747	post vacant)
May 1747–Oct. 1751	Willem IV (*great-grandnephew of Willem II*)
Oct. 1751–May 1795	Willem V (*son*) (deposed)
(May 1795–June 1806	French occupation)

Kings/Queens

June 1806–July 1810	Lodewijk I (Louis Bonaparte, *brother of Napoléon I of France*) (abdicated)
July 1810	Lodewijk II (Napoléon-Louis Bonaparte) (*son*)
(July 1810–Nov. 1813	French annexation)
(Nov. 1813–March 1815	Provisional government)

RULERS OF THE NETHERLANDS *(continued)*

March 1815–Oct. 1840	Willem I (*son of Willem V*) (also Guillaume I of Luxembourg) (abdicated)
Oct. 1840–March 1849	Willem II (*son*) (also Guillaume II of Luxembourg)
March 1849–Nov. 1890	Willem III (*son*) (also Guillaume III of Luxembourg)
Nov. 1890–May 1940	Wilhelmina (*daughter*) (1st) (exiled) Regent: Nov. 1890– Aug. 1898 Queen Emma
(May 1940–May 1945	German occupation)
May 1945–Sept. 1948	Wilhelmina (2nd) (abdicated)
Sept. 1948–April 1980	Juliana (*daughter*) (abdicated)
April 1980–	Beatrix (*daughter*)

Prime Ministers

March–Nov. 1848	Gerrit Schimmelpenninck
Nov. 1848–Nov. 1849	Jacob de Kempenaer/Dirk Donker Curtius (1st)
Nov. 1849–April 1853	Jan Thorbecke (1st)
April 1853–July 1856	Floris van Hall (1st)/Dirk Donker Curtius (2nd)
July 1856–March 1858	Justinius van der Brugghen
March 1858–Feb. 1860	Jacob Rochussen/Pieter van Bosse (1st)
Feb. 1860–March 1861	Floris van Hall (2nd)/ Schelte van Heemstra
March 1861–Jan. 1862	Julius van Zuylen van Nijevelt (1st)/James Louden
Feb. 1862–Feb. 1866	Jan Thorbecke (2nd)
Feb.–June 1866	Isaac Fransen van de Putte (1st)
June 1866–June 1868	Julius van Zuylen van Nijevelt (2nd)/Jan Heemskerk (1st)
June 1868–Jan. 1871	Pieter van Bosse (2nd)
Jan. 1871–Aug. 1872	Jan Thorbecke (3rd)
Aug. 1872–Aug. 1874	Isaac Fransen van de Putte (2nd)/Gerrit de Vries
Aug. 1874–Nov. 1877	Constantinius van Lynden van Sandenburg (1st)/Jan Heemskerk (2nd)
Nov. 1877–Aug. 1879	Johannes Kappeyne van de Coppello
Aug. 1879–April 1883	Constantinius van Lynden van Sandenburg (2nd)
April 1883–April 1888	Jan Heemskerk (3rd)

RULERS OF THE NETHERLANDS *(continued)*

April 1888–Aug. 1891	Aeneas Mackay
Aug. 1891–May 1894	Cornelius van Tienhoven (Lib. P.)
May 1894–July 1897	Johan Roëll (Lib. P.)
July 1897–Aug. 1901	Nicolaas Pierson (Lib. P.)
Aug. 1901–Aug. 1905	Abraham Kuyper
Aug. 1905–Dec. 1908	Theodoor de Meester (Lib. P.)
Dec. 1908–Aug. 1913	Theodoor Heemskerk (*son of Jan Heemskerk*) (Anti-Rev. P.)
Aug. 1913–Sept. 1918	Pieter Cort van der Linden (Lib. P.)
Sept. 1918–Aug. 1925	Charles Ruys de Beeren-brouck (1st) (Cath. P.)
Aug. 1925–May 1929	Hendrickus Colijn (1st) (Anti-Rev. P.)
May–Aug. 1929	Dirk de Geer (1st)
Aug. 1929–May 1933	Charles Ruys de Beeren-brouck (2nd) (Cath. P.)
May 1933–Aug. 1939	Hendrickus Colijn (2nd) (Anti-Rev. P.)
Aug. 1939–May 1940	Dirk de Geer (2nd)
(May 1940–May 1945	German Occupation)
May–July 1945	Pieter Gerbrandy (Anti-Rev. P.)
July 1945–July 1946	Willem Schermerhorn (Soct. P.)
July 1946–Aug. 1948	Louis Beel (1st) (Cath. P.)
Aug. 1948–Dec. 1958	Willem Drees (Soct. P.)
Dec. 1958–May 1959	Louis Beel (2nd) (Cath. P.)
May 1959–July 1963	Jan de Quay (Cath. P.)
July 1963–April 1965	Victor Marijnen (Cath. P.)
April 1965–Nov. 1966	Joseph Cals (Cath. P.)
Nov. 1966–April 1967	Jelle Zijlstra (Anti-Rev. P.)
April 1967–July 1971	Petrus de Jong (Cath. P.)
July 1971–May 1973	Barend Biesheuvel (Anti-Rev. P.)
May 1973–Dec. 1977	Johannes den Uyl (Lab. P.)
Dec. 1977–Nov. 1982	Andreas van Agt (Chris. Dem. P.)
Nov. 1982–	Rudolphus Lubbers (Chris. Dem. P.)

The Constitution distinguishes between departmental and nondepartmental ministers. The latter, who are also known as ministers without porfolio, are generally appointed to achieve a desirable balance among political parties. Since 1948 the Constitution has provided for the appointment of state secretaries. Appointment as a state secretary is a political and not a civil service appointment. A state is not a member of the Council of Ministers but may be invited to take part in it in an advisory capacity. Although subject to the authority of the departmental minister, a state secretary is accountable to parliament for his actions, without prejudice to the responsibility of his superior. A state secretary must resign if his minister steps down, but the reverse is not the case.

Ministers of state are appointed by the queen on recommendation of the Council of Ministers. Minister of state is actually an honorary title conferred on distinguished retired politicians whose wisdom and experience are useful in the conduct of public affairs.

The Council of Ministers usually meets once a week. Decisions are reached by a majority vote, and on issues where there is no clear majority, a decision is deferred until the next meeting. The prime minister has a casting vote. Specific issues are dealt with by various standing committees, such as the Civil Services Council, the Economic Affairs Council and the Science Policy Council.

The Council of State is the senior advisory body to the crown. It must be consulted on all draft legislation, and over the years it has acquired additional functions. The council's powers are governed by the Council of State Act of 1861, the Constitution, the Charter for the Kingdom and the Council of State Act of 1962. The first act created the Administrative Disputes Section in 1861. In 1976 the Judicial Section was established, and under the Administrative Jurisdiction (Government Orders) Act, members of the public can appeal to the council against decisions of national, provincial or municipal authorities.

The queen presides over the Council of State but delegates its day-to-day affairs to the vice president. There are 24 other members, who are nominally appointed for life but who must retire on reaching age 70. An additional 10 part-time members may be appointed by the crown for deliberations on specific issues. The Council of State is divided into sections, each of which is concerned with one ministry. Each section consists of three members. A separate committee advises the council on matters of general legislation.

The Council of State gives its recommendations upon all proposals before the States General, all drafts of general administrative orders and all international agreements. The council examines the constitutionality and legality of all proposals. Where required by the national interest, it may call for legislative action on a specific issue, either in the form of a parliamentary bill or general administrative order.

The council's Administrative Disputes Section is responsible for advising the ministers on the legal and policy aspects of appeals requiring a decision by the crown. Members of the section are nominated by the Minister for Home Affairs on the council's recommendations and after consulting with the Minister of Justice. The section is generally divided into a number of chambers (at present 10), each with three to five members and a chairman. After hearing the interested parties, the section submits its report to the crown together with a draft royal decree. If the crown decides not to accept the recommendations, the decision and its reasons are published in the Bulletin of Acts, Orders and Decrees together with the section's findings.

The council's Judicial Section hears appeals against rulings of central, provincial and local authorities, provided the decision in question does not have general application and is not justiciable under civil law. Certain categories, such as tax matters and appointments, are precluded from the section's purview. The decision may be overturned by the section if (1) it conflicts with an act of parliament or the Constitution, (2) if the administrative body had acted *ultra vires*, (3) if the administrative body had ignored some evidence that had a bearing on the case and (4) if proper and fair procedures had been violated. The members of this section are appointed in the same manner as those of the Administrative Disputes Section. At present the section is composed of five chambers.

The Constitution provides for a General Chamber of Audit, whose membership and functions are regulated by the Government Accounts Act of 1976. The chamber consists of three members, each of whom is selected by the crown from a list of three people drawn up by the Lower House. Each member has a deputy. Members and their deputies enjoy broadly the same legal status as members of the judiciary. Members are appointed for life (subject to retirement at 70) and may be suspended or dismissed only by the Supreme Court. Their salaries are also fixed by law.

The chamber is divided into seven divisions, and each division into sections that correspond to the various ministries. There are also separate sections dealing with state enterprises and salaries, work study, policy study and computerization. The chamber performs three functions. It determines whether funds have been disbursed in accordance with statutory regulations and do not exceed the limits laid down by parliament, (2) it investigates malfeasance by public officials and (3) it examines whether the government's policy objectives are being met by the expenditure and recommends policy changes if they are not. The chamber submits an annual report to the queen and the States General by April 1.

There are at present 14 ministries, but the number is not fixed.
1. Ministry of General Affairs. It is always under the prime minister and includes the Information Department, Foreign Information Service, Advisory Council on Government Policy and the Office of the Minister for Netherlands Antilles Affairs.

2. Ministry of Foreign Affairs. Includes Ministry for Development Cooperation.

3. Ministry of Justice. Includes Directorates General of Police, Prisons, Child Care and Protection, Private Law, Constitutional and Criminal Law, Court and Legal Administration, and Alien Affairs.

4. Ministry of Home Affairs. Includes the Directorates General of Home Administration, Public Order and Safety, and Public Service Staff Policy.

5. Ministry of Education and Science. Includes Directorates General of Primary Education, Secondary Education, Education and Inspection Services, Higher Education and Scientific Research, and Science Policy.

6. Ministry of Finance. Includes Directorates General of Budget, Fiscal Affairs and Taxes.

7. Ministry of Defense. Includes the Defense Staff and the Directorates General for Personnel, Equipment, and Economics and Finance.

8. Ministry of Housing and Physical Planning. Includes three departments: Central Housing, Gevernment Buildings and Construction Industry; the National Land-Use Planning Agency, and Land and Public Registry.

9. Ministry of Transport and Public Works. Includes Directorates General of Transport and of Shipping, Road Safety Department, Road Transport Department, Civil Aviation Authority, Royal Netherlands Meteorological Institute, Public Works Department, IJsselmeer Polders Development Authority, Postal and Telecommunications Services, Dutch Railways and KLM (Royal Dutch Airlines).

10. Ministry of Economic Affairs. Includes Directorates General of Foreign Economic Relations; Industry; Prices, Planning and Regional Policy; Energy Supply; and Commerce, Crafts and Service Trades; Economic Information Service; Economic Surveillance Department.

11. Ministry of Agriculture and Fisheries. Includes Directorates General of Agriculture and of Food; and Land Division, Soil and Forest Management.

12. Ministry of Social Affairs. Comprises Directorates General of Labor of Manpower of General Policy Matters and of Social Services.

13. Ministry of Cultural Affairs, Recreation and Social Work. Comprises Directorates General of Cultural Affairs; Nature Conservation, Recreation and the Media; and Community Development.

14. Ministry of Health and Environmental Protection. Comprises Directorates General of Public Health and Environmental Protection.

Because of the increasing complexity of policy-making and administration, permanent standing committees have been created for oversight of issues that require continuing attention. There are seven such standing committees in the Council of Ministers: (1) Economic Affairs Council, (2) European Affairs

Council, (3) Civil Service Council, (4) Physical Planning and Environmental Protection Council, (5) General Defense Council, (6) Welfare Council and (7) Science Policy Council. All these councils are chaired by the prime minister, but interministerial cooperation is coordinated by a minister.

There are other advisory bodies, composed entirely or predominantly of civil servants.

CABINET LIST

Queen	Beatrix
Prime Minister	Ruud Lubbers
Vice Prime Minister	Rudolf de Korte
Min. of Agriculture	Gerrit Braks
Min. of Defense	Willem van Eekelen
Min. of Development Coopera-tion	Piet Bukman
Min. of Economic Affairs	Rudolf de Korte
Min. of Education	Willem Deetman
Min. of Finance	Herman Ruding
Min. of Foreign Affairs	Hans van den Broek
Min. of Home Affairs	Cees van Dijk
Min. of Housing, Physical Plan-ning and Environment	Ed Nijpels
Min. of Justice	Frederik Korthals Altes
Min. of Netherlands Antilles Af-fairs	Jan de Koning
Min. of Science	Willem Deetman
Min. of Social Affairs	Jan de Koning
Min. of Transportation and Pub-lic Works	Neelie Smit-Kroes
Min. of Welfare, Health and Cul-ture	Leendert Brinkman
Sec. of State for Defense	Jan van Houwelingen
Sec. of State for Economic Affairs (Foreign Trade)	Yvonne van Rooy
Sec. of State for Economic Af-fairs (Retail Trade)	Albert Evenhuis
Sec. of State for Education	Nel J. Ginjaar-Maas
Sec. of State for Finance	Hendrik E. Koning
Sec. of State for Foreign Affairs	Rene van der Linden
Sec. of State for Home Affairs	Dieuwke de Graaf-Nauta
Sec. of State for Housing	Ennaeus Heerma
Sec. of State for Justice	Virginie Korte-van He-mel
Sec. of State for Social Affairs (Social Security)	Lou de Graaf
Sec. of State for Welfare, Health and Culture	Dick van Dees

CABINET LIST *(continued)*

President, The Netherlands
Bank   Willem Duisenberg

FREEDOM & HUMAN RIGHTS

As a parliamentary democracy, all human rights are ensured by law and respected in practice. The Netherlands attaches great importance to human rights in both domestic policies toward foreign workers and in foreign policy in dealing with states that violate human rights. First asylum is provided for refugees from East European countries and permanent resettlement for a limited number of persons ("invited refugees") principally from Vietnam and Iran. Support for human rights also is a key tenet of Dutch foreign policy, and the Netherlands has repeatedly condemned violations of human rights in Eastern Europe and Suriname as well as in South Africa.

The problem of integrating racial and ethnic minorities remains the most difficult issue related to human rights confronting the government. Following incidents of violence against these minorities, particularly Turks and Moroccans, the government introduced strong legislation against racial violence. Further, noncitizens who have resided in the Netherlands for more than five years are granted the right to vote in municipal elections.

Women enjoy full legal and political equality. In economic life, the entry of substantial numbers of women into the labor force occurred somewhat later in the Netherlands than in most Western countries. As a result, their average wage rates still lag behind those of men.

CIVIL SERVICE

Known as quangos, the civil service advisory any boards number an estimated 300, of which 60% are standing and 40% are temporary. The total number of civil servants is about 200,000, of whom 10% are employed within the ministries.

LOCAL GOVERNMENT

The Netherlands is divided into 11 provinces, varying considerably in size and population. The general administration of each province is carried out by the Provincial Council, the Provincial Executive and a queen's commissioner. The Provincial Council is the provincial legislature, with its members elected by universal suffrage on a system of proportional representation for a term of four years. The strength of the Provincial Council is proportional to the population and ranges from 50 to 86. Provincial Executive members are in charge of day-to-day administration. They are elected by the Provincial Council from among its members for a term of four years. Each Provincial Council has at least six members. They receive a salary and are eligible for pension. Their duties are specified in the Provinces Act and include control of the Water Boards. The Provinces Act also provides for the establishment of committees, which may include specialists who are not Provincial Council members. Certain administrative powers are generally delegated to these committees. The head of the provincial administration is the queen's commissioner, who also functions as chairman of the Provincial Council and as head of the Provincial Executive, in which he has a regular vote as well as a casting vote. Under the Provinces Act he reports to both the minister for home affairs and the Provincial Executive. One of the major responsibilities of the queen's commissioner is to draw up a list of candidates from which the queen appoints burgomasters.

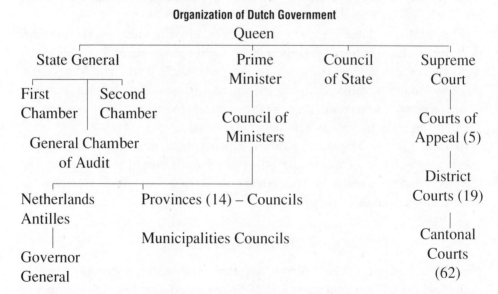

Organization of Dutch Government

The Provincial Councils and Executives may pass independent ordinances but also are required to enforce acts of parliament and central government ordinances. The crown has the power to suspend provincial measures that are contrary to law or public interest or that conflict with central government regulations.

The Constitution provides for the municipality as the only form of administrative unit at the local level. All towns, villages and hamlets are part of one of approximately 820 municipalities in the country. They are governed by the Municipalities Act of 1851, which has been repeatedly amended.

AREA AND POPULATION

| Provinces | Capitals | Area | | Popu-lation |
		Sq. km.	Sq. mi.	1984 estimate
Drenthe	Assen	2,654	1,025	427,300
Friesland	Leeuwarden	3,336	1,288	597,200
Gelderland	Arnhem	5,006	1,933	1,735,800
Groningen	Groningen	2,335	902	561,500
Limburg	Maastricht	2,170	838	1,083,500
Noord-Brabant	's-Hertogen-bosch	4,957	1,914	2,103,000
Noord-Holland	Haarlem	2,668	1,030	2,307,400
Overijssel	Zwolle	3,811	1,471	1,042,100
Utrecht	Utrecht	1,332	514	929,400
Zeeland	Middelburg	1,785	689	355,500
Zuid-Holland	's-Graven-hage	2,907	1,122	3,139,200
Municipalities				
Almere	—	148	57	33,000
Dronten	—	333	129	22,200
Lelystad	—	271	105	55,100
Zeewolde	—	223	86	800
TOTAL		33,936	13,103	14,394,400

Source: Official government figures.

Municipalities are administered by three bodies: the Municipal Council, the Municipal Executive and the burgomaster himself. The Municipal Council is the town legislature, and its strength varies from seven to 45. Council members are elected for a term of one year by the municipal electorate, consisting of Dutch subjects 23 years and older who normally reside in the town. Council meetings are generally open to the public, and they are required to be so when the budget or tax proposals are being discussed.

The Municipal Executive is composed of the aldermen and burgomaster. The Municipal Council elects the aldermen from among its members every four years. The strength of the council may vary from two to six. Although the Municipal Executive is collectively responsible for the administration, in practice each alderman is assigned a particular responsibility, such as education or finance. Aldermen receive a fixed annual salary and are eligible for pension.

The Municipalities Act also empowers the Municipal Council to set up committees endowed with advisory or regulatory powers and to which non-Municipal Council members may be appointed. Many of them are standing committees, but some are ad hoc ones created to deal with or study special needs and issues.

Burgomasters are appointed by the crown for a renewable period of six years. In the case of provincial capitals or municipalities with over 50,000 inhabitants, the appointment is subject to the approval of the Council of Ministers. In the case of smaller towns, with a population of under 5,000, a burgomaster may head two municipalities if they are adjacent. He presides over both the Provincial Council and the Municipal Executive, but in the former he has no vote, while in the latter he has a double vote in case of a tie. He is assisted by the municipal clerk, who countersigns all official documents. As head of the municipal police force, the burgomaster has a particular responsibility in maintaining public order and civil peace.

The relationship between provinces and the municipalities is similar to that between the central government and the provinces, except that municipal authorities are accountable to both the provincial government and the central government. This accountability is defined in law, but in practice the provinces and the state do not readily intervene in municipal activities. Municipal authorities are required to provide provincial executives with information about their decisions. Municipal ordinances must be submitted to provincial executives if they contain penal clauses. Provincial executive approval also is required for the municipal budget and other financial measures. This approval may be refused if the measure is contrary to law or public interest. Municipal authorities must also seek the approval of the crown before introducing, changing or abolishing any municipal taxes. The crown also may suspend or annual a municipal decision by a royal decree stating the reason or reasons for the action.

Over the years both the size of individual municipalities and their number have changed through readjustment of boundaries, amalgamation and creation of new towns. These changes require an act of parliament and are subject to the approval of the States General. The net result of these changes has been a reduction in the number of municipalities, from 1,209 in 1851 to 994 in 1960 and to 820 in the 1980s. New municipalities are created only in cases where land has been reclaimed. One such example is Dronten, which became a municipality in 1972. Because of the shifting populations, there is an increasing tendency to redraw municipal boundaries, and even more to amalgamate neighboring towns. Even where amalgamation has not been affected, municipalities have combined to offer common services in matters such as refuse disposal, health care, fire protection, water purification, caravan sites and energy. This form of cooperation was encouraged by the Joint Provisions Act of 1950. Under this act, preregions have been set up to which participating municipalities may delegate part of their functions. Two further regional bodies, the Rhine Estuary Authority and the Eindhoven Agglomeration, have been set up by separate acts of parliament. The Union of Netherlands Municipalities, to which all the municipalities and the 39 preregions belong, plays an important role in promoting intermunicipal cooperation and in representing municipal interests before the central government.

Water Control Boards are very old Dutch institutions, many predating towns and some going back to the 12th century. They are public bodies incorporated by law and charged with water management within a specified area. They are established by Provincial Councils and not by the state, and for that reason their powers, duties and functions vary from province to province. The size of the boards also varies, and their number has declined through amalgamation, from 2,600 in 1950 to about 600 today.

Most boards are administered by an Executive and a General Council elected by the local landowners. Many contain representatives of industrial polluters, who are required to pay a levy to the board. The Executive generally is elected by the General Council except in coastal areas such as IJsselmeer, where the members are appointed by the crown.

Water Control Boards have traditionally been responsible for protection of the land against water, construction and maintenance of dams, dikes and locks; regulation of water level; drainage; and, in some instances, for roads and waterways. Water quality has recently been added to the boards' functions. Although the crown has supreme authority over national water management, actual supervision of the boards is left to the provincial authorities. Thus all major decisions by the boards require the approval of the Provincial executive. The boards' activities are financed by a water tax and levies imposed under the Pollution of Surface Waters Act.

Provincial finances are derived from three sources: annual grants from the Provinces Fund; grants and allocations for special purposes, such as roads; and provincial taxes. The size of the grant from the Provinces Fund is calculated on the following basis: 40% according to population, 22.5% according to size and 2.5% according to the length of provincial roads. The remaining 35% is divided into 11 equal parts.

About 90% of municipal revenues come from central government sources, including grants from the Municipalities Fund and grants and allocations for special purposes. Grants from the Municipalities Fund are regulated by the 1960 Financial Apportionment Act, which is reviewed annually. In addition to a per capita amount, each municipality receives an amount based on surface area, ratio of built-up to rural areas, the net cost of social services and the costs of municipal schools. Municipalities with special problems, such as a low tax base, being an inner city or rapid population growth are eligible for an increased per capita grant. Municipalities also receive supplementary grants and allocations from the budgets of the various ministries.

FOREIGN POLICY

Officially neutral before World War II, the Netherlands reversed its foreign policy after 1945 to become a founder and active participant in the major West European and Atlantic alliances—NATO, the Benelux Union, the Western European Union and the European Communities. The country also made a smooth transition to the postcolonial era after granting independence to Indonesia (1949) and Suriname (1975).

A major foreign affairs issue with strong domestic repercussions relates to the deployment of nuclear missiles. Pressures from the lower house led the government in 1984 to delay a decision in the hope that a meaningful arms-control agreement could be reached with the Soviet Union. The defection of two Christian Democratic members in 1983 considerably weakened the Ruud Lubbers coalition government.

Another foreign policy concern since 1970 is development cooperation with the Third World. The budget allocation for development assistance grew from $70 million in 1965 to $1.718 billion in 1986, or 0.27% of the GNP, the highest in Europe outside Denmark, Sweden and Norway. One feature of its aid policy is direct aid to the poorest countries and those in acute need. More emphasis also is being placed on improving the quality of aid by linking it to specific programs. In line with its tradition of freedom and tolerance, The Netherlands has adopted a stronger stance than some of its allies against South Africa's policy of apartheid, despite its historic association with the dominant race in that country. Its defense of human rights extends to a strong opposition to the Pinochet regime in Chile and the Bouterse dictatorship in Suriname.

PARLIAMENT

The Dutch parliament, known as the States General, consists of an Upper House (Eerste Kamer) and a Lower House (Tweede Kamer).

Initially, during the period of the Republic of the United Netherlands (1588–1795), the States General constituted a single permanent chamber comprising representatives of the various provinces. A bicameral system was introduced in 1815 under the new Constitution, with members of the Upper House chosen by the king and members of the Lower House chosen by the Provincial Councils. The Constitution of 1848 introduced the system of direct elections to the Lower House, but suffrage was limited to taxpayers. The revised Constitution of 1917 gave full suffrage to men, followed in 1919 by full suffrage for women.

Members of the Upper House, also known as the Senate, are elected indirectly for six-year terms by each Provincial Council. Every three years half the numbers step down. The current strength of the Upper House is 75. The speaker, appointed by the queen from among the membership, holds office for a one-year term only.

The 150 members of the Lower House are elected directly for four-year terms. As in the Upper House, the speaker holds office for a one-year term only. The minimum age for membership in both houses is 25. Unlike Great Britain, ministers and state secretaries are not permitted to sit in either house as a member. If a minister or state secretary is elected to either house, he is required to relinquish either his seat or his office within three months.

Parliamentary sessions begin on the third Tuesday in September with a speech from the throne. The Upper and Lower houses meet in joint session for both the opening and prorogation, when the speaker of the Upper House presides. Parliament may be dissolved at any time within its normal lifetime.

Legislation may be initiated by either the Lower House or by the government, but most often the latter. Government bills are drafted by civil servants and submitted by the concerned minister to the Council of Ministers together with an explanatory memorandum. After approval by the Council of Ministers, it is sent to the Council of State for its recommendations. Along with these recommendations, the bill is then submitted to the queen, who forwards it to the speaker of the Lower House with a royal message. The speaker places the bill before the appropriate standing committee, which produces a provisional report and then a final report for consideration of the full house. The bill is now ready for public debate in the Lower House. During the debate, members consider the bill first in its entirety and then clause by clause. The Lower House has the right to propose amendments, which may or may not be adopted.

Once a bill has been passed by the Lower House, it is sent to the speaker of the Upper House, where it undergoes much the same procedure with the important difference that the Upper House has no right of amendment. For this reason individual clauses are not discussed and only the general bill is debated. After its passage through the Upper House, the bill is sent to the queen for her signature and to the relevant minister for countersignature. Finally, the bill is published in the *Staatsblad*, or Bulletin of Acts, Orders and Decrees.

Members of the Lower House have the right to initiate legislation, although few private bills end up as Acts of Parliament. The procedure for private bills differs from that of a government bill. The former are drafted by a member or group of members with an explanatory memorandum, and the sponsors are responsible for leading the bill through the Lower and Upper houses. Only then is it sent to the Council of Ministers, which refers it to the Council of State as required by law. Thereupon it is sent to the queen for her signature and to the concerned minister for his countersignature and is published in the *Staatsblad.*

Amendments to the Constitution follow a special procedure. After passage of an amendment through the States General and publication in the *Staatsblad*, both the Upper and Lower houses are dissolved and new elections are held to give the electorate an opportunity to voice its opinion on the amendment. The newly elected States General then may accept or reject the proposal in its entirety by at least a two-thirds majority.

UPPER HOUSE Election, June 9 1987	Seats
Christen-Democratisch Appel (CDA)	26
Partij van de Arbeid (PvdA)	26
Volkspartij voor Vrijheid en Democratie (VVD)	12
Democraten 66 (D66)	5
Politieke Partij Radikalen (PPR)	1
Communistische Partij van Nederland (CPN)	1
Pacifistisch Socialistische Partij (PSP)	1
Staatkundig Gereformeerde Partij (SGP)	1
Reformatorische Politieke Federatie (RPF)	1
Gereformeerd Politiek Verbond (GPV)	1
Total	75

Parliamentary control over the Executive is exercised through the right of the Lower House to consider, approve or reject each item of revenue and expenditure in the national budget, the right of interpellation of individual ministers, the right to institute inquiries independently of government, and the right to pass motions to express the house's wishes or opinions or lack of confidence in the Council of Ministers.

All Dutch citizens 18 years or older have the right to vote under the Constitution of 1917 and the Franchise Act of 1919. The Constitution of 1983 enfranchises Dutch citizens living abroad. It also permits aliens to vote and to run as candidates in municipal elections. In local elections voters must normally be resident in the province or municipality in which they vote, and candidates must be resident once elected. Compulsory voting, introduced in 1917, was abolished in 1970. In all elections a system of proportional representation is used, under which the distribution of seats among all parties corresponds as closely as possible with the distribution of votes—in the country as a whole for national elections, in the province for provincial elections and in the municipal-

| **LOWER HOUSE** | | |
| General election, May 21, 1986 | | |
	Votes	Seats
Christen-Democratisch Appel (CDA)	3,172,918	54
Partij van de Arbeid (PvdA)	3,051,678	52
Volkspartij voor Vrijheid en Democratie (VVD)	1,596,991	27
Democraten 66 (D66)	562,466	9
Staatkundig Gereformeerde Partij (SGP)	159,740	3
Politieke Partij Radikalen (PPR)	115,203	2
Pacifistisch Socialistische Partij (PSP)	110,182	1
Gereformeerd Politiek Verbond (GPV)	88,381	1
Reformatorische Politieke Federatie (RPF)	83,582	1
Total	N.A.	150

ity for municipal elections. To make this possible, each of the above units is treated as a single constituency.

For elections to the Lower House, the country is divided into 18 districts. Elections are preceded by the nomination of candidates, and in the case of normal full-term elections, nomination day is the second Tuesday in April, and the election follows 43 days later. If interim elections are held because of the dissolution of the Lower House before its full term, the crown sets the date for the nomination of candidates within 40 days of the dissolution decree. On nomination day, parties hand in their list of candidates at the main polling station in each electoral district. Each list may include the names of not more than 30 candidates signed by at least 25 voters and accompanied by a declaration from the candidates that they accept the nomination. The name of a candidate may not appear more than once on a list in an electoral district. Each party determines the order in which the candidates appear on the lists, which are treated as single units for seat allocation purposes. Different parties may submit unified lists linked together in an order of preference. Each list must be ratified and validated in The Hague by the Electoral Council, which publishes them. When a party not currently represented in the Lower House submits a list of candidates, it must deposit 1,000 guilders with the Treasury for each electoral district. This deposit is returned if the party obtains at least three-quarters of the electoral quota (arrived at by dividing the number of votes cast by the number of seats: the electoral quota is only 0.67% of the national vote).

Each voter receives a card authorizing him or her to vote either in person or by proxy. Although voting machines are used in some municipalities, the voters normally cast their ballots by coloring with a red pencil a white circle in a black square against the name of the candidate of their choice on the ballot paper. A vote for a candidate also counts as a vote for his or her party list. When the polls have closed, counting of the ballots begins in public. First the total number of votes cast at each polling station is ascertained along with the votes for each candidate and each party list. The provisional results are then announced on radio and television. The final results are tallied and published by the Electoral Council after all objections have been considered and disposed of.

Parliamentary seats are allocated among the parties that have reached or exceeded the electoral quota (calculated by dividing the total number of valid votes by 150, the number of seats in the Lower House). The number of votes cast for each list of candidates is divided by the electoral quota, and the quotient determines the party's initial allocation of seats. Individual candidates achieving more than half the quota, including preferential votes (in the proportional representation system), are placed, in order of popularity, at the top of their party list, the others remaining in the order in which they originally appeared on the ballot papers. The seats to which a party is entitled are filled on the basis of this order of preference. The first round of allocations does not normally fill all 150 seats, and those not filled are then apportioned among the parties, using the method of the highest average. The number of votes cast for each party is divided by one more than the number or seats allocated to it. The averages thus arrived are listed in descending order, and the remaining seats are allotted to the parties heading the list until all the seats are filled.

Elections to the provincial and municipal councils follow more or less the same procedure except that for the former the deposit for unrepresented parties is 250 guilders, while no deposit is required for the latter. Nomination day for provincial elections is the second Tuesday in February, that for municipal elections is the third Tuesday in April. In both cases the election follows 43 days later.

The 75 members of the Upper House are elected indirectly (i.e., not by the voters at large) for six-year terms by each Provincial Council. Elections to the Upper House normally are held within three months of the Provincial Council elections. Nomination day is the Tuesday that falls in the period May 10–16, with the election following 34 days later.

In addition, the Netherlands elects 25 members to the European Parliament. They serve five-year terms. They are elected on the basis of universal suffrage with the addition of Dutch subjects in other EC member countries and nationals of EC member states resident in the Netherlands.

POLITICAL PARTIES

The first Dutch political party was the Antirevolutionary Party (ARP), founded in 1878, followed by the Social Democratic Labor Party (SDAP) in 1894, the Roman Catholic National Party (RKSP) in 1896, and the Christian Historical Union (CHU) in 1908. During the interwar years, marked by the rise of communism in the Soviet Union and Nazism and Fascism in other parts of Europe, the political situation in the Netherlands remained generally stable; however, there was increasing fragmentation on both the left and the right. The Liberals were divided into three separate groups; the Calvinist Party made its appearance in 1918, and the Communist Party gained a permanent foothold in the Lower House. After World War II, the process continued. The Labor Party (PvdA) emerged from the Netherlands People's Movement (NVB). Liberals broke away from Labor to form the People's Party for Freedom and Democracy (VVD). The Catholic People's Party (KNP) emerged as successor to the Roman Catholic National Party. On the right, the Catholic National Party and on the left Pacifist Socialist Party were able to achieve representation in the Lower House.

Until 1959 the Netherlands was governed by a series of red/Catholic coalitions, made up of the Catholic People's Party, the Labor Party and the Christian Historical Movement, reinforced in 1952 by the Antirevolutionary Party. The last Socialist government, headed by Willem Drees, fell in 1958, and the denominational parties entered into a coalition with the VVD until 1965 and with Labor from 1965 to 1966. This last coalition, under the veteran Joseph Cals, was brought down by Catholic dissidents, an event that led to a breakaway from the Catholic People's Party.

Three new parties appeared on the scene in the 1960s: the farmers' Party (BP); the Radical Party (PPR), composed of Catholic dissidents; and Democrats (D'66). The rise of the new parties reflected the changes in society, especially the rising influence of the youth counterculture, impatient with the slow processes of political consensus. On the right, denominational parties suffered a severe erosion in their popular base *pari passu*, with a steady dechristianization of public life; on the left, the older stalwarts lost ground to the "new left," encompassing not merely the nonreligious or anticlerical but also the militantly radical.

From 1972 onward, coalition governments have become more unstable than in the past, electoral fortunes of all parties have tended to ebb; new parties that notched spectacular gains in one election lost heavily in the next. Negotiations for the formation of governments began to set records: 163 days in 1972–73 and 208 days in 1977. The alignment of parties has remained unchanged with the notable exception of a merger of three denominational parties. The new parties have not been able thus far to dislodge the older ones or materially affect the composition of political power. Cabinet-forming strength still remains vested in the three established groups: the CDA, the Labor Party and the VVD, of which the CDA always has been the bellwether.

The Catholic Democratic Appeal (Christen Democratisch Appel, CDA) is an amalgamation of three denominational parties that have been powerful in this century: the ARP, the CHU and the Catholic People's Party (KVP). The CDA was formed in 1980 following a decade of electoral reverses for denominational parties in general. Although the constituent parties have harmonized their programs and strategies, the CDA is not yet a unitary party, and each party remains a distinct entity.

Of the three constituent groups, the ARP is the most conservative, having been founded to oppose the ideas of the French Revolution. The CHU, the smallest of the three, is less populist but in some ways more progressive. The KVP is moderate and centrist, ready to join with the conservatives on the right or the Labor Party on the left. The CDA favors economic orthodoxy, application of Christian principles to political life and wholehearted support of NATO and Western alliances.

Democrats 66 (Democraten '66, D'66) was founded in 1966 to work for constitutional reform. After initial successes, the Party lost momentum, but it recovered slightly in 1981 when it became the fourth-largest party. D'66 is predominantly an urban liberal-radical party with natural ties to the Labor Party and (PvdA) advocates the abolition of proportional representation and direct election of the prime minister. A major party plank is environmental protection. While its social policies are progressive, its economic orientation is closer to that of the CDA. Much of the D'66 membership of 10,000 is in Amsterdam, and its supporters tend to be younger and more educated than average.

The Labor Party (Partij ven de Arbeid, PvdA) was founded only in 1946, but it traces its roots back to the Social Democratic Workers Party, founded in 1894 as an orthodox Marxist party. After World War II it shed much of its doctrinaire rigidity and expanded its appeal to include progressive Christians. The PvdA served in various coalitions, always with the KVP, until 1973, when the party's first prime minister, Johannes den Uyl, led a broad center-left coalition that lasted for a full term. Gaining from the weakening of the denominational parties, the PvdA became the largest single party in the Lower House in 1982.

The PvdA is the best organized of Dutch parties, with over 800 local groups. The party's ideology is no longer described as Marxist but as "personal socialism," a vague label that may mean anything between Christian humanism and militant socialism. The "new left" took over the party leadership in the 1960s and steered it again to the left, with opposition to cruise missile deployment as a major policy element. This leftward drift, similar to that which overtook the West German Socialists, led some of the more moderate Old Guard to bolt the party and form Democratic Socialist Party in 1970. Its membership base of 120,000 is drawn from urban white-collar as well as blue-collar workers, middle-class professionals and anticlericals.

The People's Party for Freedom and Democracy (Volkspartij voor Vrijheid en Democratie, VVD) inherited the mantle of the old Liberal Party, which went into eclipse following the extension of the franchise and adoption of proportional representation in 1917. It was reborn in 1948 and gained rapidly in the 1970s to become a natural coalition partner for the governments led by the CDA. The name Liberal is misleading because in many senses the VVD is a conservative party, far to the right of the others on most domestic issues. It is wedded to free enterprise, opposes any government economic intervention and vehemently supports the deployment of cruise missiles. Curiously, it also supports Social Security programs and worker participation in management. The party's membership base is estamated at 100,000, primarily of the upper and middle classes.

There are five principal minor parties. The Farmers Party (Boerenpartij, BP) was founded in 1958 and entered the States General in 1963. Its title is misleading because it is essentially a protest party opposing big business and high taxes. The Communist Party (Communistische Partij, CP) was founded in 1918 as a breakaway from the Social Democratic Workers' Party. Its peak electoral performance was in 1946, when it gained 10.6% of the vote; it has never participated in government. The party broke with Moscow in 1964 and has generally adopted a Eurocommunist line. The Democratic Socialists (Democratische Socialisten, DS) is breakaway from the PvdA and represents the more moderate socialists. The Pacifist Socialist Party (Pacifistisch Socialistische Partij, PSP), founded in 1957, is a splinter party that has never participated in government. It may more properly be described as a pressure group representing the more radical "new left" positions. The Radical Political Party (Politieke Partij Radikalen, PPR) is an offshoot of the former KVP and comprises the more youthful Catholic activists opposed to nuclear energy and armament. In addition, there are three Calvinist parties: the Reformatoric Political Federation, founded in 1975; the Reformed Political Association, founded in 1948; and the State Reform Party, founded in 1918. All are breakaways from the ARP. Two of the smallest parties are the anti-immigrant Center Party and the Evangelical People's Party.

ECONOMY

The Netherlands a developed three-market economy in which the private sector dominant. After a difficult period of adjustment in the 1970s and early 1980s, the Dutch economy has undergone significant shifts in direction. The postwar years just prior to the oil crisis were marked by largely uninterrupted growth. The expansion had been most visible in industry, particularly in chemicals and petroleum refining, and much of the capacity was concentrated in densely populated areas. The discovery of large gas reserves in the North Sea also built national confidence. But as wealth and incomes grew, there was some erosion of the political and social consensus that had undergirded the early stages of expansion. National debates turned on far-reaching issues, such as conservation, quality of life and management of scarce resources. It is significant that the Report of the Club of Rome and Global 2000 received for more public attention in the Netherlands than in the rest of Europe. Well into the latter part of the 1970s, Dutch governments were far more concerned with accommodating social and environmental demands than in pursuing purely economic strategies. The period also witnessed more active government intervention in areas such as labor relations, wage fixing, income support and geographical redistribution of industry.

During the 1970s the Dutch economy both gained and lost from its prime natural resource: gas. Higher energy prices boosted investment programs in other areas of the economy and financed more generous and broader social services. But there were unwanted side effects. The exchange rate appreciated, and although this dampened the inflationary impact of the two oil shocks, competitiveness was reduced in the export-oriented sector. The increased flow if gas revenues favored consumption rather than investment. There was an expansion in services and a contraction in manufacturing—a phenomenon that came to be known as the "Dutch Disease." But the advent of gas was not the only reason for the weakening of the economy. Overoptimistic social and political expectations based on rosy projections of gas revenues led to a chronic budget deficit. Tax pressures rose, and where they fell on business or led to higher wage demands, profits were squeezed. Despite rising unemployment, real wages held up strongly in all sectors and thereby increased the pressure on profits in exposed sectors, where international competition prevented firms from hiking prices in line with costs. Rising prosperity made certain kinds of employment less desirable, creating a permanent underclass of alien workers.

It took the second oil crisis, of 1979, and the subsequent collapse in domestic demand and investment to preduce a shift in the policies and attitudes of the country's economic managers. Dutch government economists embarked on a program of reducing inflation, the size of the public sector and the budget deficit, as well as restoring profitability and increasing employment, all at the same time. More generally, there dawned a better public appreciation of the limits to growth, the need for profits, more reasonable labor demands and the undesirable side effects of unbridled prosperity. The government's task was made easier by the recovery in world trade accompanied by increasing competitiveness in Dutch industry. Rising export demand more than offset the effects of reduced public spending from 1983 to 1985, while age moderation and higher output have raised profits. Since 1984 there has also been a decline in registered unemployment, partly as a result of a change in registration practices. Nonetheless, the level of unemployment remains high, particularly considering the existence of hidden unemployment.

Historically, the Netherlands has been a trading and an agricultural nation, in that order. Industralization had a late start, and it got under way on a full scale only after 1945. The postwar period was characterized by a rapid expansion of the industrial sector with a marked increase in the share of trade in the total output. While all manufacturing subsectors contributed to this growth, chemicals, petroleum refining and food processing dominated. This partly reflected the discovery of gas and the growth of Rotterdam as an entrepôt center for oil, which led to greater downstream facilities. Structural change in manufacturing was greater in the Netherlands than in most of its neighbors during this period. Although agriculture remained relatively more important than the OECD average, the relative sectoral size of manufacturing reached the same level as in other industrialized countries in Western Europe. Industry was highly capital- and energy-intensive, and consequently labor productivity was among the highest in the EEC area.

The structure of trade reflected the fact that the Netherlands was an open economy with the largest share of imports and exports in the GDP in the OECD area. Exports at the beginning of the 1970s were concentrated in food and food products (roughly one-quarter), chemicals (roughly one-eighth), mineral fuels and fabricated materials. Between one-fifth and one-sixth of exports was made up of machinery and transportation equipment. Trade surpluses were found in food products, chemicals, planes and ships; deficits occurred energy, machinery (excluding electrical machinery) and motor transportation. Another characteristic of the Dutch economy was the importance of relatively few large companies, as a result of a number of mergers in the 1960s. In 1970 a total of 30 firms accounted for 53% of industrial employment. Within this group, five resident multinationals employed approximately one-quarter of the industrial work force. These firms dominated the export trade in their sectors—petroleum refining, chemicals and electrical goods. They also undertook 80% of research and development.

While the 1970s was a period of transition, the 1980s was one of consolidation for the Dutch economy. The two oil shocks had a major impact on the economy. Higher energy costs pushed the prices of energy-intensive products, in which the Netherlands had a relative specialization both in industry and in trade. Lower demand led to overcapacity in a number of sectors, such as artificial fibers, chemicals and petroleum refinery products. The export market slowed down more markedly than in other OECD countries. At the same time, the Netherlands was unable to benefit from the increased demand from developing and OPEC countries, which were mostly for heavy industrial and transport goods, in which the Dutch were less specialized. Increased competition from newly industrialized countries in a number of sectors, such as textiles and clothing, and from Japan in electronics and shipping, placed pressure on many enterprises and accelerated their decline in some cases.

However, the rise in gas production during this period compensated for these constraints. The growth of gas exports strengthened the current balance and led to an appreciation of the currency and a further weakening in the competitive position of exposed industries. Between 1970 and 1980 the share of mineral fuels in exports more than doubled. The value of gas output rose from 1.25% of the GDP in 1970 to 7% in the early 1980s. By the end of this period, more than 60% of this was drawn off into the government. Higher gas revenues permitted an expansionary fiscal policy, a substantial part of which was absorbed by increased public-sector wages, and social services. Taxes and Social Security contributions rose sharply, cutting into profits and leading to even higher wage demands. The overall impact of these factors set the stage for a sharp contraction in economic activity during the early 1980s. Contributing to this development was a growing rigidity in the labor market, the practice of wage indexation, and an overall fall in the aggregate profit share of value-added at a factor costing the nongas sector from 16% in 1969–73 to 9% in 1982–83. The squeeze on profits was particularly marked in industry and agriculture, which were unable to pass their wage costs on to prices because of intense international competition. While business investment fell by 5%, private and public consumption increased their share of the GDP by 4%. The share of imports and exports in the GDP also rose sharply. Increased cost pressures accelerated the decline of textiles, clothing, footwear, basic metals and shipbuilding. The share of exports rose, reflecting the higher value of gas exports. The deceleration of domestic demand forced firms supplying investment goods to search for foreign markets. Even among medium-size firms there was an increasing internationalization of production facilities. By 1978 some 1,400 Dutch firms participated in 4,800 foreign enterprises, and 2,600 foreign companies had acquired interests in 2,200

Dutch companies. Of the 100 largest companies, only 20 were exclusively established in the Netherlands.

These changes combined to produce marked shifts in the relative size of the sectors. In the decade preceding 1983, the level and share of output and employment accounted for by the public sector rose, while those of the private sector fell. Within the market sector, the share of manufacturing in total output fell by 8%. Employment fell by 300,000 man-years in manufacturing, 50,000 man-years in agriculture and 165,000 man-years in construction between 1970–71 and 1983–84. As a result of consolidation and rationalization, manufacturing became even more capital-intensive. All these factors contributed to a rise in productivity, although at a slower pace than in the past.

Since 1983–84, the Dutch economy has made an impressive recovery. Competitiveness of industry has steadily improved, along with output and profits. Investment has picked up, and production facilities have been consolidated in many industries. Inflation is low by international standards, wage demands are restrained and industrial relations are stable. Between 1983 and 1986 the GNP grew by 1.8% annually, compared with -0.4% during 1979–82, 2.3% between 1975–78 and 3.5% during 1971–74. Private spending grew by 2.6% in 1986. The fall in employment in the private sector has been halted, although unemployment remained high, at 765,000, in 1986.

PRINCIPAL ECONOMIC INDICATORS

Gross National Product: $135.8 billion (1985)
GNP per capita: $9,290
GNP average annual growth rate: 1.8% (1983–86)
GNP per capita average annual growth rate: 2.0% (1980–85)
Average annual rate of inflation: 3.5% (1980–85)
Consumer Price Index: 1980=100
　　All items: 122.90 (1986)

Average annual growth rate of (1980–85)
　　Public consumption: 0.6%
　　Private consumption: -0.2%
　　Gross domestic investment: 0.9%

PUBLIC FINANCE

The Constitution requires prior approval of both houses of parliament for all government expenditures, based on a fiscal year that follows the calendar year. Expenditure estimates must be detailed in legislation, together with sources of revenue, and separate acts of parliament must be passed for each section of the

GROSS DOMESTIC PRODUCT

GDP nominal (national currency): 394.9 billion
GDP real (national currency): 336.8 billion
GDP per capita ($): 9,620

Average annual growth rate of GDP, 1980–85: 0.7%
Average annual growth rate of GDP per capita, 1965–85: 2.0%

GDP by type of expenditure (%)
  Consumption
    Private: 59
    Government: 16
  Gross domestic investment: 20
  Gross domestic saving: 25
  Foreign trade
    Exports: 58
    Imports: -54

Cost components of GDP (%)
  Net indirect taxes: 9
  Consumption of fixed capital: 10
  Compensation of employees: 55
  Net operating surplus: 25

Sectoral origin of GDP (%)
  Primary
    Agriculture: 4
  Mining: 0
  Secondary
    Manufacturing: 25
    Construction: 7
    Public Utilities: 2
  Tertiary
    Transportation and communications: 7
    Trade: 15
    Finance: ⎱
          ⎰ 29
    Other Services: ⎰
  Government: 15

Average annual sectoral growth rates, 1980–85
  Agriculture: 7.8%
  Industry: 0.4
  Manufacturing: 1.4%
  Services: 0.2%

national budget covering a single government department. Separate budgets are prepared for social insurance funds and public corporations. An important feature of the Dutch budget is that it makes no distinction between current and capital expenditures. The minister of finance places all budget proposals before the Lower House on the third Tuesday in September, soon after the queen opens parliament with her speech from the throne.

BALANCE OF PAYMENTS, 1986 ($ million)	
Current accounts balance:	4,648
Merchandise exports:	73,557
Merchandise imports:	−66,558
Trade balance:	6,999
Other goods, services and income credit:	28,271
Other goods, services and income debit:	−28,988
Other goods, services and income net:	−717
Private unrequited transfers:	−643
Official unrequited transfers:	−991
Capital other than reserves:	−2,483
Net errors and omissions:	−2,550
Counterpart items:	740
Liabilities constituting foreign authorities reserves:	55
Total change in reserves:	−409

FOREIGN AID	1965	1970	1975	1980	1981	1982	1983	1984	1985	1986
Total $ million	70	196	608	1,630	1,510	1,472	1,195	1,268	1,136	1,738
As % of GNP	0.36	0.61	0.75	1.03	1.08	1.07	0.91	1.02	0.91	1.00
To low income countries as % of GNP	0.08	0.24	0.24	0.26	0.30	0.37	0.31	0.26	0.29	0.27

The chief characteristic of the budgetary policy followed by the Dutch government since the early 1960s is that the total budget is drawn up less on the basis of annual tax revenues than on forecasts of medium-term economic trends. Central to the policy is the concept of budget margin—that is, the extra sum available, as compared with the preceding year, for additional expenditure or tax cuts. Each year's margin is determined on the basis of four factors: the structural or trend rate of growth in tax revenues, discounting any cyclical rise and fall; the expected annual growth in nontax revenues; the growth in the acceptable structural budget deficit; and increases in tax rates when expenditures prove inadequate.

The trend rate of growth in tax revenues is a function of the underlying growth rate of national income, discounting cyclical fluctuations. Tax revenues always increase faster than national income, largely because of the progressive nature of the tax system and shifts in the pattern of distribution and disposal of incomes. Nontax revenues include interest payments, profits of public corporations, levies, tariffs, capital repayments and proceeds from broadcast advertis-

BUDGET ESTIMATES (million guilders)		
Revenues	1986	1987
Income tax	38,250	40,730
Corporation tax	13,300	12,400
Import duties	2,100	1,855
Excise duties	8,170	9,035
Turnover tax	30,500	33,400
Motor vehicle tax	2,770	2,910
Tax on legal transactions	1,885	2,405
Other taxes	4,670	5,053
Shares in profits from Nether-lands Bank	1,975	1,600
Interest from loans (Housing Act dwellings)	6,670	5,587
Capital transfers, Government Telecomm. Service	4,345	4,747
Natural gas revenues	16,400	7,850
Others	16,799	16,535
Total	147,834	144,107
Expenditures	1986	1987
Social Security and public health	30,807	29,773
Education and culture	29,852	31,764
Defense	13,739	13,658
Transportation and public works	11,436	10,987
Housing, town and country planning	14,615	14,415
Interest on public debt	21,785	21,918
Agriculture and fishery*	8,006	8,299
Local authorities' shares in taxes	13,063	12,091
European Communities' shares in taxes	4,905	4,869
Public order and security	5,582	5,646
Foreign relations	5,380	5,341
Foreign aid	4,528	4,568
Trade and handicraft	9,272	8,373
Others	1,443	515
Total	174,413	172,217

* The Netherlands' share of the levies of the EEC's Agriculture Equalization Fund is included in the expenditure on agriculture and excluded from the European Communities' shares in taxes. **1988** total expenditures (estimate, million guilders): 168,000.

ing. The size of the acceptable structural budget deficit is determined on the basis of medium-term forecasts of the average excess of savings in the economy.

CENTRAL GOVERNMENT EXPENDITURES, 1986
(% of total expenditures)

Defense: 5.2
Education: 11.1
Health: 10.8
Housing, Social Security, welfare: 39.8
Economic services: 10.7
Other: 22.5
Total expenditures as % of GNP: 56.6
Overall surplus or deficit as % of GNP: -1.7

CENTRAL GOVERNMENT REVENUES, 1986
(% of total current revenues)

Taxes on income, profit and capital gain: 24.3
Social Security contributions: 37.9
Domestic taxes on goods and services: 20.6
Taxes on international trade and transactions: 0.0
Other taxes: 2.3
Current nontax revenue: 14.8
Total current revenue as % of GNP: 51.6
Government consumption as % of GNP: 16.0
Annual growth % of government consumption: 0.8
(1980–86)

The structural budget policy has significant economic and administrative advantages over the use of annually fluctuating growth figures. It promotes balanced economic growth by dampening cyclical fluctuations. In periods of expansion, government expenditures rise less rapidly, while in periods of recession, public expenditures rise to stimulate the economy.

Together with the national budget, the minister of finance places before the Lower House a budget memorandum, including an analysis of the state of the Dutch economy and an outline of the government's socioeconomic goals and strategies. The Central Planning Bureau's macroeconomic forecast, published at the same time as the budget memorandum, covers both domestic and international economic developments. The size of the Dutch budget has increased considerably over the years, from less than 1 billion guilders before World War II to 100 billion guilders in 1979 and 179 billion guilders in 1986. Public spending now accounts for over 60% of national income.

Since 1973 the budget memorandum has included not only the following year's revenues and expenditures but also estimates for four subsequent years, as required by the Government Accounts Act. Although each minister is responsible for his departmental budget, overall responsibility rests with the minister of finance, who must ensure that total expenditures do not exceed acceptable levels. The finance minister receives his fellow ministers' budget proposals not later than May 1 each year. Differences or objections are discussed and resolved either at general cabinet meeting or in discussions between the minister of finance and the minister concerned. The budget is presented to the Lower House in September and later to the Upper House; only the former has the right to amend the proposals. Parliament begins discussing the various sections of the budget (in the form of separate bills) in October. In practice, the discussions take on the character of a policy debate on all aspects of a ministry's work. As a rule, the budget does not complete its passage through Parliament until several months after the start of the fiscal year. However, ministers are empowered to undertake necessary expenditures within certain limits pending enactment of the budgetary legislation. The actual expenditure of moneys is subject to the supervision of the independent General Chamber of Audit.

The budget memorandum groups the figures for government expenditures under departmental headings (or functions), an arrangement that facilitates international comparisons. One that is peculiar to the Netherlands is water control. Among the state's more recent responsibilities are environmental protection and overseas development. In the latter field, Dutch spending measured as a percentage of national income is among the highest in the world, amounting to over 1% of the GNP. Dutch municipalities receive about 90% of their income from the Municipalities Fund. Other special-purpose payments, most of which relate to education, are included in the national budget. Municipalities facing special problems receive supplementary grants. A certain percentage of the national taxes is paid into the Municipalities Fund but is not shown as such in the national budget.

Of government revenues, 70% is derived from taxes; 20% from nontax revenues; and 10% from loans, Treasury bills and the like. Nontax revenues include interest payments on loans for public-sector housing, revenues from public corporations, fines, pilotage fees, proceeds of the state lottery, revenues from state-owned land, receipts from the post office, broadcasting licence fees, advertising revenue from radio and television, and natural-gas revenues.

The central government regularly borrows on the capital market. Issue, repayment and registration of government debt instruments are organized through the Ministry of Finance agency and the National Debt Office. Government debt instruments are traded on both public and private capital markets. In addition, the Treasury bills are sold on the money market. Outstanding government debt is of the order of 80 billion guilders, and amortization and interest payments amount to 3 billion and 6 billion guilders annually, respectively. The national debt represents some 30% of the national income, about the same percentage as in 1974.

Tax laws may be divided into two groups: general and specific. The general covers all forms of taxation and deals with such items as procedures for making returns, lodging appeals, sanctions against evaders, and inspection of documents. The two general tax laws are the Customs and Excise Act and the State Taxes Act. Two others acts are the Direct Taxes (Collection) Act and the Administrative Jurisdiction (Taxation) Act. The general legislation also applies for the most part to taxes levied by authorities other than the Central Government. The taxes covered by specific legislation include taxes on expenditures (such as VAT and car tax) and taxes on income, profits and capital (such as income tax, corporation tax, wealth tax and inheritance tax). The 1964 Income Tax Act defines three types of taxable income: business profits, earned and investment income, and capital gains. The tax rates are progressive, with a built-in system of personal allowances.

The 1986 budget followed the policy set in 1982 to rein back the size of the public sector and reduce the budget deficit. At the central and local government levels, the deficit in the Social Security accounts led to a net deterioration in the government accounts. This change reflected a shift in the government-financed part of unemployment support to the Social Security system. Although partly balanced by moving child allowances in the other direction, increased spending and lower rates of contribution resulted in the Social Security system showing a deficit of 3.3 billion guilders. Government tax revenues rose by roughly 3%, slightly faster than the growth in national income. Budgetary policy for the remaining years in the 1980s will be aimed at streamlining the public sector, reducing the size of borrowing requirements and keeping the "collective burden" of taxes and Social Security contributions low.

CURRENCY & BANKING

The Dutch unit of currency is the guilder, often abbreviated as "f" or "fl," which is an abbreviation of florin (from the Italian city of Florence, where they were first struck in 1252). The guilder is divided into 100 cents. The 5-cent piece is known as a *stuiver*, the 10-cent piece as a *dubbeltje*, the 25-cent piece as a *kwartje* and the 2½-guilder piece as a *rijksdaalder*. The gold ducat also is a Dutch coin, but it bears no indication of value and is not legal tender. Bank notes are issued in denominations of 5, 10, 25, 100 and 1,000 guilders.

In the early 1980s the total value of notes and coins circulating in the Netherlands was 21 billion guilders (of which 1 billion was in coins), while bank deposits exceeded 41 billion guilders. The total money supply was thus 61 billion guilders, or approximately 25% of national income.

In recent years the exchange rate of guilders per dollar has been as follows: 2.624 (1982); 3.064 (1983); 3.549 (1984); 2.772 (1985); 2.192 (1986); 1.956 (1987).

Two peculiarities of the Dutch money circulation are the dominance of the giro system and the relative unpopularity of checks and credit cards. Two giro networks exist side by side in the Netherlands: that operated by the post office, known as the Post Check and Giro Service (PCGD), and the bank giro system. About one-third of all giro accounts are held by the PCGD, one-fifth by cooperative banks and the remainder by commercial banks.

The central bank is the Nederlandsche Bank, which originally was a private institution with the sole right of issuing bank notes. All shares in the bank were acquired by the state in 1948. The relationship between the Nederlandsche Bank and the government is regulated by the Banking Act primarily, and also by other legislation, such as the Credit Control Act and the Exchange Rate of the Guilder Act. The activities and responsibilities of the central bank include regulation and stabilization of the value of the currency, issuance of bank notes, facilitation of bank transfers and conduct of monetary transactions with other countries. It also controls monetary policy directly by placing a ceiling on credit, and it is lender of last resort.

The banking system comprises commercial banks, cooperative banks, savings banks, investment banks and mortgage banks. The post office operates two banking systems: the PCGD and the National Savings Bank.

Historically, Dutch banks were merchant banks emphasizing short-term credit. However, as a result of the mergers of the 1960s, distinctions among the various branches have become blurred, and commercial banks now offer a wide range of banking services both in the domestic market and in international capital markets. The cooperative banks, which originally specialized in agricultural lending, have taken on more of the characteristics of commercial banks. Savings banks, too, have greatly expanded their range of services without, however, entering the industrial or commercial field.

One of the major developments in banking in the 1960s was the growing number of mergers and takeovers. They have reduced the number of independent and commercial banks from 114 to 18, six of which now account for almost 90% of all deposits. The largest commercial bank is the Algemene Bank Nederland (ABN), followed by the AMRO (Amsterdam-Rotterdam) Bank and the RABO Bank. All three banks are in the top 30 among world banks. The Dutch Savings Bank Association has some 80 members, with total deposits of 20 billion guilders.

Under the Credit Control Act, the central bank regulates the credit system. The central bank is particularly concerned with the solvency and liquidity positions of the banks it supervises. The task of regulating the cooperative and savings banks is partly delegated to the RABO Bank and the Union of Savings Banks, respectively. Deposits of small depositors are guaranteed up to 25,000 guilders.

Investment institutions also are governed by legislation. All their dealings must be in share certificates included in the Register of Shareholdings and Certificates, and the institutions themselves must meet certain requirements and obligations regarding their organizational and financial structure. Insurance companies also are subject to strict regulations, which distinguish between life and nonlife business. The two classes of business cannot be carried on by the same organization. Insurance companies are required to publish all important financial data. The insurance market is an open one, in which nearly one-third is foreign.

Unlike in most other countries, the Dutch money market is restricted to banks that function as both buyers and sellers. The capital market is dominated by a network of private financial institutions. The public capital market is the Amsterdam Stock Exchange, on which new bonds and shares are issued and existing securities traded. It is run by a private body, the Association for Security Transactions, in which the banks are prominent. Active stocks are quoted at all times in guilders, while in the case of other stocks there is a pause of half an hour in the middle of the day's trading, during which brokers may submit orders for the second half of the day, taking account of the prices ruling in the first half. Since 1978 Amsterdam has been the home of the European Options Exchange, where dealings take place in call and put options on various European and U.S. securities. The foreign exchange trade takes place in Amsterdam and Rotterdam bourses, where representatives of domestic bankers and brokers meet every afternoon.

Netherlands is a member of the European Monetary System (EMS). EMS currencies float within narrow limits against others in the system. Each member country sets a target rate for its currency, expressed in terms of the European Currency Unit (ECU), and these rates are used as a basis for central rates between each of the currencies and all the others. Fluctuations are limited to plus or minus 2⅜% of the central rates. When a currency reaches the upper or lower limits (or under certain other circumstances), the central banks intervene in each other's currencies, selling the strongest and buying the weakest.

```
┌─────────────────────────────────────────────────────┐
│              FINANCIAL INDICATORS, 1986               │
│                                                       │
│  International reserves minus gold: $15 billion        │
│     SDRs: 830                                          │
│     Reserve position in IMF: 886                       │
│     Foreign exchange: 13.285 billion                   │
│  Gold (million fine troy oz.): 43.94 million           │
│  Ratio of external debt to total reserves: N.A.        │
│                                                       │
│  Central bank                                          │
│  Assets:                                               │
│     Foreign assets: 57.75 billion guilders             │
│     Claims on government: 3.21 billion guilders        │
│     Claims on bank: 5.95 billion guilders              │
│     Claims on private sector: N.A.                     │
│                                                       │
│  Liabilities                                           │
│     Reserve money: 42.7%                               │
│     Government deposits: 4.7%                           │
│     Foreign liabilities: N.A.                           │
│     Capital accounts: N.A.                              │
│                                                       │
│  Money supply                                          │
│  Stock in billion national currency: 88.8              │
│  M¹ per capita: 6,130 guilders                          │
│  U.S., liabilities to: $10.819 billion                  │
│  U.S., claims on: $3.716 billion                        │
│                                                       │
│  Private banks                                         │
│  Assets                                                │
│     Loans to government: 12.1%                          │
│     Loans to private sector: 47.4%                     │
│     Reserves: 0.4%                                      │
│     Foreign assets: 40.1%                              │
│  Liabilities: deposits: 498 billion guilders           │
│     of which                                           │
│     Demand deposits: 12.0%                             │
│     Savings deposits: 36.3%                            │
│     Government deposits: 0%                            │
│     Foreign liabilities: 36.5%                         │
└─────────────────────────────────────────────────────┘
```

FINANCIAL INDICATORS, 1986

International reserves minus gold: $15 billion
   SDRs: 830
   Reserve position in IMF: 886
   Foreign exchange: 13.285 billion
Gold (million fine troy oz.): 43.94 million
Ratio of external debt to total reserves: N.A.

Central bank
Assets:
   Foreign assets: 57.75 billion guilders
   Claims on government: 3.21 billion guilders
   Claims on bank: 5.95 billion guilders
   Claims on private sector: N.A.

Liabilities
   Reserve money: 42.7%
   Government deposits: 4.7%
   Foreign liabilities: N.A.
   Capital accounts: N.A.

Money supply
Stock in billion national currency: 88.8
M^1 per capita: 6,130 guilders
U.S., liabilities to: $10.819 billion
U.S., claims on: $3.716 billion

Private banks
Assets
   Loans to government: 12.1%
   Loans to private sector: 47.4%
   Reserves: 0.4%
   Foreign assets: 40.1%
Liabilities: deposits: 498 billion guilders
   of which
   Demand deposits: 12.0%
   Savings deposits: 36.3%
   Government deposits: 0%
   Foreign liabilities: 36.5%

AGRICULTURE

A mild climate, relatively fertile soil and generally adequate supply of water form the bases for a great variety of agricultural products and a strong farming sector in the Netherlands. The soil is extremely varied, ranging from light sand to heavy marine clay, the former in the higher regions in the East, Center and South and the latter mainly in the North and the West. The alluvial clay deposits on the banks of the major rivers are very suitable for arable farming and for growing fruit. The peat soil found in various places in the West and North is suitable for grassland and for growing vegetables. The coastal areas favor horticulture. In addition to these advantages, Dutch agriculture is sustained by a highly skilled and well-trained farm population, an efficient marketing system and strong state support.

GROWTH PROFILE
(annual growth rates, %)

Population, 1985–2000: 0.3
Crude birth rate, 1985–90: 11.6
Crude death rate, 1985–90: 8.9
Urban population, 1980–85: 0.9
Labor force, 1985–2000: 0.5
GNP, 1975–85: N.A.
GNP per capita, 1965–85: 2.0
GDP, 1980–85: 0.7
Inflation, 1980–85: 3.5
Agriculture, 1980–85: 7.8
Industry, 1980–85: 0.4
Manufacturing, 1980–85: 1.4
Services, 1980–85: 0.2
Money holdings, 1980–85: 6.0
Manufacturing earnings per employee, 1980–85: 2.1
Energy production, 1980–85: -0.3
Energy consumption, 1980–85: -0.1
Exports, 1980–85: 3.4
Imports, 1980–85: 2.6
General government consumption, 1980–85: 0.6
Private consumption, 1980–85: -0.2
Gross domestic investment, 1980–85: 0.9

RANKINGS

1. Total land area: 121
2. Current population: 51
3. Annual population growth rate: 153
4. Birth rate: 182
5. Death rate: 132
6. Population density: 17
7. Urbanization: 23
8. Annual urban population growth rate: 117
9. Senior citizens in population: 18
10. Homogeneity Index: 35
11. Most powerful nations: 25
12. Age of nations: 22
13. Civil Disorder Index: 94
14. Index of democratization: 2
15. Foreign aid per capita: N.A.
16. Most powerful nations: 29
17. Men and women under arms: 41
18. Defense expenditures: 11

RANKINGS *(continued)*

19. Defense expenditures as % of GNP: 57
20. Gross National Product: 12
21. GNP per capita: 13
22. Per capita GNP annual growth rate: 80
23. Average annual rate of inflation: 86
24. Strongest currency: 1
25. External public debt: N.A.
26. External public debt as % of GNP: N.A.
27. Balance of trade: 112
28. Exports per capita: 9
29. Imports per capita: 6
30. Terms of trade: 45
31. Share of food in imports: 39
32. Agriculture's share of GDP: 94
33. Agricultural Production Index: 16
34. Food Production Index: 9
35. Tractors: 23
36. Fertilizer consumption: 28
37. Production of roundwood: 106
38. Fish catch: 34
39. Industry's share of GDP: 37
40. Energy Production: 21
41. Energy consumption per capita: 17
42. Coal production: N.A.
43. Crude petroleum production: 49
44. Electrical energy consumption: 31
45. Economically active population: 85
46. Women in the labor force: 92
47. % of labor force in agriculture: 137
48. % of labor force in industry: 8
49. % of labor force in services: 29
50. Railway trackage: 12
51. Length of roads: 7
52. Passenger cars: 13
53. Inland waterways: 1
54. Cargo handled by ports: 4
55. Civil aviation: passengers: 11
56. Tourist arrivals: 14
57. Tourist receipts: 13
58. Male life expectancy: 5
59. Female life expectancy: 3
60. Physical Quality of Life Index: 3
61. Physicians: 21
62. Male literacy rate: 4
63. Female literacy rate: 4
64. Study abroad: 44
65. Educational expenditures as % of GNP: 15
66. Radio receivers: 69
67. Television sets: 23
68. Daily newspaper circulation: 18

RANKINGS *(continued)*

69. Annual movie attendance: 70
70. Number of museums and attendance: 14

Source: *New Book of World Rankings*

In 1986 there were 134,000 farms with an average size of 0.15 sq. km. (15 ha.). The total area of land under cultivation is 21,030 sq. km. (2.103 million ha.), constituting 48.2% of the land area. Of the total cropland, 11.6% are under permanent crops, 87.7% under temporary crops and 0.7% fallow. Of the total cultivable land, 56.7% are meadows and pastures. Dutch farms tend to be larger than the European norm. Only 11.2% are under 0.01 sq. km. (1 ha.), while 21.6% are between 0.01 and 0.05 sq. km. (1 and 5 ha.), 16.6% between 0.05 and 0.1 sq. km. (5 and 10 ha.), 23.1% between 0.1 and 0.2 sq. km. (10 and 20 ha.), 23.9% between 0.2 and 0.5 sq. km. (20 and 50 ha.), and 3.6% over 0.5 sq. km. (50 ha.). Family-owned and operated farms make up 47%, rented farms 12.3% and communal and other farms 40.1%.

Only 8% of the male working population is directly employed in agriculture (compared with 17% in 1950). However, farm productivity has been steadily rising since the end of World War II, helped partly by the general economic growth and partly by Dutch membership in the EEC. Nevertheless, exogenous problems, such as high interest rates and rising energy costs, have tended to depress the state of Dutch agriculture, as in all other industrialized countries.

The total area available for agriculture has declined, from 23,350 sq. km. (2.335 million ha.) in 1950 to 20,200 sq. km. (2.020 million ha.) in the mid-1980s. Particularly since the early 1960s, more and more land has been taken over for nonagricultural purposes. By 1990, total agricultural land area is expected to decline still further, to 18,860 sq. km. (1.886 million ha.). Arable farming declined from 40 to 35% between 1950 and 1980, while grassland farming grew from 56 to 59% and horticulture from 4 to 6% during the same period. This is due mainly to a decline in mixed farms and increasing specialization.

Another major problem is the size of the farm. Many farms are still smaller than 0.1 sq. km. (10 ha.) and therefore uneconomical to operate. Since 1960, economic pressures have forced more than half the number of farms under 0.1 sq. km. (10 ha.) to close. On the other hand, there is a trend toward farm consolidation, actively encouraged by the government. However, this trend is slowing because the supply of freehold farmland is diminishing, partly because of reduced job opportunities in the nonfarm sectors and the increased demand on farmland for nonagricultural purposes.

Since the supply of land is limited, land prices have been skyrocketing, although they are subject to the 1981 Agricultural Land (Exchange) Act. High

Farm Size, 1980	
0.01–0.05 sq. km. (1–5 ha.)	30,955
0.05–0.1 sq. km. (5–10 ha.)	26,101
0.1–0.2 sq. km. (10–20 ha.)	37,259
0.2–0.3 sq. km. (20–30 ha.)	18,783
0.3–0.5 sq. km. (30–50 ha.)	12,015
0.5–1 sq. km. (50–100 ha.)	3,469
Over 1 sq. km. (100 ha.)	378

land prices also have led to increasing use of leasing as a means of financing farmland. In 1980, a total of 41% of agricultural land was leased.

The decline in agricultural population has been accompanied by a significant gain in productivity. Between 1958 and 1975, productivity rose by 7.5% in agriculture compared with 5.5% in industry, and agricultural productivity continued to outpace industrial productivity by 4 to 1.5% even in the mid-1980s. Mechanization has accounted for the sustained growth in per-worker yields. In 1950 there were 24,500 tractors and 210,000 farm horses, while 30 years later there were 173,000 tractors but only 12,000 farm horses. During the same period, the number of combine harvesters increased from 3,000 to 5,700.

Because mechanization calls for high investment, agricultural credit plays an important role in financing expansion. In most cases farmers have recourse to the cooperative agricultural credit bank Rabobank, which has more than 3,100 branches throughout the country. Loans may be secured either through mortgage or through a guarantee from the Agricultural Guarantee Fund.

Not only has the area under crops declined by over 2,000 sq. km. (200,000 ha.) between 1950 and 1980, but also changes have taken place in the size of the area devoted to different crops. The areas under sugar beet, and to a lesser extent wheat and potatoes, have increased, and there has been a striking expansion in the area under fodder maize. At the same time, the areas under rye, barley and oats have declined. These changes are related partly to changes in commodity prices and partly to EEC policies. Particularly in the case of cereals, the rise in aggregate production reflects the introduction of more productive and disease-resistant varieties.

Two important crops receive special Common Market protection. The first are cereals, which enjoy a threshold price and an intervention price. The second is sugar, which is protected by an intervention price. However, sales of sugar within the Common Market are subject to a fixed quota, and the remainder is sold without support on the world markets.

Livestock farming provides more than 66% of the gross value of agricultural production. Milk production more than doubled between 1950 and 1980 primarily because of a rise in milk yield per cow, from 3,820 kg. (8,422 lb.) per

Product (1,000 metric tons)	1950	1960	1970	1980
Wheat	294	590	643	882
Barley	231	291	334	258
Rye	422	460	172	39
Oats	382	387	201	94
Potatoes	4,408	4,173	5,648	6,267
Sugar beet	2,904	4,676	4,739	5,931
Fodder maize	—	—	—	5,931

year in 1950 to 5,035 kg. (11,100 lb.) in 1980. Along with the size of the dairy cattle, the area of grassland has also grown over the past 25 years, to 12,400 sq. km. (1.24 million ha.). In 1950 there was an average of 115 dairy cows per 1 sq. km. (100 ha.); by 1980 there were almost 200. Over 1 million head of adult cattle are slaughtered every year, 80% of them female, along with 1 million calves. Pig meat production has also increased during the past few years as a result of specialization, the introduction of breeds with a high grain/meat conversion ratio, and intensification of production throught larger units per farm. The production of broilers and eggs has been restricted as a result of excess production in other EC countries.

Between 1950 and 1980 the contribution of horticulture to the gross value of Dutch agricultural production rose from 14 to 23%. Although the total area under horticulture has not increased appreciably, many small market gardens have disappeared, resulting in an increase in the cultivated area per holding. Cultivation under glass has more than doubled, to 87.6 sq. km. (8,760 ha.). Cultivation patterns are changing. Certain crops are no longer grown in certain areas—for example, strawberries to the north of the North Sea Canal. Bulb growing, traditionally carried on in the neighborhood of Lisse and Hillegom, is now also found in North Holland and West Friesland. The range of products has changed, too. Fruit growing has declined in importance. Other sectors (vegetables, flowers and plants, and trees and shrubs), on the other hand, have shown considerable growth. Auctions play an important part in sales and the price structure. There are about 55 auctions for market garden produce and 12 for flowers, the former regulated by the Central Horticultural Auction Markets Bureau and the latter by the Netherlands Flower Auction Association.

The Netherlands is one of the least wooded countries in Europe. Woodland covers some 3,000 sq. km. (300,000 ha.), or 8.5% of the total land area. The official afforestation plan will bring another 300 sq. km. (30,000 ha.) under forest by 1990, one-third of it in the Randstad and one-third in the IJsselmeerpolder of southern Flavoland. Dutch forests are for the most part young and consist mainly of a limited number of varieties. About 25% of woodlands are state-owned, 50% are privately owned, 16% are owned by municipalities and provinces, and the remainder belong to nature conservancy organizations. Management of state-owned forests is the responsibility of the State Forest Service.

The Netherlands is a net exporter of food products, which account for 22% of exports and 15% of imports. The principal imports are oil seeds, crude oil and fats, cereals and animal feed, while the principal exports are livestock products and horticultural products. The food industry processes about 60% of the products of Dutch agriculture and horticulture. Per capita food consumption shows marked differences and growth rates for the various products. In general, consumption of bread, potatoes and milk and milk products has gone down during the past 20 years, while that of cheese, meat, fresh fruit and vegetables has gone up.

By far the largest proportion of Dutch national territory—approximately 78%—is used for agriculture and forestry. Thus agricultural modernization is a key element in land management policies. The Agricultural Land Management Office concludes agreements with local farmers for implementation of sound land management programs. It also directs land consolidation programs combining scattered plots of land into larger parcels, resiting and renovating obsolete rural structures, safeguarding existing vegetation and planting new vegetation. Since land consolidation began in 1924, projects covering 8,300 sq. km. (830,000 ha.) have been completed.

Another instrument of agricultural policy is the Agricultural Development and Rationalization Fund. Among its programs is the interest subsidy scheme under which farmers and market gardeners may receive an interest subsidy on loans to finance an approved development plan. It also administers a subsidy scheme for investment in energy-saving facilities, a subsidy scheme for a "manure bank," and the Land Bank. Rationalization programs are regulated by the Liquidation Compensation Decree, which compensates farmers and market gardeners who wish to liquidate their holdings. The fund also provides financial assistance to elderly workers on farms.

Elementary agricultural education consists of four-year full-time courses in 133 schools. Intermediate secondary education is provided in 50 secondary schools, which offer two- and three-year courses. Advanced secondary agricultural education is provided in 11 colleges, which offer four-year courses, including six months of practical work. Agricultural training at the university level is provided at the Agricultural University at Wageningen, which also conducts the International Agricultural Center. Basic and applied agricultural research is carried out in some 30 institutions run by the Ministry of Agriculture and Fisheries as well as in the Agricultural University in Wageningen and at institutions affiliated with the Organization for Applied Scientific Research in the Netherlands. Research programs are coordinated and supervised by the National Agricultural Research Council.

Extension services and guidance to farmers are provided by 38 regional extension offices, each with a staff of 25 to 30 specialists, or one for about 300 undertakings. The regional extension offices are controlled by the Provincial Directorates for Agricultural Development. There also is a national extension service. Employers' and workers' organizations also dispense advice and counsel to farmers.

Agricultural and horticultural products must satisfy standards of health and quality specified in the Agricultural Quality Control Act. Use of pesticides and chemical additives are governed by the Pesticides and Allied Substances Act, which conforms to EEC directives. The Netherlands also is bound by the EEC's Common Agricultural Policy (CAP), which regulates subsidies, production quotas, prices, exports, imports, modernization, consolidation and related matters. More than 75% of agricultural exports are shipped to EEC countries (34% to West Germany alone).

The Netherlands is a major contributor to agricultural development cooperation with the Third World. Within the Ministry of Agriculture and Fisheries, the Directorate for Agricultural Aid to Developing Countries coordinates programs in this area. The Netherlands provides substantial food aid to developing countries through the EEC's International Food Aid Convention and the World Food Program as well as directly and through private Dutch charitable organizations.

The Dutch fishing industry is more than 2,000 years old, going back to the beginnings of the Christian era. They were the first to exploit the rich herring fishing grounds off the northeastern coast of Great Britain long before the British did themselves. The Dutch also claim to have invented the modern techniques of herring fishing. However, since the end of World War II, the North Sea herring catch has been so severely limited that fishermen have turned to other fish—cod; coalfish; and, above all, mackerel. Two recent developments also contributed to this shift. The first is that the Netherlands accepts the maximum quotas for each species and area fixed by the International Council for the Exploration of the Sea. The Netherlands also follows the EEC conventions on fishing limits and stocks. In the light of these constraints, the Dutch government set up the Development and Rationalization Fund for the Fishing Industry to restructure the industry. The government has encouraged diversification of the catch, as a result of which a shrimp fleet has been built up. Shrimp fishing takes place over a wide area stretching along the Belgian coast, the eastern Scheldt, and the Wadden Zee and as far as the German island of Sylt. Another new effort is mussel and oyster cultivation, concentrated in the eastern Scheldt near the fishing center of Yerseke in Zeeland, where the water is particularly pure. The main fishing ports where fish auctions are held are Breskens, Den Helder, Den Oever, Harlingen, Lauwersoog, Stellendam, Urk, Vlissingen and IJmuiden. Because of biological limitations, fishing is not considered to be a growth industry.

Freshwater fishing is done in inland waterways and Lake IJssel by both professional fishermen and amateur anglers. The main types of freshwater fish are eel, pike and pike perch, the last two found especially in Lake IJssel. The development of feshwater fishing is inhibited by pollution of surface waters.

In 1980 there were 269 motor trawlers and luggers and 363 motor cutters. Of landed fish, 31% were sole, 11.5% mackerel, 11.5% plaice and 12.7% cod. Herring made up only 1% compared with 41% in 1959.

AGRICULTURAL INDICATORS, 1986

Agriculture's share of GDP: 4.1
Average annual growth rate: 4.5% (1980–85)
Value added in agriculture: $7.130 billion
Cereal imports (000 tons): 4,435
Index of Agricultural Production (1974–76=100): 129 (1983)
Index of Food Production (1979–81=100): 111 (1983–85)
Index of Food Production per capita (1979–81=100): 109 (1984–86)
Number of tractors: 188,000
Number of harvester-threshers: 5,700
Total fertilizer consumption: 673,400 tons
Fertilizer consumption per 0.01 sq. km. (1 ha.) (100 oz.): 7,812
Number of farms: 134,000
Average size of holding (ha.): 15
Size class %
   Below 1 ha.: 11.2
   1–5 ha.: 21.6
   5–10 ha.: 16.6
   10–20 ha.: 23.1
   20–50 ha.: 23.9
   50–over 200 ha.: 3.6

Tenure %
   Owner-operated: 47
   Rented: 12.9
   Other: 40.1

Activity %
   Mainly crops: 31.4
   Mainly livestock: 55.6
   Mixed: 13

AGRICULTURAL INDICATORS, 1986 *(continued)*

% of farms using irrigation: 59
Farms as % of total land area: 48.2

Land use %
   Permanent crops: 11.6
   Temporary crops: 87.7
   Fallow: 0.7
   Meadows and Pastures: 56.7
   Woodland: N.A.
   Other: N.A.

Yields (kg./ha.)
Grains: 7,497
Roots and tubers: 41,207
Pulses: 5,249
Milk kg./animal: 5,592

Livestock
Cattle: 5,076,000
Horses: 58,000
Sheep: 800,000
Pigs: 12,908,000

Forestry
Production of roundwood: 990,000 cu. m. (756.881 cu. yd.)
   of which industrial roundwood %: 90.3
Value of exports ($000): $894,194

Fishing
Total catch (000 tons): 462
   of which marine %: 99.2
Value of exports ($000): 500,500

MANUFACTURING

The Netherlands is relatively young among industrialized countries. It was only after World War II that the foundations of its industrial strength were laid. Some factors that favored large-scale industrial development were the high rate of population growth, the decline of agriculture, the decline in traditional exports, wage restraint policies and liberalization of international trade. Government policies also created the necessary conditions for rapid industrialization. These included support of extensive R&D programs, an open-door policy toward foreign business, provision of fiscal incentives for investment under the Investment Account Act, promotion of measures to raise productivity and encouragement of labor market flexibility. Dutch commitment to R&D was particularly significant and provided the basis for an alliance between industry and technology. Besides the Central Organization for Applied Scientific Research

(TNO), a number of other organizations were involved in this effort, including the Government Industrial Advisory Service, the Netherlands Energy Development Corporation, the Netherlands Aerospace Development Agency and the Netherlands Maritime Institute. The annual growth of manufacturing production in recent years has been 3 to 4%. Manufacturing contributes 38% of the national income, and manufactured products account for 70% of annual exports. The bellwethers of the manufacturing sector are metallurgy, chemicals and electronics. At least four of the world's largest multinationals are headquartered in the Netherlands: Royal Dutch Shell, Unilever, Philips and Akzo.

The western Netherlands, with its great ports of Rotterdam and Amsterdam, has long been the hub of Dutch industry. Many basic and heavy industries are in this region. Metal, electronic, textile and chemical industries are in the East and South. Until recently the northern part was comparatively underdeveloped, but the discovery of natural gas has changed the situation. Government policy is to disperse industry to achieve a more balanced spread of employment throughout the country. Strong incentives are offered for industries established in the North, including grants of up to 25% of investment costs.

The major industrial subsectors are iron and steel; nonferrous metals; the electrotechnical industry; aerospace, transportation and engineering; food, drinks and tobacco; chemicals; clothing and textiles; paper and cardboard; printing; and leather goods. The largest steelmaker is Estel, a West German-Dutch corporation formerly known as Royal Netherlands Blast Furnaces and Steel (or Hoogovens). The nonferrous sector includes Aluminium Delfzigl in Groningen and Pechiney Nederland in Vlissengen (Zeeland), and the zinc smelters of Billton Company and Budel. The electrotechnical industry is led by Philips, the aerospace industry by Fokker, the food and drinks industry by Unilever and the shipbuilding industry by Rijn-Schelde-Verolme. The weakest sectors are shoes, clothing and textiles, as well as shipbuilding, brickmaking and coal mining.

The Netherlands has 219 firms that have over 500 employees. The number of large firms has steadily declined since 1974 as well as the number of their employees. Firms with less than 50 employees have generally done much better than the larger ones, and enterprises with 10 to 20 employees have shown consistent growth. Nevertheless, very large firms continue to dominate, accounting for 43% of the employment, while small firms account for only 6%. Certain industries are characterized by large establishments—for example, chemicals, metallurgy, electronics and shipbuilding. On the other hand, most establishments in the clothing and leather industries tend to be small. Small firms also are more numerous in printing, metals, food and furniture.

Eindhoven, Rotterdam and Amsterdam form the leading trio of the Dutch industrial centers. Nearly 100,000 of the country's 800,000 industrial jobs in 1984 were in the zone between the Maasvlakte and Gorinchem, while there were another 90,000 industrial jobs in the region of the North Sea Canal, including the conurbation of Amsterdam, IJmond and the Zaan District. The chains of towns in North Brabant and the industrial zones of North and South Holland form the first level of industrial development, followed by the regions of Twente and South Limburg (with 40,000 industrial jobs) as the second level, and the Peat Colonies in the Northeast and a number of urban centers, such as Utrecht, Amersfoort, Arnhem, Nijmegen and The Hague, as the third level.

Since 1970 the government's industrial policy has gone through several phases. As the size of the manufacturing sector fell sharply, official policy for an orderly contraction of industrial capacity was overtaken by events. Calls for more selective growth policies, a more adaptable production structure and higher investment in new technology were rendered irrelevant by the worsening business environment and lower profits. In any case, selective growth policies never became effective. Official sectoral policy now concentrates on improving the business climate by reducing the tax load and the public deficit.

There are no specific provisions in the Netherlands commercial code dealing with the status of foreign enterprises. Their status is exactly the same as enterprises entirely owned by Dutch citizens. There are no provisions that establish a required ratio of foreign to Dutch capital in a company. No difference is made between Dutch and foreign companies in the issue of public or private shares. There are no provisions requiring the appointment of Dutch nationals to a board of directors, to the management or to the staff of a company. Such a liberal policy has attracted extensive foreign investment; the U.S. unvestment alone is close to $10 billion, with manufacturing in first place and the petroleum industry next in order of importance.

Foreign as well as domestic investors are eligible for a wide range of investment incentives under three basic instruments: the Investment Account Law (WET Investerings Rekening, WIR), the Selective Investment Law (Selective Investerings Regeling, SIR) and the Investment Premium Law (Investerings Premie Regeling, IPR). Under the WIR, designed to encourage investment in fixed or capital assets, the government provides free tax bonuses that are offset against tax assessment. The SIR applies to investments in underdeveloped areas outside the Randstad, particularly Zuid Holland, the southern part of Noord Holland and the western part of Gelderland. IPR investment premiums are granted to "dynamic service enterprises of more than regional importance." In all cases, premiums are granted only to entrepreneurs who are subject to Dutch taxation. The Dutch government has established an industrial commission to attract foreign investment, with offices in New York and Tokyo as well as The Hague.

```
┌─────────────────────────────────────────────────────┐
│              MANUFACTURING INDICATORS                │
│                                                      │
│  Average annual growth rate, 1980–85: 1.4%           │
│  Share of GDP: 34% (industry)                        │
│  Labor force in manufacturing: 32% (industry)        │
│  Value added in manufacturing: (million 1980 $),     │
│      1984: N.A.                                       │
│      Food and agriculture: 19                        │
│      Textiles: 4                                      │
│      Machinery: 28                                   │
│      Chemicals: 13                                   │
│  Earnings per employee in manufacturing              │
│      Growth rate, 1980–85: 2.1%                      │
│      Index (1980=100): 108 (1985)                    │
│  Total earnings as % of value added: 58              │
│  Gross output per employee (1980=100): 113 (1985)    │
│  Index of Manufacturing Production (1980=100): 107   │
│  (1984)                                              │
└─────────────────────────────────────────────────────┘
```

ENERGY

Dutch energy consumption patterns have changed radically since the two oil shocks of the 1970s. Between 1973 and 1978, for example, consumption increased by only 1% per year and between 1980 and 1985 actually declined, by 0.1%. A series of mild winters and slower economic growth helped in achieving this saving. Natural-gas discoveries made the Netherlands a net exporter of energy in the 1970s and early 1980s, but this situation is expected to change, since the gas reserves are expected to diminish rapidly and new discoveries have not yet been made.

Petroleum currently supplies over 48% of the country's energy needs. Domestic output has become insignificant after reaching a peak of 2.4 million tons in 1965. Approximately two-thirds of the imports comes from the Persian Gulf. There are six domestic refineries (BP, Shell, Kuwait State Oil Company [formerly Gulf], Esso, Chevron and Mobil), with a capacity of over 90 million tons per year. Of the crude oil imported for processing, over one-third is reexported in the form of oil products. Domestic oil consumption is expected to rise as gas supplies decline.

Natural gas is currently the main energy source. Production in 1984 was 77,442,000 metric tons of coal equivalent, down from 109,028,000 metric tons in 1975. Gas reserves, both confirmed and potential, are estimated at 2.227 billion cu. m. (1.703 cu. yd.), of which 321.8 million cu. m. (246.0 million cu. yd.)

are under the Dutch sectors of the continental shelf. Most of the gas still comes from the Slochteren field. It is extracted by the Netherlands Petroleum Company and sold to the Netherlands Gas Union, which distributes half to domestic users and half to industrial undertakings and power stations. In view of the depletion of existing reserves, export of gas is being curtailed. Some gas is imported from Norway and Algeria to maintain supplies. The rate of gas extraction from Groningen is also being reduced in lengthen its life as a strategic reserve.

Net production of electricity in 1985 was 63.632 billion kwh., or 4,398 kwh. per capita. The majority of the power stations use either oil or natural gas. Electricity is produced for the national grid by 16 provincial and municipal power companies. Electricity distribution is in the hands of 16 generating concerns

---

ENERGY INDICATORS

Total energy production: 97,631,000 metric tons
Average annual energy growth rate (1980–85): -0.3
Public Utilities' share of GDP: 1.7%
Energy consumption per capita (000 kg. oil equivalent): 5,138
Energy imports as % of merchandise imports, 1985: 21
Average annual growth rate of energy consumption, 1980–85: -0.1

Electricity
  Installed capacity: 17,650,000 kw.
  Production: 62.78 billion kw.-hr.
    % Fossil fuel: 94
    Hydro: 0
    % nuclear: 6
  Consumption per capita: 4,584 kw.-hr.

Natural gas
  Proved reserves: 1.885 trillion cu. m. (1.441 trillion cu. yd.)
  Production: 80.592 billion cu. m. (61.615 billion cu. yd.)
  Consumption: 31.205 billion cu. m. (23.857 billion cu. yd.)

Petroleum
  Proved reserves: 195 billion bbl.
  Years to exhaust proved reserves: 7
  Production: 26 million bbl.
  Consumption: 234 million bbl.
  Refining capacity: 1,468,000 bbl. per day

Coal
  Reserves: 240 million metric tons
  Production: 0
  Consumption: 9.9 million metric tons

and some 75 undertakings, most of them municipally owned. There are two nuclear power stations: a 50-megawatt plant in Dodewaard and a 450-megawatt power station in Borssele in Zeeland. Electricity consumption is increasing by 3% annually.

MINING

A part from salt in the East, the Netherlands is not rich in minerals. Coal mining, which was concentrated in Limburg Province, was discontinued in 1974 following the government's decision to close down noncompetitive enterprises. Coal needed by the steel industry is now imported.

LABOR

In 1985 the Dutch labor force was estimated 4.501 million, down from 4.619 million in 1982. The general participation rate is 60 to 84% for men and 32% for women. The female participation rate is one of the lowest in Europe, and further, 80% of women workers are employed in the trades and services. The percentage of the work force in agriculture has been relatively stable since 1980, but that in manufacturing has been declining.

With a modest upswing in economic conditions in the mid-1980s, unemployment, which had risen steadily from 1980 to a high of 822,400 in May 1984 (14.9%), declined to 761,000 (12.7%) in 1985. The decline is attributable not to renewed economic growth but to a change in regulations eliminating the requirement of workers over age 57½ to register at employment exchanges. Many discouraged job-seekers also tend to withdraw from the labor market. The role played by part-time workers in reducing unemployment is difficult to determine because of a peculiarity in Dutch labor statistics. Unemployment data are not obtained from surveys but rather from registration lists at labor exchanges. This system misses, on the one hand, those who are not registered because they are not eligible for benefits and, on the other, those who have unreported or part-time jobs that do not have to be listed.

The labor force growth is projected at 1.5% through the year 2000. Labor unions do not believe that this growth can be absorbed by any level of economic expansion and consequently are pushing for work-time shortening. The government, on the other hand, places more emphasis on training schemes and part-time work, pointing out that the bulk of the unemployed is made up of youth and those with low levels of education and inadequate training.

The "pillared" society of the Netherlands is evident in the history of Dutch trade unionism. The three modern federations developed in the early 20th century. The Christian (Protestant) Trade Union Federation (CNV) began in 1909, calling for social reform in accordance with the Gospel. The Catholic Trade Union Federation (NKV) founded in 1909, developed from the Bureau of Roman Catholic Trade Unions and based on the papal encyclical *De Rerum Novarum* of 1891. For more than 50 years the NKV was dominated by the Catholic hierarchy, but in 1964 it asserted its independence. The third federation, the Netherlands Federation of Trade Unions (NVV), was founded in 1905 and traces its origins to the Socialist International. The NVV was anti-Communist until 1971, when it opened its ranks to Communists. The NVV is affiliated with the International Confederation of Free Trade Unions, and the CNV and the NKV with the World Confederation of Labor. Each is affiliated separately with the European Trade Union Confederation and the OECD Trade Union Advisory Committee.

Radical changes have occurred in union membership since 1964. In 1959 the NVV began promoting a merger of the three federations into one body, and its efforts led to a "Common Action Program" in 1967. In 1976 the NVV and the NKV agreed to a new federation known as the FNV, and they merged fully in 1981. The CNV remains outside, but nevertheless the three present a common front in bargaining. All three are represented in the Social and Economic Council, along with the Labor Central for Clerical and Managerial Personnel (MHP). Membership figures at the end of 1985 were 903,000 for the FNV, 298,000 for the CNV and 107,000 for the MHP.

Union membership has been steadily declining for the past several years, both in absolute numbers and as a percentage of the total work force. Traditionally representing well over 40% of Dutch workers (low by West European standards), organized labor has fallen to about 31%. The FNV lost most heavily; the CNV also lost proportionately; only the MHP has held its strength. The reasons for the decline are not completely clear even to union leaders. The loss of jobs in the sectors of traditional labor strength, such as construction, mining and heavy industry, is a partial reason; the postwar breakup of old institutional allegiances is another. Paradoxically, the single most significant cause may have been the very success of the labor movement in having enacted far-reaching social and economic legislation. Workers' rights are so well entrenched in law and so well protected by state agencies that unions have little more to offer their members. Also working against unions is the absence of labor organizers at the national or local levels. Unions rely upon demonstrations and rallies to bring in new members. In the absence of crises, union membership tends to decline.

The merger of the old Socialist and Catholic federations into the FNV has had two largely unforeseen results. First, by compelling a significant number of Catholic unions (primarily of teachers and policemen) to join the CNV to retain their confessional nature, it converted the Protestant CNV into a labor federation representing a wider Christian tradition. Second, and more significantly, it created space for a third, nonconfessional and non-Socialist movement, a space soon occupied by the MHP, with the bulk of its members in the private sector.

In virtually every sector of the Dutch economy, union negotiating positions are undermined by organized-labor fragmentation. For example, in banking, unions represent only 10 to 15% of employees, yet are divided into four unions. However, the unions' position in contract negotiations is both regulated and protected by law. Attempts to circumvent the unions is frowned upon. Union-negotiated contracts are certified by the labor minister as applicable industry-wide.

Another characteristic of Dutch trade unionism is the preponderance of the public sector. Of the total union membership of 1.5 million, 47% (or 700,000) are public sector workers, although they comprise only 22% of the total work force. Well over one-third of the FNV membership comes from the public sector; the FNV civil service union, AbvaKabo, is now the largest union, with 242,000 members. In the CNV some two-thirds are public sector employees, while of the three MHP-affiliated unions, one, with 30,000 members, is entirely public sector. Additionally, there is a fourth federation, the independent Civil Servants Central, composed of 110,000 civil servants. Finally, there are a dozen or more small, unaffiliated unions of public sector employees, such as the KLM Airline Employees. Despite such numerical strength, civil servants find themselves constantly subjected to pay freezes, retrenchment and privatization of government services.

One of the major issues in Dutch labor relations is what is known as work shortening—specifically, the institution of a 36-hour workweek (to be reduced to a 32-hour workweek by 1990 and to a 25-hour workweek eventually). The concept is designed to reduce the unemployment rate by bringing in new workers for the hours thus saved. The 36-hour workweek is the battle cry for the unions in contract negotiations.

The Ministry of Labor is assisted by a number of statutory organizations, of which the Socioeconomic Council (SER) is by far the most important. Set up by the Industrial Organization Act of 1950, the SER is an advisory body with regulatory powers. Of the SER's 45 members, 15 are appointed by the government, 15 represent the employers and 15 represent the unions (10 for the FNV, 4 fot the CNV and 1 for the MHP). The composition of the government appointees reflects, as far as possible, the current political balance in parliament. SER members hold office for two-year terms. The government is required to consult the SER before taking any important measures affecting the economy or the labor force. The SER's standing committees include those for works councils, mergers, economic development, international economic and labor affairs, consumer affairs, social insurance and the labor market. The SER may exercise its regulatory powers autonomously, as in the case of the preparation of a mandatory mergers code. However, the only sanction it may impose is to publish the names of offenders.

A new Works Council Act came into force in 1971, and it was radically amended in 1979. The act applies not only to companies but also to all undertakings in which people are employed under contract. A works council must be established in every undertaking with more than 100 employees, unless exempted from doing so by the SER or the appropriate industrial commission. Members of a works council are elected by the employees and may number up to 25. Any person who has been employed for more than one year may run for election, and any worker of more than six months' standing may vote. Elections, which take place every two years, are based on the proportional representation system, giving equal opportunity to unions and nonorganized labor groups. Each works council must have a constitution that lays down procedures and regulates internal matters. Meetings of the councils take place during working hours in the employers' premises, and council members receive normal pay for time spent in meetings. Works council members may not be discriminated against or dismissed. Works councils must meet at least six times a year in the presence of the manager of an enterprise, and the general conduct of affairs must be discussed at least twice a year. Annual accounts and other financial information must be made available to the council.

Management must consult the council before making major decisions affecting the future of an enterprise, such as mergers, closures, reorganization, relocation, takeovers, contraction or expansion, and investments. The council must also be consulted regarding any proposal affecting working conditions, such as profit sharing, pensions, hours of work, holidays, health, safety and welfare. Other matters requiring works council agreement include training schemes, assessment of employees, recruitment, dismissal and promotion policies, and complaints procedures. The council may appeal against any decision reached against its recommendation with the Companies Division of the Amsterdam Court of Appeal. Management may approach the appropriate industrial commission for approval of any proposed measures to which the works council has withheld its agreement. A further appeal may be made, to the minister for social affairs. Cantonal courts can determine whether firms meet their obligations under the Works Council Act. In addition to works councils for individual enterprises, there are central and group councils for all undertakings run by a single employer or for groups of individual enterprises.

Under the Civil Code, works councils in large public and private companies have a right to a say in the composition of the supervisory boards in such com-

Union Membership			
	1983	1984	1985	1986
FNV	989,239	942,825	915,815	902,672
CNV	330,511	311,275	301,502	298,108
MHP	110,042	110,181	109,412	106,920

Wages (averaged at 2.75 guilders per dollar)			
Average hourly wage	1983	1984	1985
All workers	18.42	18.48	N.A.
White-collar	19.67	19.78	
Blue-collar	15.99	16.05	
Average weekly wage			
All workers	762	765	N.A.
White-collar	812	820	
Blue-collar	666	668	
Weekly minimum wage	472.80	458.70	N.A.

Sources: *Sociale Maandstatistiek* (March 1986) and *Statistical Bulletin No. 6* (February 6, 1986).

Strikes				
	1981	1982	1983	1984	1985
Disputes	11	12	9	11	45
Workers involved	8,600	69,766	20,307	16,158	22,570
Lost work-days	24,114	215,441	118,162	29,181	89,390

panies. A company is classified as large when its issued capital and reserves total at least 10 million guilders and it has at least 100 employees. In such companies supervisory boards of not less than three members must be appointed not by the shareholders but by the supervisory board itself, but both the works councils and the shareholders may object to any appointment. The supervisory boards have special powers in addition to general functions of supervising management policy and the general conduct of company affairs. First, the board appoints and dismisses the managers of the company; finalizes the annual accounts for approval of shareholders; and approves certain management decisions, such as share issues, mergers, amendments to the articles of association, investments, winding up the company, large-scale layoffs and major reorganization. The works council has the right to make recommendations on certain of these matters. Special provisions apply to companies that form part of a conglomerate.

The Civil Code provides for investigations into the affairs of public companies (NVs), cooperative organizations and private companies (BVs). A request for such an investigation may be made by a trade union to the Companies Divi-

---

LABOR INDICATORS, 1986

Total economically active population: 4,501,000
As % of working-age population: 69
Female participation %: 35.6
Activity %:
  Total: 41.2
  Male: 54.2
  Female: 28.5

Employment status (%)
  Employers and self-employed: 7.8
  Employees: 77.4
  Unpaid family workers: 2.0
  Other: 12.8

Sectoral employment (%)
  Agriculture, forestry, fishing: 5.2
  Mining: 0.2
  Manufacturing, construction: 28.8
  Electricity, gas, water: 0.9
  Trade: 17.6
  Transportation, communications: 6.3
  Finance, real estate: 8.9
  Services: 34.1

Average annual growth % of labor force, 1980–2000: 0.5

Unemployment %: 12.7
Labor under 20 years: 5.5
Earnings in manufacturing: 16.93 guilders per hour (1983)

Hours of work per week
  Manufacturing: 40.4

---

sion of the Amsterdam Court of Appeal after the management and the works council have been given a chance to resolve the problems.

Industrial commissions comprising equal number of management and trade union representatives are established to implement the Works Council Act. Their work consists principally in granting exceptions to individual employers for the requirement to set up works councils, in approving the constitutions of works councils and in approving appropriate management decisions for which works council permission has been denied.

Like labor unions, employer associations have, until recently, followed the same confessional divisions—Catholic, Protestant and nondenominational.

In the 1960s, the two Christian groups merged to form the NCW (Nederlandsche Christelijk Werkgeversverbond), with 125 affiliates while the VNO (Verbond Van Nederlandsche Ondernemingen), the nonconfessional group, represents 86 organizations. The Netherlands Employers' Federation is a consultative body that links the VNO and the NCW. Employer organizations have a generally harmonious relationship with trade unions, although they tend to support conservative positions in politics.

The Labor Foundation, an autonomous body, is the core of the collective bargaining process, Established in 1950, it consists of 18 members equally divided between employer and employee organizations. Its purpose is to provide guidelines for contract negotiations for maximum limits applicable nationally. Its deliberations normally begin in September after the receipt of the SER report on the state of the economy. In 1970 the Wage and Salary Act was passed, giving the government power to intervene in collective bargaining when needed to protect its economic policies. After opposition to the act culminated in a general strike, the government has rarely used this power. Collective bargaining has become a bilateral affair on a single-industry basis. Historically, the federations have paid little attention to the union role in individual plants, thus discouraging local initiatives. This, too, is changing, with greater local militancy and less reliance on top national leaders.

There is no separate provision for mediation, conciliation, arbitration or settlement of grievances. These matters are incorporated in collective agreements that have the force of law. If disputes are not settled between employers and the unions at the plant level, they are taken to the Wage Technical Service of the Ministry of Social Affairs. The local courts are the agents of last resort. Strikes are few and far between, and national unions refuse to support wildcat strikes.

The major pieces of labor legislation are the Van Houten Act of 1874, prohibiting employment of children under 12; the Factories Act; and the Industrial Safety Act. The standard workday is eight hours and the maximum workweek is 40 hours. Weekend and night work are not permitted except in special circumstances, when permits are issued by the Ministry of Social Affairs. Workers are entitled to 15 days of paid vacation per year. Children under 15 may not work, and women under 18 may not be employed on certain hazardous jobs.

Wage rates are determined by collective bargaining for each industry. The national minimum wage rates, first established in 1966, have been periodically revised upward. Young people receive a lower minimum wage than adults. Since 1982, wage developments have been dominated by private sector agreements to trim salary increases and a shortening in working hours to permit increased recruitment. In the public sector, wage policy has remained restrictive. The near stability of wage levels is reflected in lower costs per unit of output. In manufacturing, this decline was estimated at 4.3% in 1984 and a further 2% in 1985.

Manpower policy is formulated by the independent, tripartite Council for Employment. Considerable importance is attached not only to full employment but also to enhancement of the quality of available work. Manpower policies comprise measures to influence trends in supply and demand and efforts to reduce disparities between the types of employment sought and opportunities actually available. Adverse structural trends in the labor market do not affect all groups and occupations equally. Women, young people and older workers are historically the disadvantaged groups in the sector. Therefore, manpower policies are concerned as much with growth as with the distribution of employment, regionally as well as among age groups and sexes. Primary responsibility in manpower and labor supply areas lies with the Directorate General for Manpower. It is represented at the district and provincial levels by chief inspectors and directors and by the district heads of the Supplementary Employment Offices. The role of these latter offices lies principally in the services they provide for firms and job-seekers, such as occupational guidance, career information service, placement service and employment medical advisory service. Adult training centers have been established in areas of unemployment, offering short-term training in needed skills. The Ministry of Social Affairs also sponsors supplementary employment schemes in cooperation with regional public service commissions. An active ingredient of manpower policy is the elimination of regional disparities in the supply and demand of labor. This is achieved through allocation of funds under the supplementary employment schemes, in the provision of training facilities and in a system of relocation allowances to encourage geographical mobility. Another tool of manpower policy is the very restrictive policy on immigration of non-EEC workers. Recruitment of foreign workers has virtually ceased, and the majority of immigrants now admitted are dependents of people already in the country. All foreign workers are required to possess employment permits obtained through their prospective employer, and a residence permit.

FOREIGN COMMERCE

The Dutch economy remains particularly sensitive to external trade because imports and exports are very large in relation to the GNP, each valued at more than two-fifths of the annual output. Further, most of its important trade partners are within the EMS, with its relatively fixed exchange rates. This limits the degree to which a fall in the world value of the guilder would result in increased purchase of Dutch goods.

In addition to its membership in the EEC, the Netherlands has close ties to Belgium and Luxembourg through membership in the Benelux Economic Union. The Netherlands also has free trade in industrial products with members of the EFTA.

Since 1984 the exports of goods in volume terms has grown rapidly, helped by the recovery in world trade. Markets for Dutch goods grew by 8.1% in 1984 and by 5% in 1985. The competitive position of the manufacturing industry improved further as domestic costs fell, even though the dollar depreciated. Manufactured exports grew by 2⅜% more than markets in 1984 and were particularly strong in food products, metals and metal manufactures. Exports such as gas slowed after 1985. Food exports were affected by changes in the Common Agricultural Policy (CAP).

Import volumes also have been growing at a rapid pace. Higher imports of raw materials and semimanufactured goods have been related to positive stock-building after a rundown over several years.

There was a sharp rise in the trade surplus of 5.5 billion guilders in 1984 and a further 0.9 billion guilders in 1985. A terms-of-trade gain added another 3 billion to 5 billion guilders to the trade surplus in value terms. Although imports rose in 1985, import prices fell sharply, and terms-of-trade gains added another 2 billion to 2.5 billion guilders to the trade surplus.

TRANSPORTATION & COMMUNICATIONS

Transportation and communications play a key role in the Dutch economy because of the country's location. Of the maritime freight that pass through EEC ports, more than a quarter is handled by Dutch ports, with Rotterdam—the world's busiest port — taking the lion's share. Just under half the Rhine traffic via Lobith and about one-quarter of the international road haulage within the EEC are handled by Dutch carriers. In addition, a large number of Dutch firms are engaged in transportation-related services. The transportation sector contributes more than 7% to the national income.

The national rail service is the Nederlandse Spoorwegen (NS), a limited company wholly owned by the state. It operates a network of 3,000 km. (1,865 mi.) of track, of which 1,800 km. (1,119 mi.) are electrified, and 306 km. (190 mi.) carry only freight traffic. The frequent river crossings, necessitated by the many stretches of water, place a considerable strain on the system. Among the new rail links is that between The Hague and Amsterdam via Schiphol International Airport; the link was completed in 1981 and integrated into the national system in 1986.

More than half the freight traffic is transnational in origin or destination. Since 1963 the NS has shown a loss every year on its passenger operations, which is made up by government subsidies under the EEC harmonization decision. In terms of safety equipment and rolling stock the NS is a modern rail system. The age of the steam locomotive came to an end in 1958, and the last wooden carriages were taken out of service in 1956, making the NS the first European all-steel carriage system. Diesel-hydraulic rolling stock has been in-

```
┌─────────────────────────────────────────────────┐
         FOREIGN TRADE INDICATORS, 1986

  Exports: 194.218 billion guilders
  Imports: 184.791 billion guilders
  Balance of trade: 9.427 billion guilders
  Annual growth rate, 1980–85 exports: 3.4%
  Annual growth rate, 1980–85 imports: 2.6%
  Ratio of international reserves to imports (in months): 3.8
  Value of manufactured exports: $35.149 billion
  Commodity concentration: N.A.
  Terms of trade (1980=100): 104
  Import Price Index (1975=100): N.A.
  Export Price Index (1975=100): N.A.
  Import of goods as % of GDP: 52.18
  Export of goods as % of GDP: 54.96
  Average annual growth rate
     Export Price Index (1975–81): N.A.
     Import Price Index (1975–81): N.A.
```

Direction of Trade (%)

	Imports	Exports
EEC	63.9	74.9
U.S.A.	7.9	4.7
Industrialized market economies	73.6	84.4
East European Economies	2.5	1.3
Developing economies	21.4	12.7

Composition of Trade (%)

	Imports	Exports
Food	17.4	24.9
Agricultural raw materials	11.6	1.2
Fuels		
Ores and minerals	0.6	15.4
Manufactured goods	71.6	58.5
of which chemicals	13.4	17.1
of which machinery	19.5	19.8

troduced on a number of lines in the North. On lines carrying heavy commuter traffic, double-decker trains have been placed in service.

The Netherlands has over 4,300 km. (2,672 mi.) of canals and navigable rivers. Of the traffic on these waterways, some 78% is international, largely along the Rhine. Freight is transported along the Rhine via Lobith under the terms of the Mannheim Convention, which established it as an international waterway.

The Dutch merchant fleet is the 18th largest in the world and contributes 30% of the country's invisible earnings (from ships, tourism and other services). Of the total GRT of 4,586,000, a total of 950,000 are oil tankers and 782,000 ore and bulk carriers. The shipping industry forms the basis for a large number of associated activities, including shipbuilding. Scientific research is carried out by the Maritime Research Institute. Rotterdam and Amsterdam are two of the largest ports in the world; the former is considered the busiest in the world, handling over 70 ships and 700,000 tons of cargo every day of the year.

The national flag carrier is KLM (Royal Dutch Airlines), the oldest airline operating under its original name; it was founded in 1920. The KLM network of 366,790 km. (227,961 mi.) serves 119 destinations in 75 countries. It has a fleet of 52 jet aircraft, including 16 Boeing 747s. The country's aviation industry is led by Fokker, whose Friendship and Fellowship aircraft are popular planes. The National Aerospace Laboratory in Amsterdam conducts research in aeronautics and astronautics. The principal airport, near Amsterdam, is Schiphol, Europe's fourth largest airport. The nation's second busiest airport is Zestienhoven, near Rotterdam. Pilots are trained at the National Aviation School at Eelde Airport near Groningen.

The road system comprises 108,360 km. (67,346 mi.) of roads, of which 92,525 km. (57,505 mi.) are paved and 15,835 km. (9,841 mi.) gravel. On the major highways, the maximum speed is 100 km. per hour (62 miles per hour) for private cars and 80 km. per hour (50 miles per hour) for commercial vehicles. The dutch road system is notable for its bridges and tunnels. The most notable bridges are the Van Brienenoord Bridge over the Nieuwe Maas at Rotterdam, the steel suspension bridge over the Waal at Ewijk, the second bridge over the Rhine at Arnhem and a new bridge with 10 100-m. (328-ft.) spans over the Hollands Deep at Moerdijk. The tunnel under the Maas in central Rotterdam is a model of Dutch tunnel engineering.

Public transportation in urban areas is provided by municipal and regional undertakings, which run both tram and bus services. There are 27 regional transportation undertakings with close to 5,000 buses on a network of 20,000 km. (12,430 mi.) linking 2,500 towns and villages. Nine of the largest towns and cities have their own municipal transportation undertakings, which operate 1,446 buses and 772 trams. The Dutch are fond of cycling, and the bicycle and the moped are ubiquitous throughout the country. Most urban roads have cycle tracks.

The Postal and Telecommunications Service is a government agency without corporate status. It is governed by the State Enterprises Act of 1928. In addition, the Posts Act and the Telegraphs and Telephones Act grant the service a monopoly in respect of certain postal and telecommunications services. The country is divided into 12 postal regions with 2,600 post offices. The post office also performs other services, such as giro and savings bank transactions, issuing of motor vehicle licenses and selling tickets for public transportation.

The main element in the telecommunications system is the telephone service, which accounts for 90% of its turnover. Over 90% of Dutch households now have a telephone, although in number of telephones per capita, the Netherlands ranks below the United States, Sweden, Switzerland, Canada and three other countries in the world. All domestic calls and 99% of international calls are dialed directly. Netherlands is a member of Intelsat and Eutelsat. For most international telephone traffic the Netherlands uses its Burum earth station, operating in conjunction with the geostationary satellites over the Atlantic and Indian oceans as well as the Belgian earth station at Lessive for traffic via the Atlantic Ocean satellite. Teleconferencing service includes a video facility. There are over 36,000 telex connections. There are facilities for data transmission between computers and/or terminals both via the telephone system (DATEL) and over fixed links or rented lines. A public data network came into operation in 1982 and is linked with British, French and German data networks. Radiotelephone services are available both as a public service and in closed networks used by emergency services, the police, taxi companies, etc. Also growing in importance is the mobile radiotelephone service, which links subscribers' cars with the public telephone network. The interactive videotex system known as Viditel makes information available to the public through the telephone system, using a specially adapted television receiver.

In normal years expenditures by Dutch visitors abroad are more than double tourist receipts in the Netherlands. Tourism is actively promoted by the Netherlands Tourist Office, which issues the popular Holland Culture Card.

DEFENSE

The queen is the commander in chief of the armed forces. Under her, the defense structure consists of the Ministry of Defense, presided over by a minister of cabinet rank. Each of the three armed services—the Royal Netherlands Army, the Royal Netherlands Navy and the Royal Netherlands Air Force—has its own board, headed by the chief of general staff, the chief of naval staff and chief of air staff, respectively. The Royal Netherlands Military Constabulary is a separate unit. There is a joint chiefs of staff and joint agencies for the three services. The highest administrative consultative body is the Defence Council, headed by the minister of defense and two state secretaries.

The headquarters of the Royal Netherlands Army (RNA) is divided into six commands: the I Netherlands Army Corps, the National Territorial Command, the National Logistics Command, the Army Training Command, the Army Medical Command and the Army Communications Command. The I Netherlands Army Corps is responsible for the defense of the North German Plain; the National Territorial Command, for the defense of Dutch territory. The peacetime strength of the army is 68,000, of whom 43,000 are conscripts. The Dutch army is a volunteer-conscript force, which means that most units

```
┌─────────────────────────────────────────────────┐
│            TRANSPORTATION INDICATORS            │
│                                                 │
│ Roads                                           │
│ Length km.: 110,327 (68,554 mi.)                │
│ Paved %: 86                                     │
│                                                 │
│ Motor vehicles:                                 │
│ Automobiles: 4,772,000                          │
│ Trucks: 352,700                                 │
│ Persons per vehicle: 2.8                        │
│ Road freight ton-km.: 20.241 million (12.580    │
│ million ton-mi.)                                │
│                                                 │
│ Railroads                                       │
│ Track km.: 2,956 (1,837 mi.)                    │
│ Passenger km.: 9.220 million (5.734 million mi.)│
│ Freight ton-km.: 2.203 million (1.369 million   │
│ ton-mi.)                                        │
│                                                 │
│ Merchant marine                                 │
│    Vessels: 1,344                               │
│    Total deadweight tonnage: 5,949,400          │
│       Oil tankers: 950,000                      │
│                                                 │
│ Ports                                           │
│    Cargo loaded: 80,676,000 tons                │
│    Cargo unloaded: 244,056,000 tons             │
│                                                 │
│ Air                                             │
│    Km. flown: 118.4 million (73.6 million mi.)  │
│    Passengers: 5.655 million                    │
│    Passenger-km.: 18,240 billion (11.336        │
│ billion passenger-mi.)                          │
│    Freight-km.: 1.485 billion (923 million      │
│ freight-mi.)                                    │
│    Mail-ton-km.: 66.8 million                   │
│                                                 │
│ Airports with scheduled flights: 6              │
│                                                 │
│ Pipelines                                       │
│    Crude: 418 km. (260 mi.)                     │
│    Refined: 965 km. (600 mi.)                   │
│    Natural gas: 10,230 km. (6,358 mi.)          │
│                                                 │
│ Inland waterways                                │
│ Length-km.: 4,374 (2,718 mi.)                   │
│ Cargo ton-km.: 6,597 billion (4.100 billion     │
│ ton-mi.)                                         │
└─────────────────────────────────────────────────┘
```

consist of a cadre of professional soldiers and a number of conscripts. Conscription is based on Section 194 of the Constitution. All male citizens are liable for national service on the first February of the year in which they reach 18 years with certain exemptions, such as enrollment in Holy Orders and conscientious objection. After an initial period of full-time service lasting 14 months, the conscripts are assigned to a reserve (mobilizable) unit of the Army Corps of Territorial reserves. Reserve personnel are called up for refresher training from

```
┌─────────────────────────────────────────────────┐
│              COMMUNICATION INDICATORS             │
│  Telephones                                       │
│  Total: 8.84 million                              │
│  Per 100: 57.5                                    │
│  Phone traffic                                    │
│  Local: 2.949 billion                             │
│  Long distance: 2.279 billion                     │
│  International: 98.037 million                     │
│                                                   │
│  Post Office                                      │
│     Number of post offices: 2,806                 │
│     Domestic mail: N.A.                           │
│     Foreign mail: 4.696 billion                   │
│                                                   │
│  Telegraph                                        │
│  Total traffic: 879,000                           │
│  National: 485,000                                │
│  International: 394,000                            │
│                                                   │
│  Telex                                            │
│  Subscriber lines: 36,600                         │
│  Traffic (000 minutes): 405,179                   │
├─────────────────────────────────────────────────┤
│       TOURISM AND TRAVEL INDICATORS, 1989         │
│  Total tourist receipts: $1.531 billion           │
│  Expenditures by nationals abroad: $3.014 billion │
│  Number of hotel beds: 94,000                     │
│  Average length of stay: 3.1 days                 │
│  Tourist nights: 6.143 million                    │
│  Number of tourists: 2.992 million                │
│     of whom from                                  │
│     U.S.A.: 475,600                               │
│     France: 204,301                               │
│     West Germany: 601,100                         │
│     United Kingdom: 542,900                       │
└─────────────────────────────────────────────────┘
```

time to time. Each year some 45,000 Dutchmen are called to the colors, representing about 40% of their age group.

Initial basic training is conducted in central establishments and in units. Each tank and armored infantry and other supporting unit has an organic training company. A conscript remains a private soldier throughout his service. A reserve officer starts his national service earlier and holds the rank of *underofficer* during active service. All officers and NCO's in the active army are regulars. Potential regular army officers spend four years at the Royal Military Academy at Breda and later may attend the Army Staff College at The Hague, which offers a one-year course guaranteeing them a command tour as a lieutenant colonel. The Royal Military School at Weert provides instruction for NCO's. There also is the Institute for Military Leadership at Hilversum.

Former conscripts remain in the reserves until they are 35, although some NCO's continue until 40 and some officers until 45.

Together with British, West German and Belgian Army corps, the I Netherlands Army Corps makes up the NATO Northern Army Group (NORTHAG). The peacetime strength of this corps is about 35,000, divided into 10 independent combat brigades. These brigades can be combined to form three divisions. Of these, the 1st Division (known as December 7) and the 4th Division—each of which has one armored brigade and two armored infantry brigades—are largely operational. The four other brigades and the staff of the 5th Division are almost entirely mobilizable. Each brigade is composed of five units of battalion strength (500 to 800 men) and four or five units of company strength (100 to 200 men). Tank battalions and armored infantry battalions make up the maneuver units of a brigade, and a field artillery battalion provides them with fire support. Further support comes from a reconnaissance company, a company of armored engineers, an antitank company and a battery of mechanized antiaircraft artillery. Additional backup services are provided by an ordnance unit, a medical unit, a signals group, a light aircraft group, the Logistics Command and the Military Constabulary.

The National Territorial Command links the 11 provincial military commands, the three most northerly of which are combined to form the Regional Military Command (North). They are responsible for various operations, such as accommodations, storage, munitions, transportation and security. The security companies are assisted by units from the National Reserve Force.

A soldier in the RNA carries a Browning pistol, an Uzi submachine gun and a FALFN rifle. All units have machine guns at their disposal, sometimes mounted on vehicles. Combat vehicles are equipped with Oerlikon 25 mm. automatic cannon, and the infantry and cavalry have mortars. Antitank weapons include rocket launchers and medium- and long-range TOW missiles. Some armored vehicles are equipped as TOW carriers. Tank battalions are equipped with West German Leopard I and Leopard II tanks, which have replaced the older Centurion tanks. The artillery battalions use 155 mm. howitzers and 175 mm. guns. The army corps light aircraft group has Alouette III and Bolkow helicopters flown by pilots of the Royal Netherlands Air Force.

Lapel insignia on the uniform show the branch and often also the regiment to which a soldier belongs. The colors and standards often are inherited. The Commando Corps wears a green beret. Of the 11 infantry corps, three are guards regiments. The cavalry has four Hussar regiments. There also is a mechanized horse artillery regiment dating from 1783.

The army is undergoing a process of reorganization in which military superstructures have been slimmed, new training organizations created, logistics streamlined and interservice programs integrated. Conversion to an all-regular army also is being considered. Much of this is taking place against a backdrop of the spread of unconventional and anti-establishment challenges from younger conscripts. The countercultural movement has been very strong in the Netherlands since the 1960s and finds some of its strongest voices within the armed forces. Large numbers of Dutch soldiers have long hair, untidy uniforms and undisciplined behavior, all of which strike outside observers as undermining morale and authority. Another unusual feature is the presence of three trade unions within the armed forces, of which the Vereniging voor Dienst Plichtige Militairen is the main one and also the most militant.

The Royal Netherlands Navy comprises two escort groups for the Atlantic Ocean, one for the English Channel and one for the North Sea. Each group consists of a guided missile or air defense frigate, a supply ship and six other frigates. With the exception of the air defense frigates, all vessels have helicopters on board. The submarine unit consists of six submarines with conventional propulsion; the submarines work in collaboration with the British Navy and sometimes operate from the British Faslane Base. The Naval air arm comprises two squadrons of maritime patrol aircraft stationed at Valkenburg Naval Air Base and two helicopter squadrons stationed at De Kooy Base. The Royal Netherlands Marine Corps has two amphibious task forces, one of which is trained to operate in the Arctic.

The Royal Netherlands Air Force is part of the Allied air defense system and comes under the wartime command of the commander of Allied Air Forces, Central Europe. The operational units comprise a number of squadrons of combat aircraft and several guided-missile groups. The Tactical Air Force Command has nine squadrons. The air defense system includes a U.S. Air Force squadron operating from Soesterberg Air Base. All the guided-missile groups are stationed in West Germany. Most of the flight training takes place in Canada and the United States. The Tactical Air Command operates the Light Aircraft Group, based at Soesterberg and Deelen, with over 100 helicopters. The group is at the disposal of the I Netherlands Army Corps.

The Netherlands has never had a significant armaments industry, and the percentage of national output devoted to defense is very small compared to that of other developed nations. Most military equipment is purchased abroad, particularly from West Germany.

The Netherlands does not have an autonomous defense policy, and this is reflected in the small size of its defense forces and the poor morale of rank-and-file soldiers. The prominence of counterculture and anti-establishment groups in the army, frequent structural reorganizations and financial stringency have reduced the effectiveness of defense forces in general. There has been some improvement in this respect since the 1970s.

MILITARY BUDGET, PERSONNEL & EQUIPMENT

Defense budget, 1985: $3.816 billion

Armed forces: 105,975 (including 1,450 women, 48,773 conscripts and 4,400 Royal Military Constabulary)

Reserves: 176,300

Army: 67,000

    Units: 1 corps headquarters; 3 mechanized division headquarters; 2 armed brigades; 4 mechanized infantry brigades; 1 SSM battalion; 3 helicopter squadrons

    Equipment: 1,146 tanks; 744 armored personnel carriers; 467 howitzers; 333 mortars; antitank guided weapons; air defense guns; 93 helicopters and aircraft.

Navy: 16,694

    Bases: Den Helder, Flushing, Curaçao

    Units: 5 submarines; 11 destroyers; 32 frigates; patrol craft; Mine countermeasures vessels

Naval air arm: 3 maritime reconnaissance aircraft; 1 antisubmarine warfare helicopter squadron; 1 search and rescue helicopter squadron

Marines: 2,800; 2 amphibious commando groups

Air Force: 16,810

Units: 7 fighter squadrons; 1 reconnaissance squadron; 1 transport squadron; 14 SAM squadrons

---

EDUCATION

Little is known of the existence of schools or an educational system in the Netherlands prior to the 16th century. The founding of the Universities of Leiden (1575), Groningen (1614) and Utrecht (1636) gave considerable impetus to learning, but there was no educational legislation as such until the 19th century. After the creation of the unified state known as the Batavian Republic, the first piece of educational legislation was enacted in 1801. The central government determined both the structure and the content of education through school supervisors at the local level. In the first half of the 19th century educational standards in the Netherlands were among the highest in Europe. The Constitution of 1848 guaranteed freedom of education and thus made it no longer a state monopoly. Because public schools were neutral in matters of religion, both Catholics and Protestants sought to create parallel school systems of their own to advance their doctrinal positions. This led to the *schoolstrijd* (schools issues), which troubled Dutch politics from 1848 until 1917, when private schools were made eligible for state grants. Since then public schools have become a minority. For every 26 state primary and secondary schools there are 74 private ones. Private schools include the Waldorf schools, based on Rudolf Steiner's ideas; Jena plan schools; and Montessori and Dalton schools.

Major Sectors	Percentage
Public	26
Catholic	41
Protestant	26
Nondenominational private	7

Since education is a social right, any individual or group can found a school as long as the following criteria are met. Primary schools can be founded only by a legal body; minimum attendance must be guaranteed; teachers must be properly qualified; and the timetable and curriculum must be drawn up in accordance with state regulations. Arrangements for founding secondary schools are slightly different and need the approval of the Ministry of Education and Science.

Education is compulsory between ages 5½ and 16 by virtue of the Compulsory Education Act of 1900. Under the act, it is the responsibility of the parents or guardians to register their child with a school at 5½ and to ensure regular attendance until 16. Under the 1919 Factories Act, children of school age are not allowed to work. Education is totally free during the compulsory education period and also during the nursery school period. Fees are paid from the fifth grade upward in secondary schools. If several children from one family attend the same school, there is a discount of 25% for two children, 40% for three children and 50% for four or more children. At some schools there are additional payments for extras such as field trips and library. Tuition fees are levied by both higher vocational institutions and universities, but not more than 1,000 guilders per year.

The legal basis of Dutch education is found in the following enactments:

1. the Preprimary Education Act of 1955

2. the Primary Education Act of 1920, regulating financial arrangements, supervision and curricula

3. the Nursery and Primary Education Bill of 1970, raising the school-leaving age from 12 to 16

4. the Nursery and Primary Education Bill of 1976, integrating primary and nursery schools

5. the Special Education Decree of 1967, dealing with education of disabled children

6. the Secondary Education Act of 1963

7. the University Education Act of 1961, regulating the nine state and four private universities

8. the University Administration (Reform) Act of 1970

9. the Apprenticeship Training Act of 1966

10. the Compulsory Experiments Act of 1969

11. the Educational Experiments Act of 1970

Enrollment is essentially 100% in each of the six primary grades. The number of 16-year-old males and females in full-time education is close to 90%.

About 50% of male and 40% of female 18-year-olds are in full-time education. The number of females in university classes is markedly less than that of males.

The school year begins about September 1 and runs for 42 school weeks in primary schools and for some 40 school weeks in secondary schools. Instruction takes place six days a week in most schools, although a growing number have adopted a five-day week. The school week consists of 26 hours for primary grades and between 32 and 36 hours for secondary classes. Schools are closed for approximately 10 days at Christmastime, 12 days during Easter and for at least one month in summer. The language of instruction is Dutch.

Students receive report cards several times a year. Marks are given on a 10-point scale, as follows: 10 = excellent; 9 = very good; 8 = good; 7 = satisfactory; 6 = passing; 5 = barely passing; 4 = unsatisfactory; 3 = very unsatisfactory; 2 = poor, 1 = very poor.

Nursery education (Kleuteronderwijs) is regulated by the New Primary Education Act of 1977. As a general rule, a child is admitted into nursery school on his or her fourth birthday and leaves it when seven. Although nursery education is not compulsory, practically all four- and five-year olds attend a nursery school. Nursery education is free. Children usually attend nursery school for three hours in the morning from Monday through Friday and for two hours in the afternoon on Monday, Tuesday, Thursday and Friday. They have over 12 weeks of holidays over the year. Since 1976, nursery and primary education have been integrated.

Primary education (Lager Onderwijs) is compulsory for its full course of six years and consists of 1,000 teaching hours (except for the first two years, when 800 hours suffice). Primary teachers are qualified to teach all subjects, and special teachers are rare, except for physical education. Schools are free to draw up their own timetables on the basis of an approved curriculum. A child's progress is assessed each year, and if found unsatisfactory, he or she is given remedial teaching. Additional facilities are provided for disadvantaged children, such as those from lower socioeconomic backgrounds or ethnic minority groups. Special education is governed by the Act on Special Education and Secondary Special Education, which came into force in 1985. There are about 975 special schools and 725 private ones. The teaching of the handicapped goes back to 1790, when the first School for the Deaf in the Netherlands opened its doors, followed by the School for the Blind in 1808 and a School for Mentally Retarded children in 1896. In all there are 20 types of special schools. A number of pedagogic experiments have been tried at the first level, including the Enschede experiments, directed against poor performance, and the Amsterdam FLOS (Flexible Organization of the School), which permits five to 11-year-olds to study at their own pace and using special learning packages. The Rotterdam Project is concentrated in deprived areas and relates educational innovation to social environment.

Secondary education (Voortgezet Onderwijs). Excluding the technical or vocational secondary sector, there are four types of secondary schools:

1. LAVO (Lager Algemeen Voortgezet Onderwijs): lower general secondary education for years one and two; phased out during the 1970s.

2. MAVO (Middelbaar Algemeen Voortgezet Onderwijs): intermediate general secondary education for years one to four

3. HAVO (Hoger Algemeen Voortgezet Onderwijs): higher general secondary education for years one to five

4. VWO (Voorbereidend Wetenschappelijk Onderwijs): pre-university secondary education for years one to six

Since 1970, when the compulsory school-leaving age was raised to 16, virtually all pupils go on to full secondary education from primary school. About 60% go to VWO, HAVO or MAVO and 40% to a vocational school. HAVO and VWO select their students on the basis of primary-school proficiency certificates and either an entrance examination or an achievement or psychological test, such as that produced by CITO (National Institute for Educational Measurement). During the first two bridge years in the secondary school, there is further assessment, after which misfits are redirected to appropriate other tracks.

The idea of a single type of secondary education has been accepted in principle and, as a first step in this direction, a common transition or bridge year from primary to secondary school has been instituted in combined schools (scholengemeenschappen). A few combined schools have extended the transition from one to three years to provide an integrated school for 12- to 15-year-olds.

VWO is provided at three types of school: gymnasiums, atheneums and lyceums. All three types offer six-year courses with direct entry from primary school and prepare pupils for university entrance. The distinction between gymnasiums and atheneums is that the former must teach Greek and Latin. A lyceum is a combination of a gymnasium and an atheneum with a common first year. After the fourth of fifth years, the gymnasiums and atheneums are divided into A and B tracks. B has mathematics and science as the core subjects in both types of schools, while A at a gymnasium has classical languages and at an atheneum modern languages and economics. Each course culminates in a leaving examination in seven subjects, five of which are compulsory and two chosen by the student. Dutch is always compulsory. In addition to these examination subjects, there are compulsory lessons in social studies, physical education and some arts. Since 1973, schools have been permitted to dispense with the A and B tracks and instead substitute one in which pupils have a free choice of five (four in the case of gymnasiums) of the seven examination subjects, with Dutch and one of the three modern languages as compulsory. A gymnasium must always include at least one classical language in the leaving examination. This type of curriculum is used in 50% of pre-university education.

MAVO covers the last four years of compulsory education and culminates in a certificate that gives access to a senior secondary vocational school or HAVO. HAVO schools, introduced in 1968, offer a five-year course. In the first three years there is a common course, while in the fourth and fifth years there is a choice of subjects, with a leaving examination in six subjects.

Vocational education is divided into eight major types, each given at junior, senior and higher levels:

1. technical and nautical education
2. domestic science and home economics
3. agricultural education
4. trade and crafts education
5. economic and commercial education
6. teacher education
7. sociopedagogic education for careers in youth work, adult education, social work, community development, personnel work, child care, health care, librarianship and mass media
8. art education

Junior vocational schools (LBO) offer a four-year course in which the first two years offer general training and the last two a specialized one. Senior vocational schools train 16- to 20-year-olds for middle-grade management, the independent practice of a profession or further education and training. The main courses given are in building, mechanical, engineering, electrical and civil engineering. The courses last four years, one of which is a practical year.

Higher vocational education at the postsecondary level is given in technical colleges in courses that last four years. The third year is spent in the industry under school supervision.

Apprentices sign an agreement with their employers by which they receive practical training in the firm and general and vocational training in a school. This agreement is a legal contract. The normal admission requirement is the junior vocational school certificate. In most cases apprentices attend school for one day a week for a full school year. Practical training is divided into elementary and advanced courses, with the former lasting one year. At the end of the practical training, apprentices take a national examination.

The Netherlands has two types of universities: the *universiteit* and the *hogeschool*. The distinction is that the former is required to have at least three faculties: medicine, mathematics and natural science. There are four state universities, one municipal and two denominational. The four state universities *(rijskuniversiteiten)* are those of Leiden, Groningen, Utrecht and Rotterdam. The municipal university is the University of Amsterdam. The two denominational universities are the Free University of Amsterdam (Protestant) and the University of Nijmegen (Catholic). The University of Limburg, founded in 1975, has as yet only a faculty of medicine and thus does not fall under the strict category of *universiteit*. There are five *hogeschools*: the three Universities of Technology at Delft, Twente and Eindhoven; the Agricultural University of Wageningen; and the Catholic University of Tilburg, which specializes in economics, law, social sciences and theology. There are also seven colleges of theology. Relevant certificates showing completion of pre-university courses are required for admission except in the case of mature students over 25, for whom there is an entrance examination. Where only a limited number of places are available, seats are allocated on the basis of a weighted lottery.

Generally, university courses are divided into three parts: the *propadeutisch* part (one year), the *kandidaats* part (one to two years) and finally the *doctoraal* part (two three years), for a total of four to six years. Holders of the *doctoraal* certificate are entitled to the designation *doctorandus (drs.)*; if they have studied law, to the designation *meester (mr.)*. Thereafter they may obtain the title of doctor by thesis. Graduates of the Universities of Technology are entitled to the designation *ingenieur (ir.)*.

While men and women have equal access to university education, the proportion of women at the university level has been historically low and has not exceeded 42%.

Under the University Administration (Reform) Act of 1970, the principal agencies of university administration are:

1. the University Council, composed of representatives of the academic staff, nonacademic staff and students as well as outside specialists

2. the Executive Board of three to five members, including the *rector magnificus*, one or two members elected by the University Council from among the academic staff and one or two appointed by the crown

3. the Faculty Board/ Faculty Executive Committee, both chaired by the dean

4. the Committee of Deans, chaired by the *rector magnificus* and responsible for teaching and research affairs and the award of doctorates

Unlike universities in other countries, Dutch universities do not have terms or semesters but only academic years. Under the Two-Tier University Education Act of 1982, the maximum time for which students may be registered is six years, although students may still take examinations after this period.

The academic staff consists of professors, professors extraordinary (professionals lecturing on a part-time basis), lecturers and research assistants. Deans of students are attached to all universities.

The administration of education is largely decentralized. All municipalities and district councils have their own directors of education, and the largest municipalities have professional educators in charge of the curricula. Central control over education is exercised by the minister of education and science, who is advised by the Education Council in respect to elementary and secondary education and by the Academic Council in respect to universities. He is assisted by one or more state secretaries who are, like himself, politically responsible to parliament and by a permanent staff consisting of a director general, two secretaries general and one inspector general.

The central government inspectorate plays an important role in coordination, administration and setting standards in curricula. However, in practice the government refrains from approving or rejecting the curricula of private primary schools, which are in the majority, but insists on being notified of the selection of instructional materials. For preprimary education the country is divided into 28 district, each with an inspector supervised nationally by two chief inspectors. For primary education there are four regions, each under a chief inspector, and that are divided into 69 inspectorates. Secondary education is supervised by 41 inspectors, of whom 17 are in charge of general secondary education. There are also inspectors for technical, vocational and special education. The state meets virtually all the costs of education at all levels of education, both public and private. Institutional budgets at the secondary and postsecondary levels have to be approved by the Ministry of Education and Science.

Scientific research and science policy are the responsibility of the minister of education and science. He has a number of policy instruments at his disposal:

fact-finding committees, special research programs, sector councils and two funds: the Development Fund and the Investment and Reprogramming Fund. Major official advisory agencies in this area include the Advisory Council for Science Policy, the Royal Dutch Academy of Sciences, the Dutch Organization for Applied Scientific Research and the Organization for Pure Research.

Traditionally adult education has taken place through private initiative. It is not considered to be part of the educational system and actually is under the Ministry of Cultural Affairs, Recreation and Social Affairs. Each of the larger towns supports a social-cultural center called *volksuniversiteit*, offering facilities for nonvocational pursuits as well as evening classes. Correspondence courses have existed since about 1890 and are now well established; they are regulated by the Recognition of Correspondence Course Institutes Act of 1973. The Netherlands has no open university, but one has been under consideration for some time. Residential courses are provided in 42 government-aided institutes. There is a small literacy program for the few Dutch citizens who are illiterate and also for non–Dutch-speaking ethnic minorities.

Consistent with their tradition of freedom, the Dutch tolerate a variety of teacher education programs and institutions with various levels of teaching, different admissions criteria and great disparity in salaries. At the preschool level, prospective teachers are trained at special intermediate-level vocational and technical schools. Primary-school teachers enter a teacher-training academy for a three- or four-year course. Secondary-school teachers are divided into three categories. Third-degree teachers are the lowest and receive little special training; second-degree teachers are trained in teachers colleges for four years; first-degree teachers have a university degree in their subject field and are trained for five years at the university level. In-service training is at an embryonic stage, and there are no national programs.

EDUCATION INDICATORS

Literacy
  Total %: 99.9
  Male %: 99.9
  Female %: 99.9

First level
  Schools: 9,467
  Students: 1,193,338
  Teachers: 75,998
  Student-teacher ratio: 15:1
  Net enrollment ratio: 90
  Female %: 49

Second level
  Schools: 1,409
  Students: 822,615

EDUCATION INDICATORS *(continued)*

Teachers: 53,375
Student-teacher ratio: 15:1
Net enrollment %: 85
Female %: 48

Vocational
Schools: 2,031
Students: 640,737
Teachers: 54,560
Student-teacher ratio: 11.7:1
Vocational enrollment %: 40.4

Third level
Institutions: 456
Students: 305,126
Teachers: 30,396
Student-teacher ratio: 10:1
Gross enrollment %: 31
Graduates per 10,000 ages 20–24: 2,645
% of population over 25 with postsecondary education:
7.2
Female %: 42

Foreign study
Foreign students in national universities: 3,453
Students abroad: 5,735
  of whom in
    U.S.A.: 1,282
    France: N.A.
    West Germany: 1,850
    Belgium: 1,872

Public expenditures
Total: 28.124 billion guilders
% of GNP: 7.7
% of national budget: N.A.
% current: 87.1

GRADUATES, 1984

Total: 14,835

Education: N.A.
Humanities and religion: 2,277
Fine and applied arts: N.A.

Law: 2,348
Social and behavioral sciences: 2,723
Commerce and business: 384
Mass communication: N.A.
Home economics: N.A.
Service trades: N.A.
Natural science: 1,360
Mathematics and computer science: 174
Medicine: 2,035

GRADUATES, 1984 (continued)

Engineering: 1,727
Architecture: N.A.
Industrial programs: N.A.
Transport and communications: N.A.
Agriculture, forestry, fisheries: 774
Other: 1,033

Generally, teaching is a respected profession, and teachers at all levels earn more than their counterparts in comparable positions in manufacturing. Compared to a West European average of 70%, only 44% of primary-school teachers are women. The percentage is less at the secondary level, at 37%.

As in other sectors, fragmentation has hindered the establishment of large national teachers' unions. The Netherlands Association of Teachers was formed in 1972 through the merger of four teachers' associations. Its membership is drawn primarily from secondary schools and it has a somewhat conservative reputation. The General Union of Teachers is a slightly more liberal organization.

LEGAL SYSTEM

The Dutch legal system is based on civil law, with some influence of English common law. Trial by jury is unknown in the Netherlands. Whereas procedures for the administration of justice are mainly embodied in the Code of Civil Procedure and the Code of Criminal Procedure, provisions relating to administrative procedure are embodied in a variety of statutory measures. Some of these procedures—in particular, all fiscal proceedings—are dealt with by ordinary courts, while the rest are handled by special administrative tribunals, whose members are appointed either for life or for a specific period. Each type of tribunal has its own statutory rules. The judiciary is independent of the executive, but judges are retired on reaching age 70.

The ordinary administration of justice devolves upon 62 cantonal courts, 19 district courts, five courts of appeal and the Supreme Court, with about 800 judges in all. The cantonal and district courts are courts of first instance. District courts may also hear appeals from cantonal courts. Appeals from the district courts lie with the courts of appeal.

The cantonal courts have jurisdiction in all civil cases where the claims do not exceed 5,000 guilders and in criminal cases involving misdemeanors only. Each cantonal court is presided over by a single judge. District courts have jurisdiction in all civil cases outside the jurisdiction of the cantonal courts, in divorce and bankruptcy cases, and in criminal cases relating to both felonies and misdemeanors. District court judges are assigned to one more divisions, in each of which one or three judges sit. Courts presided over by a single judge may be a children's court, a police court or an economic police court. Police courts handle simple and straightforward criminal cases where the principal punishment may not exceed six months' imprisonment. The president of a district court may also issue injunctions and settle urgent civil cases by a simplified procedure.

The courts of appeal have divisions in each of which three judges sit, except in fiscal cases. The Arnhem Court of Appeal has an agricultural division with five members, of whom two are lay experts.

The Supreme Court at The Hague has several divisions, each consisting of five judges. It hears appeals in "cassation" involving nonobservance of procedural formalities or incorrect application of the law. It does not review findings of fact and reviews cases "in the interests of law." Its decisions do not set aside the judgments of the inferior courts but only affect subsequent judgments.

Criminal proceedings may be instituted only by the Department of Public Prosecutions, composed of the procurator general and the advocates general at the Supreme Court, five procurators general, advocates general and solicitors general at the courts of appeal, and 19 chief public prosecutors, public prosecutors and traffic magistrates attached to district and cantonal courts, for a total of 250. The department is structured hierarchically in the same manner as the judicial system. Outside the system is the procurator general, who is independent and is appointed for life. He is consulted by the Supreme Court in all cases brought before it and may initiate an appeal "in the interests of law" on his own initiative. The entire department has considerable independence. Dutch law recognizes the principle of opportuneness as opposed to the principle of legality. This means that a public prosecutor is not bound to prosecute except on the express order of a court of appeal, the minister of justice or the procurator general.

Members of the armed forces are governed by the Code of Military Criminal Law, under which offenses are tried by courts-martial. Appeals lie to the Courts-martial Appeals Court and then, in cassation (or on points of law), to the Supreme Court.

Dutch law makes ample provision for the settlement of administrative disputes. Appeals against decisions relating to the enforcement of fiscal laws lie with the fiscal division of the courts of appeal. Other tribunals hear appeals against social insurance legislation, civil service regulations and economic legislation. For disputes not covered by a special provision, the Administrative Jurisdiction (Government Orders) Act provides for appeal to the Judicial Section of the Council of State.

The criminal justice system is based on the following instruments:

- the Criminal Code and the Code of Criminal Procedure
- the Prisons Act and the Prisons Rules

- the Criminal Psychopaths Regulations
- the Aftercare of Discharged Prisoners Regulations

No child under 12 years may be charged with a criminal offense. Those between 12 and 17 years come under the juvenile justice system.

Persons suspected of having committed serious offenses may be remanded to custody by order of the examining magistrate for a maximum period of six days; this order may be renewed once only. After the preliminary examination, the prosecutor may apply to the court for a warrant to hold the accused in custody for 30 additional days. The preliminary examination is conducted by an examining magistrate, who does not sit on the court that tries the case. On the conclusion of the preliminary examination the public prosecutor decides whether to prosecute.

The principal penalties laid down in the Criminal Code are imprisonment, detention and fine. In addition to the principal sentence, the judge may impose an additional sentence or special order or both. Legal provisions on punitive sanctions specify the maximum term of imprisonment and the maximum fine that may be imposed by the court. Capital punishment was abolished in 1870.

Additional sentences include deprivation of certain rights, such as the rights to vote, to run for election to hold public office or to practice certain professions; confiscation of property; and disqualification from driving.

There is no information available on the prison population.

LAW ENFORCEMENT

The Netherlands has three police forces: the State Police (Rijkspolitie), the Municipal Police (Gemeentepolitie) and the Royal Constabulary (Marechaussee).

The State Police is in charge of nationwide police duties. It reports to the Inspector General of State Police, who heads the Police Directorate in the Ministry of Justice. The national territory is divided into five police inspectorates, each headed by an inspector of police directly appointed by the crown. The inspectorates are divided into districts, each consisting of a varying number of groups. The smallest unit is the *politiebureau* or precinct. Each district has its Criminal Investigation Branch. Other units include the Central Data Processing Service, which represents the Interpol, and the Center for Police Studies at Warnsveld. Expert services, such as forensic medicine, fingerprinting, drug enforcement and organized crime, are handled directly by the Ministry of Justice and not by the State Police. The State Police also is in charge of policing harbors, with the exception of Rotterdam. Inland waterways are policed by the Water Police. The Aviation Unit (Dienst Luchtvaart) polices civil airfields and mans a growing fleet of helicopters. There are police dog units in the main cities.

Training is provided at the Kaderschool for commanding officers and the Opleidingsschool for lower ranks, both at Apeldoorn. There are special courses for the Traffic Branch.

The Municipal Police forces serve in 14 municipalities, with varying personnel strengths fixed by the Ministry of Internal Affairs on the basis of population. Large cities have chief commissioners or commissioners of police appointed by the crown, while smaller municipalities have chief inspectors or inspectors of police appointed by the local burgomaster with the approval of the Ministry of Internal Affairs. The Municipal Police maintain law and order and regulate traffic, but criminal investigations are under the direction of one of the five attorneys general. Training is provided at three Gemeentepolitie Opleidings-schools—at Amsterdam, The Hague and Rotterdam.

The ratio of police officers to the civilian population is 1:670.

The duties of the Royal Constabulary, a military police force under the control of the Ministry of Defense, include border patrol, security of public buildings and the royal family, and law enforcement in rural areas and military bases. It has an efficient riot-control unit. The gendarmerie is divided into districts that correspond to the Dutch provinces. Each district has a number of brigades assigned to the more important municipalities. Amsterdam itself has two brigades. Gendarmes are trained at the Opleidingscentrum Willem III at Apeldoorn.

All penal institutions are under the control of the Prisons Department of the Ministry of Justice. The prison sentences are implemented by the director of public prosecutions. Each prison is administered by a governor assisted by a staff that includes chaplains, counselors, doctors, psychiatrists and social workers. Supervisory boards oversee the care of the prisoners but have no administrative authority. They may, however, hear complaints against the staff and review their decisions.

Penal institutions include houses of detention and prisons. Dutch penal policy emphasizes rehabilitation rather than punishment. It is designed to reduce the disadvantages of isolation and maximize chances of reassimilation into society. Prisoners are permitted to lead normal lifestyles closely approximating those outside and to maintain contacts with the world beyond the walls. To this end they are permitted to write letters unsupervised and are granted periodic leaves of absence for home visits under certain conditions. Each prison has a prisoners' committee and a prisoner-run newspaper.

Women serve sentences in the Women's Prison in Amsterdam, while the Houses of Detention in Maastricht and Groningen have separate sections for women. Adults over 23 who have not been remanded to custody because the offense is not particularly serious and who have received a short term of imprisonment are assigned to one of the semiopen prisons: Bankenbosch at Veenhuizen, Ter Peel at Sevenum, Oostereiland in Hoorn, De Raam in Grave or Westlinge in Heerhugowaard. Persons who at the time of sentencing are in custody are divided into two classes. The shorter sentences are served in Boschpoort in Breda or the Nederheide Penitentiary Training Institute in Doetinchem. Longer sentences are served in Esserheem and Norgerhaven in Veenhuizen, Noorderschans in Winschoten, Schutterswei in Alkmaar or The Hague prison. Prisoners between 18 and 23 who have not been remanded to custody are assigned to Nieuwe Vosseveld in Vught or to De Corridor Penal Training Camp in Zeeland. Short-term prisoners are sent to Vught or De Corridor, while long-term prisoners are sent to Zutphen. Allocation of prisoners is done by the Prison Allocation Center, headed by a psychologist.

After serving two-thirds of his or her sentence or spending nine months in custody, whichever is longer, a prisoner may be released on license for a period one year longer than the remaining part of the sentence. Prisoners thus released are usually assisted by a probation or after-care organization, which is required to draw up a rehabilitation plan prior to the date of release. It is also possible for social reasons for sentences of not more than two weeks to be served in installments. Changes in the Penal Code since 1925 have resulted in decreasing use of custodial sentences and increasing use of fines and suspended sentences. Less than 20% of all convictions result in unconditional custodial sentences, while over 55% result in fines only. At the same time, the duration of custodial sentences has increased in recent years. Short custodial sentences still predominate. In 1981 a total of 54.8% of prison sentences were for terms of less than one month, 17.9% for terms of up to three months, 21.5% for terms of between three months and one year and 6.1% for terms of over one year.

The Minister of Justice is responsible for granting remissions and pardons, which is a royal prerogative. A remission may consist of the reduction of a sentence, conditionally or otherwise, or its commutation to a different, usually lighter one. Rehabilitation, probation and after-care work remain largely in the hands of private voluntary organizations. Their relationship to the government is laid down in the Probation and Aftercare of Discharged Prisoners Regulations, which stipulate that such work shall be carried out only by officially recognized organizations. Their costs of staff and facilities are borne in full by the government, which also subsidizes the actual rehabilitation.

Each of them has at least one office in every court district. The rehabilitation plan is based on the personal report submitted to the court at the time of the trial and in which the offender's adjustment problems are analyzed. Direct supervision of rehabilitation activities is in the hands of Probation and After-care Boards. Under the "Early Intervention" Program, persons in police custody are provided assistance by the Probation and Aftercare Service.

HEALTH

The Dutch are remarkably healthy people, but it was not always so. Well into the first half of the 19th century, large sections of the Dutch population were undernourished and subject to periodic outbreaks of epidemics. The year 1865 is a landmark in the history of health care in the Netherlands, marking the introduction of legislation for regulating medical practice. In 1872 the Epidemics Act came into force. The Health Act of 1901 made provision for setting up the State Inspectorate of Health.

Public health is part of the portfolio of the minister of welfare, health and cultural affairs. The ministry operates within the framework of the Health Services Act, the Health Care Charges Act, the Exceptional Medical Expenses (Compensation) Act and other legislation. While the central government has overall responsibility, basic, primary and secondary health-care programs are administered by provincial and municipal authorities.

The principal official public health agencies are the State Inspectorate of Health, the National Institute of Health and Environmental Protection, and the State Institute for Drug Control. They are assisted by a number of advisory bodies, such as the National Advisory Council for Public Health, the Central Council for Health Care Charges, the Health Insurance Funds Council, the Health Council and the Hospitals Council.

Approximately 70% of the Dutch are covered by the Health Insurance Act. The health insurance funds are administered by the Health Insurance Funds Council. The act provides for three types of health insurance: compulsory, voluntary and for senior citizens.

Nearly half of all deaths are caused by cardiovascular diseases. The second greatest cause of death is cancer. Congenital disorders are the major causes of death and disorder among children, accounting for 20% of deaths of children under 14 years. Mental health accounts for 12% of the total cost of health care. Almost all mental institutions are private.

FOOD & NUTRITION

The per capita daily intake is 3,343 calories and 94.3 grams of protein.

```
┌─────────────────────────────────────────────────────────┐
│                 HEALTH INDICATORS, 1985                  │
│                                                          │
│  Health personnel                                        │
│     Physicians: 31,185                                   │
│     Per capita: 1 per 465.                               │
│     Dentists: 6,865                                      │
│     Nurses: 34,500                                       │
│     Pharmacists: 1,800                                   │
│     Midwives: 950                                        │
│                                                          │
│  Hospitals                                               │
│     Number: 815                                          │
│     Number of beds: 68,343                               │
│        Per capita: 122 per 10,000                        │
│     Admissions/discharges per 10,000: 1,148              │
│     Bed occupancy %: 80.2                                │
│     Average length of stay: 13 days                      │
│                                                          │
│  Type of hospitals                                       │
│     Government: N.A.                                      │
│     Private non-profit: N.A.                             │
│     Private profit: N.A.                                 │
│                                                          │
│  Public health expenditures                              │
│     As % of national budget: 11                          │
│     Per capita: $548.10                                  │
│                                                          │
│  Vital statistics                                        │
│     Crude death rate, 1985, per 1,000: 8                 │
│     Decline in death rate, 1965–85: Insignificant        │
│     Life Expectancy at Birth: 1985                       │
│     Males: 73                                            │
│     Females: 80                                          │
│  Infant mortality rate per 1,000 live births: 7.9        │
│  Child mortality rate ages 1–4 per 1,000: insignificant  │
│  Maternal mortality rate per 100,000 live births: 5.3    │
└─────────────────────────────────────────────────────────┘
```

MEDIA & CULTURE

The Netherlands was one of the first countries in Europe with a free and independent press. Amsterdam had two newspapers early in the 17th century. By 1830, when the first daily appeared, there was a flourishing press. The Constitution of 1848 abolished censorship entirely, leading to a virtual publishing boom. Between 1850 and 1866 the total number of daily and nondaily papers rose from 92 to 159. Following the repeal of the stamp tax on the press, the first cheap popular daily, *Het Nieuws van den Dag* (News of the Day), appeared. During the second half of the 19th century the Dutch press was shaped by—and in turn helped to shape—the country's unique phenomenon called pillarization or compartmentalization, by which confessional lines determined political and social loyalties. This system did not entirely break down until the end of World

PER CAPITA CONSUMPTION OF FOODS

Potatoes: 34.5 kg. (76.1 lb.)
Wheat: 56.0 kg. (123.5 lb.)
Rice: 4.0 kg. (8.8 lb.)
Fresh vegetables: 47.0 kg. (103.6 lb.)
Fruits (total): 132.4 kg. (291.9 lb.)
   Citrus: 80.0 kg. (176.4 lb.)
   Noncitrus: 52.4 kg. (115.5 lb.)
Eggs: 12 kg. (26.5 lb.)
Honey: 0.5 kg. (1.1 lb.)
Fish: 11.0 kg. (24.3 lb.)
Milk: 97.9 kg. (215.8 lb.)
Butter: 4.0 kg (8.8 lb.)
Cream: 2.8 kg. (6.2 lb.)
Cheese: 13.0 kg. (28.7 lb.)
Yogurt: 17.2 kg. (38.0 lb.)
Meat (total): 73.1 kg. (161.2 lb.)
   Beef and veal: 18.6 kg. (41.0 lb.)
   Pig meat: 41.3 kg. (91.0 lb.)
   Poultry: 12.8 kg. (28.2 lb.)
   Mutton, lamb and goat: 0.4 kg. (0.9 lb.)
Sugar: 41.7 kg. (91.9 lb.)
Chocolate: 4.2 kg. (9.3 lb.)
Ice cream: 3.1 l. (3.3 qt.)
Margarine: 15.0 kg. (33.1 lb.)
Biscuits: 19.7 kg. (43.4 lb.)
Breakfast cereals: 1.0 kg. (2.2 lb.)
Pasta: 2.9 kg. (6.4 lb.)
Frozen foods: 15.1 kg. (33.3 lb.)
Canned foods: 32.2 kg. (71.0 lb.)
Beer: 89.2 l. (94.3 qt.)
Wine: 14.0 l. (14.8 qt.)
Alcoholic liquors: 2.6 l. (2.7 qt.)
Soft drinks: 55 l. (58.1 qt.)
Mineral waters: 8.4 l. (8.9 qt.)
Fruit juices: 16.4 l. (17.3 qt.)
Tea: 0.6 kg. (1.3 lb.)
Coffee: 9.8 kg. (21.6 lb.)
Cocoa: 1.4 kg. (3.1 lb.)

War II, helped partially by the spread of television. The nonselective behavior of Dutch viewers helped to develop a homogenization of divergent political outlooks and regional cultures. This, in turn, brought a new ideological self-reliance to the press. Many newspapers identified with parties or special-interest groups disappeared, while others loosened or actually broke their ties with the groups they originally belonged to. Local and regional daily papers share 60% of the total circulation and national and specialized dailies the balance. Before the war all newspapers were evening papers, although some had morning editions. Since then the pattern has been reversed, although regional papers are still published mainly in the evenings. The distinction between the popular press and quality or elite papers is less clear in the Netherlands than in most Western countries, although the *NRC Handelsblad* comes closest to being an elite one. Also of high quality and influence are the *Volkskrant*, once the organ of the Roman Catholic trade union; the Protestant daily *Trouw;* and the popular *Telegraaf.* A yellow press does not exist.

Since the war the number and circulation of a group of periodicals generally referred to as "opinion weeklies" have grown. The Elsevier group publishes two of these periodicals, ranking second and third in circulation. Generally, the opinion weeklies reach the better-educated and higher-income levels.

Almost all daily newspapers are published by limited-liability companies, sometimes within holding companies. In other cases, a foundation, cooperative or association acts as the publisher. The biggest publishing company is Elsevier-NDU, with an annual turnover of close to $1 billion and with interests in newspaper, magazine and book publishing. The 1960s and 1970s witnessed a wave of mergers and takeovers resulting in strong concentration of ownership. The mergers reflected the weakening economic position of the press, hemmed in by competition from television, higher wages and declining readership. Between 1968 and 1980 the number of newspaper publishing firms declined from 35 to 24, while the share of the three biggest publishers rose from 34.7% to 47.3%. In two-thirds of the nation's 49 more or less self-contained areas only one newspaper is published without any competition. The same is the case in 14 of the 17 cities with over 100,000 inhabitant. Newspapers generally are delivered to subscribers. Newsstand sales are less important except for some national dailies, such as the *Telegraaf* and the *Algemeen Dagblad.* More than 60% of the press earnings are derived from advertising, which occupies almost half of a daily's mean 28 pages.

In 1971 the government launched the Press Fund to give financial assistance to failing publications in reorganization and restructuring and thus regaining their profitability. Other proposals and measures to preserve the diversity of the press included control of mergers, editorial statutes stipulating the rights and duties of journalists, and a financial regulation to compensate newspapers unable to attract advertising because of low circulation, limited coverage or other handicaps.

The national journalists' trade union is the NVJ (Nederlandse Vereniging van Journalisten), which is affiliated with the FNV. An estimated 75% of Dutch journalists are enrolled in this union. In 1976 the NVJ reached an agreement with the publishers on a framework that serves as a model for editorial

WEEKLY NEWS MAGAZINES, AVERAGE CIRCULATION, 1984	
Magazines	Circulation
Intermediair*	140,168
Elseviers Weekblad	115,300
Elseviers Magazine	126,350
Vrij Nederland	96,715
De Tijd	37,709
Haagse Post	33,870
Hervormd Nederland	21,175
De Groene Amsterdammer	13,599
Source: De Journalist (March 25, 1985).	

COVERAGE OF NEW AGENCIES, SEPTEMBER 1984		
News Agency	Number of newspapers	Number of Subscribers
Algemeen Ned. Persbureau ANP	49	4,531,060
Associated Press (AP)	38	4,192,463
Gemeenschappelijke Pers Dienst GPD	13	888,267
Zuid-Oost Pers	17	718,943
AD-Nieuwsdienst	5	489,231
Audet-Nieuwsdienst	5	446,161
SP Nieuwsdienst	3	384,117
Pers Unie	9	347,920
Limburgia Pers	2	182,757
Source: De Journalist (March 13, 1984).		

statutes at every newspaper, opinion weekly and general interest magazine in the Netherlands. Strikes by journalists are rare.

Freedom of the press is guaranteed in Article 7 of the Constitution:

"No one needs prior permission to publish by the printing press thoughts or feelings, except for everyone's responsibility under the law." Despite this broad guarantee, the press may be prosecuted for three categories of offenses: (1) offenses against the security of the state, peace and morals; (2) insult of members of the royal family or special groups of the population and blasphemy; and (3) defamation and calumny. Criminal actions for insult or defamation are quite rare. More common are civil actions. Journalists have no statutory right to refuse to reveal their sources in court. However, in most cases courts accept

NUMBER OF INDEPENDENT DAILY NEWSPAPER PUBLISHERS IN THE NETHERLANDS AND THEIR SALES AS A PERCENTAGE OF TOTAL SALES OF THE TEN LARGEST PUBLISHERS (to third quarter of 1983)		
Year	Independent Publishers	Share of Total sales of the Ten Largest Publishers
1955	56	39.1%
1970	34	73.8%
1975	28	82.5%
1976	28	81.7%
1977	27	82.2%
1978	27	82.1%
1979	27	81.9%
1980	24	83.5%
1981	23	85.6%
1982	23	86.1%
1983	23	86.0%
Source: 1982 Fact Sheet and 1983 NDP Annual Report.		

NUMBER OF INDEPENDENT DAILY NEWSPAPER PUBLISHERS IN THE NETHERLANDS	
Year	Number
1955	56
1970	34
1975	28
1980	24
1985	24
Source: NDP Annual Report	

public-interest pleas. The professional conduct of journalists also is subject to scrutiny by the Journalism Council, a nonstatutory body. The Media Board, representing the merger of the former Press Council, the Broadcasting Council and the Advertising Council, advises the government on media policy. In 1980 the Freedom of Information Act was passed by parliament, setting broad guidelines for providing access to state information. There is no prepublication censorship in the print media in peacetime.

The national news agency is the ANP (Algemeen Nederlands Persbureau), founded in 1934 as a cooperative venture by newspaper publishers. There are

THE PRINCIPAL NATIONAL DAILY NEWSPAPERS BY CIRCULATION (September 1984)	
Newspaper	Circulation
De Telegraaf	705,600
Algemeen Dagblad	387,635
De Volkskrant	264,100
NRC Handelsblad	170,216
Het Parool	140,300
Trouw	124,900
Source: *De Journalist* (December 17, 1984).	

REGIONAL NEWSPAPERS WITH A CIRCULATION OF OVER 100,000 COPIES (September 1983)	
Newspaper	Circulation
Haagsche Courant/Het Binnenhof	189,450
Tubantia (incl. Hengelo's Dagblad and Dagblad van het Oosten)	166,432
De Gelderlander/De Nieuwe Krant	156,882
Het Vrije Volk	148,018
De Limburger	136,170
Nieuwsblad van het Noorden	136,088
Eindhovens Dagblad/Helmonds Dagblad	124,033
Leeuwarder Courant	111,629
De Stem	108,364
Utrechts Nieuwsblad/Nieuwe Zeister Courant	107,577
Brabants Dagblad	105,766
Source: *De Journalist* (March 13, 1984).	

about 40 other bureaus and news agencies, including branch offices of foreign news agencies. The only independently operating international news agency is the Associated Press.

Broadcasting is organized according to the old pillarization or compartmentalization principle, airtime being divided among at least five groups of diverse political and religious orientations. The 1967 Broadcasting Act made the entry of new organizations into broadcasting possible through the Netherlands Broadcasting Foundation and also by setting up three categories of broadcasting organizations: "A" (those with more than 400,000 subscribers), "B" (those with between 250,000 and 400,000 subscribers) and "C" (those with between 100,000 and 250,000 subscribers). Broadcasting time is divided among the three in the ratios of 5:3:1. These groups must be nonprofit associations whose programming combines information, culture, education and entertainment in such proportion as to meet viewer needs and serve the public interest.

Under the terms of the 1983 Media Policy Document, the functions of the Netherlands Broadcasting Organization were divided among three agencies: the Program Organization, the Facilities Service and the Media Board.

There are three nationwide AM channels and three FM channels used for the transmission of five national radio programs. Among them, the five radio stations broadcast for 500 hours per week. Increasingly, the five stations are developing their own distinctive programming; Hilversum concentrating on news and current events, Hilversum 2 on light topical programs, Hilversum 3 on pop music, Hilversum 4 on classical music and Hilversum 5 on information and services for target groups.

Dutch television is on the air for more than 109 hours per week, divided into two channels, Nederland I and Nederland II. A third channel went on the air in 1987.

Regional broadcasting is conducted by regional councils such as Radio Noord, Radio Fyslan and Radio Oost, or regional cultural organizations such as Radio STAD. Cable television also is regulated by the Media Board. In 1977 the Netherlands received a frequency allocation for five satellite television channels and 16 mono and/or eight stereo radio channels. The Netherlands also participates in the European television program Olympus.

Under the Broadcasting Act, the only body permitted to broadcast radio and TV commercials is the Television and Radio Advertising Organization (STER). Commercials appear at fixed times Monday through Saturday, immediately preceding and following news broadcasts, and account for 3.6% of television broadcasting time.

The Dutch World Broadcasting Service was set up in 1947 and broadcasts programs aimed at Dutch nationals abroad and friendly nations.

About 15 fiction films are produced annually. Their production is promoted by the Production Fund for Dutch Films, which is funded by the Netherlands government and the film industry. The fund provides interest-free loans up to a maximum of 60% of the costs of the film. The remaining costs may be covered by a distribution guarantee, or by contribution from television or video companies. Of the various film festivals held annually, the most important is the Rotterdam Film Festival.

Public libraries have been in existence in the Netherlands since only the 1890s. They are governed by the Public Libraries Act of 1975. In 1985 there were 93 independent public libraries, 12 provincial interlibrary lending centers (pbc's); 378 libraries affiliated with pbc's; 588 branches of public libraries

NUMBER OF REGISTERED VIEWERS AND LISTENERS		
Year	Holders of Joint Licenses	Holders of Radio Licenses
1975	3,645,948	263,145
1976	3,753,662	242,847
1977	3,878,356	226,986
1978	4,032,822	214,011
1979	4,110,581	204,109
1980	4,181,409	194,989
1981	4,294,453	188,360
1982	4,366,921	181,652
1983	4,453,847	175,978

Source: Annual report of the Receiving Licenses Department, 1984.

(pbs's); and 105 mobile libraries. Together these have a combined stock of 38,410,000 books and nonprint items.

MEDIA INDICATORS, 1985

Newspapers
  Number of dailies: 84
  Circulation (000): 4,474
  Per capita: 310 per 1,000

  Number of nondailies: 110
  Circulation (000): 800
  Per capita: 55

  Number of periodicals: N.A.
  Circulation: N.A.

  Newsprint consumption
  Total: 429,200 tons
  Per capita: 29,993 kg. (66,122 lb.) per 1,000

Book publishing
  Number of titles, 1984: 13,209

Broadcasting
  Annual expenditures, 1983: 975.8 million guilders
  Number of employees, 1983: 6,320

Radio
  Number of transmitters: 50
  Number of radio receivers: 4.630 million
    Per capita: 322 per 1,000
  Total program hours: N.A.

MEDIA INDICATORS, 1985 *(continued)*

Television
  Television transmitters: 29
  Number of TV receivers: 4.454 million
  Per capita: 310 per 1,000
  Total annual program hours: 4,514

Cinema
  Number of fixed cinemas: 551
    Seats per 1,000: 11
  Annual attendance (million): 27
  Gross box office receipts: 212.8 million guilders

Films
  Production of long films, 1980: 7
  Import of long films: 332
  56.3% from United States
  13.3% from France
  10.5% from West Germany
  2.4% from Italy

CULTURAL & ENVIRONMENTAL INDICATORS

Public libraries
  Number: 471
  Volumes: 38,410,000
  Registered borrowers: 4,192,000
  Loans per 1,000: 12,500

Museums
  Number: 525
  Annual attendance: 14,661,000
  Attendance per 1,000: 1,020

Performing arts
  Number of performances: 33,309
  Annual attendance: 8,750,000
  Attendance per 1,000: 610

Ecological sites:
  Number of facilities: 47
  Annual attendance: N.A.

SOCIAL WELFARE

The Social Security system consists of a social insurance program supported by a welfare program. Although Social Security has its origins in laws passed early in this century, the current system entirely reflects legal provisions made since 1950. Employees' insurance is based on the principle of equivalence; the premiums paid are based on the risk, with premiums and benefits income-related up to a ceiling. The benefit is independent of income from other sources. National insurance is intended for all inhabitants; the benefit is identical for everyone un-

DUTCH FILMS AND CINEMAS					
	1980	1981	1982	1983	1984
Audience (in millions)	27.9	26.7	22	21.6	17.4
Attendance, Dutch feature films (in millions)	1.9	3.1	2.7	2.9	3.4
Gross takings (in million guilders)	213	213	189	196	160
Production, Dutch feature films	7	11	13	16	12
Number of cinemas (screens)	523	553	557	546	500

der the same conditions, but the premium is related to the income level up to a maximum. Social welfare is intended for people who in general do not meet the conditions for private social insurance, or to follow after other social insurance entitlements have been exhausted. Therefore, it forms a kind of last resort.

Social Security expenditures are financed by contributions made by employees and employers, by the central government from general revenues, and by insurance on adjustments to social insurance funds. Welfare benefits are paid out of general revenues. Contributions made by employees and employers are earmarked for particular benefits. Thus employees pay a fixed percentage of earnings in respect to each different benefit, while employers pay a fixed percentage of payroll. Contribution rates are in some cases subject to floors and ceilings and can vary across sectors of industry.

The main types of Social Security are as follows:

1. national insurance
   general old-age pensions
   widows' and orphans' benefits
   general family allowances from the third child on
   exceptional medical expenses
   general disablement benefit
2. employee insurance
   sickness benefits
   disablement insurance
   unemployment insurance
   family allowances (first and second children)
3. health insurance
4. family allowances for self-employed persons

The implementation of Social Security legislation, with the exception of the Health Insurance Act and the Exceptional Medical Expenses (Compensation) Act, is governed by two acts: the Social Insurance Bank and the Employment Boards Act, and the Social Security (Organization) Act. Another relevant act is the Social Security (Coordination) Act, under which the contributions payable are coordinated with the tax payable on wages and salaries.

The Social Security system is administered by a number of agencies, each with specific responsibilities.

1. The Social Insurance Council consists of a chairman and 21 members, one-third appointed by the minister for social affairs, one-third by employers' organizations and one-third by trade unions. The council supervises the operation of various social insurance schemes, such as disablement benefits, disablement insurance, sickness benefits and unemployment insurance.

2. Industrial Insurance Boards are recognized by the minister for social affairs and are set up by one or more workers' and employers' organizations. They administer statutory insurance schemes. Industry is divided into 25 sections, each covering one or more sectors, and one board is recognized for each section. Sectors not covered are served by a general board. Membership is compulsory for every employer. The detailed administration of the schemes is carried out by the Industrial Insurance Administration Office.

3. The Joint Medical Service was established by the Federation of Industrial Insurance Boards and is administered by a board of 12 members.

4. The Social Insurance Bank, which operates the national insurance plans, is administered by a directorate of not more than three persons and an administrative board consisting of a chairman and 15 members, one-third appointed by the minister for social affairs, one-third by employers' organizations and one-third by trade unions. The bank supervises the work of the Labor Councils and is, in turn, supervised by the Social Insurance Council. The Central Bank acts as treasurer to the bank.

CHRONOLOGY

1945—William Schermerhorn heads Socialist government.

1946—Louis Beel begins first term as prime minister in a Catholic People's Party cabinet

1948—Willem Drees heads Socialist government: Queen Wilhelmina abdicates, and Juliana is named queen; the Netherlands joins Luxembourg and Belgium in the Benelux Customs Union.

1949—the Netherlands recognizes the independence of Indonesia.

1953—Heavy storm hits the Netherlands, inundating coastal regions and killing 1,800 people.

1954—Kingdom of the Netherlands Statute is promulgated, integrating the Netherlands Antilles as an organic part of the Netherlands.

1958—Socialists are ousted and Louis Beel is back as prime minister in a Catholic People's Party cabinet; the Benelux Economic Union is launched.

1959—Jan de Quay replaces Louis Beel as prime minister in a Catholic People's Party cabinet; natural gas is discovered at Groningen.

1963—Victor Marijnen succeeds Jan de Quay as prime minister in a Catholic People's Party cabinet.

1965—Joseph Cals succeeds Victor Marijnen as prime minister in a Catholic People's Party cabinet.

1966—Jelle Zijlstra of the Antirevolutionary Party takes office as prime minister.

1967—Petrus de Jong leads the Catholic People's Party back to office as prime minister.

1969—Netherlands relinquishes control of West New Guinea (now West Irian).

1971—Barend Biesheuvel of the Antirevolutionary Party is named prime minister.

1973—Johannes den Uyl of the Labor Party is named prime minister.

1975—Suriname is granted independence.

1977—Andreas van Agt of the Christian Democratic Party begins a five-year term as prime minister; Catholic and Socialist trade union federations merge into the FNV.

1980—Queen Juliana abdicates and Beatrix succeeds to the throne.

1982—Rudolphus Lubbers of the Christian Democratic Party is named prime minister in a Christian Democratic Party-led coalition.

BIBLIOGRAPHY

Barnouw, Adriaan. *The Dutch: A Portrait Study of the People of Holland.* New York, 1940.

———*The Making of Modern Holland: A Short History.* New York, 1944.

Coleman, John. *The Evolution of Dutch Catholicism, 1958–1974.* Berkeley, Calif., 1974.

Eldersveld, Samuel J. *Elite Images of Dutch Politics: Accommodation and Conflict.* Ann Arbor, Mich., 1981.

Goudsblom, Johan. *Dutch Society.* New York, 1967.

Huggett, Frank E. *The Dutch Today.* The Hague, 1973.

Landheer, Bartholomew. *The Netherlands.* Berkely, Calif., 1944.

———*Netherlands in a Changing World.* New York, 1947.

Lyphart, A. *The Politics of Accomodation: Pluralism and Democracy in the Netherlands.* Berkeley, Calif., 1968.

Raalte, Eva. *The Parliament of the Kingdom of the Netherlands.* London, 1953.

Riley, R.C., and Ashworth, Gregory. *Benelux: An Economic Geography of Belgium, the Netherlands and Luxembourg.* New York, 1975.

Shoffer, Ivo. *A Short History of the Netherlands.* Amsterdam, 1956.

Smit, J.W. *Chronology and Factbook of the Netherlands.* Dobbs Ferry, N.Y., 1973.

Voorhoeve, Jons. *Peace, Profits and Principle: A Study of Dutch Foreign Policy.* The Hague, 1979.

Vries, Johannes de. *The Netherlands Economy in the 20th Century.* Assen, 1976.

Wels, C.B. *Aloofness and Neutrality: Studies in Dutch Foreign Relations and Policy-making Institutions.* Atlantic Highlands, N.J., 1982.

INDEX

251